1995  U.S. Pocket Stamp Catalogue

VICE PRESIDENT/PUBLISHER	Stuart J. Morrissey
EDITOR	William W. Cummings
ASSISTANT EDITOR	James E. Kloetzel
VALUING EDITOR	Martin J. Frankevicz
NEW ISSUES EDITOR	David C. Akin
COMPUTER CONTROL COORDINATOR	Denise Oder
VALUING ANALYST	Jose R. Capote
EDITORIAL ASSISTANTS	Judith E. Bertrand, Beth Brown
CONTRIBUTING EDITOR	Joyce Nelson
ART/PRODUCTION DIRECTOR	Janine C. S. Apple
PRODUCTION COORDINATOR	Meg Schultz
PRODUCTION ARTIST	Cinda McAlexander
SALES MANAGER	Bill Fay
ADVERTISING	David Lodge
CIRCULATION/PRODUCT PROMOTION MANAGER	Tim Wagner

Copyright© 1994 by

Scott Publishing Co.

911 Vandemark Road, Sidney, Ohio 45365

A division of AMOS PRESS INC., publishers of
Linn's Stamp News, Coin World, Cars & Parts
and MoneyCard Collector magazines and *The Sidney Daily News*

Colorful... Historical
UNITED STATES
Commemorative Album Pages by *White Ace*

Featuring illustrated display frames for singles of all commemoratives since the 1893 Columbians, this sectional album also has background stories that place the stamps in their historic perspective. And to highlight the stamps, there's a distinctively designed border with the multicolored pictorial illuminations that have become a White Ace trademark. But there's more to this White Ace than meets the eye, for the heavy album page card stock is acid-free, your assurance of long-lasting freshness. And the looseleaf style provides flexibility, so the album can grow with your collection. What's more, with annual supplements it always will be up-to-date. Choose this White Ace album for your U.S. Commemorative singles (or one of its companion albums for blocks or plate blocks). You will be opting for America's superlative stamp album.

WHITE ACE Commemorative Album Prices	
Commem. Singles (1893-1939) Part 1	$14.15
Commem. Singles (1940-1949) Part 2	10.60
Commem. Singles (1950-1970) Part 3	25.90
Commem. Singles (1971-1979) Part 4	23.10
Commem. Singles (1980-1986) Part 5	24.10
Commem. Singles (1987-1992) Part 6	26.60
Commem. Singles (1993) Part 7	9.95
Matching Border Blank Page Pack of 15	4.35
Gold-stamped Deluxe Binder	12.95
Commemorative album pages are available for blocks. Ask for complete list.	

ON MAIL ORDERS
....please add $3.00 for packing
(foreign by weight)

Available at YOUR FAVORITE STAMP SHOP or order direct

THE WASHINGTON PRESS
Publishers   FLORHAM PARK, NJ 07932

CONTENTS

An overview of the
world's most popular hobby 19A
How to use this book 20A

United States 3
Air Post Stamps 249
Air Post Special Delivery Stamps 263
Special Delivery Stamp 263
Registration Stamp 265
Certified Mail Stamp 265
Postage Due Stamps 267
U.S. Offices in China 271
Official Stamps 272
Newspaper Stamps 283
Parcel Post Stamps 289
Special Handling 289
Parcel Post Postage Due Stamps 289
Computer Vended Postage 290
Carrier's Stamps 295
Hunting Permit (Duck) Stamps 301

U.S. Trust Territories 307
Marshall Island 307
Micronesia 331
Palau 349

Index to advertisers 374

1,000 STAMPS $2.95

GUARANTEED WORTH OVER $30 AT INTERNATIONAL CATALOG PRICES!

Save These Valuable Postage Stamps NOW While They Last!

Reward Yourself Now! — A great opportunity to increase the value of your present collection or to start a new one. You get 1,000 all-different stamps from over 55 countries — **everything you need to enjoy the fun and fascination of collecting postage stamps** — World's Most Rewarding Hobby! *GREAT FAMILY FUN!*

Yours Free!

This fascinating illustrated booklet will enable you to tell at a glance **How to Recognize Valuable Postage Stamps** — stamps once considered relatively common and now worth up to hundreds and thousands of dollars each!

MAIL COUPON TODAY!

KENMORE, Milford OP-051, N.H. 03055
90-DAY MONEY BACK GUARANTEE IF NOT DELIGHTED!

Yes! I enclose $2.95. Rush me your 1,000 All-Different U.S.A. and Foreign Postage Stamps, **(guaranteed worth over $30 at International Catalog prices!) Plus valuable Finder's Guide and Collectors' Catalog!** I'll be glad to receive other highly-prized Selections of Stamps from your 10-Day Free Examination Shop-at-Home Approval Service from which I may purchase any or none — return balance — with option to cancel Service anytime. *(Limit One Advertised Offer Per Family)*

Name _____

Address _____

City, State, Zip _____

The contents of this book are owned exclusively by Scott Publishing Co. and all rights thereto are reserved under the Pan American and Universal Copyright Conventions.

COPYRIGHT NOTE

Permission is hereby given for the use of material in this book and covered by copyright if:

(a) The material is used in advertising matter, circulars or price lists for the purpose of offering stamps for sale or purchase at the prices listed therein; and

(b) Such use is incidental to the business of buying and selling stamps and is limited in scope and length, i.e., it does not cover a substantial portion of the total number of stamps issued by any country or of any special category of stamps of any country; and

(c) Such material is not used as part of any catalogue, stamp album or computerized or other system based upon the Scott catalogue numbers, or in any updated valuations of stamps not offered for sale or purchase; and

(d) Such use is for editorial purposes in publications in the form of articles or commentary, except for computer software or the serialization of books in such publications, for which separate written permission is required.

Any use of the material in this book which does not satisfy all the foregoing conditions is forbidden in any form unless permission in each instance is given in writing by the copyright owner.

TRADEMARK NOTICE

The terms SCOTT, SCOTT'S, SCOTT CATALOGUE NUMBERING SYSTEM, SCOTT CATALOGUE NUMBER, SCOTT NUMBER and abbreviations thereof, are trademarks of Scott Publishing Co., used to identify its publications and its copyrighted system for identifying and classifying postage stamps for dealers and collectors. These trademarks are to be used only with the prior consent of Scott Publishing Co.

Copyright 1994 by Scott Publishing Company. All rights reserved. Printed in the United States of America. No part of this book may be used or reproduced in any manner whatsoever without written permission except in the case of brief quotations embodied in critical articles and reviews. For information address Scott Publishing Co., P.O. Box 828, Sidney, OH 45365.

ISBN: 0-89487-196-X

HOW TO COLLECT
RARE STAMPS
FOR PLEASURE AND PROFIT...
JOIN AMERICA'S #1 COLLECTOR/INVESTOR PROGRAM.

Now, by investing as little as $25.00 each month you can begin a valuable portfolio of rare U.S. stamps chosen especially for you by our highly experienced staff of stamp experts. And the profit potential is proven. During the past 25 years rare stamps have far out-paced most other investments. In fact, an investment in a selected group of rare stamps would now be worth several times the original amount paid. All Stamps Mint F-VF Never Hinged or Better.

SPECIAL OFFER TO NEW MEMBERS! JOIN NOW AND RECEIVE OVER $41.00 IN FREE GIFTS!

JOSEPH KARDWELL, INC.
ORIENT, NEW YORK 11957
PHONE (516) 323-3880
FAX (516) 323-3904

Free Gift #1 — Deluxe Display Album to hold your stamp collection. $15.00 value
Free Gift #2 — Professional Stamp Tongs $3.00 value
Free Gift #3 — Monthly Subscription to "Rare Stamp News" $12.00 value
Free Gift #4 — 400 Page Catalog of Current Stamp Prices $7.95 value
Free Gift #5 — Folding Magnifying Glass $3.25 value

JOSEPH KARDWELL, INC., P. O. BOX 775, ORIENT, NEW YORK 11957

Yes, I want to join the JKI Rare Stamp Collector/Investor Program indicated below. Please send my first selection along with my 5 free gifts. I understand that I may cancel my membership at any time.   PC/95

Each month I would like to invest:
☐ $25.00 ☐ $50.00 ☐ $75.00 ☐ $100.00 ☐ $_____

☐ Check for initial purchase enclosed $_____ N.Y.S. residents add sales tax.
You will be billed for each future selection.

☐ Charge my: ☐ American Express ☐ MasterCard ☐ Visa ☐ Diners Club ☐ Carte Blanche

Card # _____ Expiration Date _____

Name _____

Address _____

City/State/Zip _____

Phone ( ) _____ Signature _____

SATISFACTION GUARANTEED OR YOUR MONEY BACK

STAMP CENTER
Presents
DUTCH COUNTRY
Public Auctions

6-8 Auctions Per Year
• CATALOGS FREE •

1600+ U.S. & WORLDWIDE Lots Every Sale

- ★ COLLECTIONS
- ★ COVERS
- ★ DEALER LOTS
- ★ LITERATURE
- ★ WHOLESALE LOTS
- ★ BULK LOTS
- ★ ACCUMULATIONS
- ★ U.S.P.S. PRODUCTS

CONSIGNMENTS ALWAYS NEEDED
Features of our Auction Services include:
- Material placed in auction promptly, normally within 60 days.
- Settlement is fast, normally within 45 days.
- Catalogs distributed nationally at least 4 weeks in advance.
- Always a high percentage of photos.
- Lots open for inspection in our spacious store for at least 3 weeks.
- Prices Realized published in following catalog.
- All consignments fully insured while in our possession.
- Only 10% seller's commission.

WE BUY COLLECTIONS, ACCUMULATIONS, STOCKS, ETC. ARE ALWAYS NEEDED . . . SHIP VIA UPS FOR IMMEDIATE OFFER AND PAYMENT.
Member: ASDA, APS, AFDCS, ASPPP, ACPS, etc.

FOR FREE CATALOG, SELLING GUIDE OR INFO . . . CALL OR WRITE:

YES
- ☐ SEND FREE CATALOG   ☐ I HAVE STAMPS TO SELL
- ☐ CONSIGNMENT DETAILS ☐ CALL ME FOR APPOINTMENT
- ☐ _____

Name _____
Address _____
City _____ State _____ Zip _____
Phone _____

STAMP CENTER • DUTCH COUNTRY AUCTIONS
4115 Concord Pike, Dept. X, Wilmington, DE 19803.
Phone (302) 478-8740 • Fax (302) 478-8779

Subscribe To
SCOTT
Stamp Monthly

Each month it's a fascinating look at the people, places and events related to stamps. Time-saving hints, remarkable stamp discoveries and quirky amusing tales focusing on bizarre facets of the hobby, you'll find it all in Scott Stamp Monthly.

12 Issues $16.95

To subscribe call
1-800-488-5351

If There is a Watermark I'll Find it... Guaranteed!

Wally Bright, lecturer to Philatelic Societies. Philatelist for more than 35 years.

My all-new... MORLEY-BRIGHT ROLL-A-TECTOR...

...will reveal the most difficult to find watermarks with unbelievable clarity. No chemicals, fluids. Never needs batteries, filters or electric current. The Roll-A-Tector is so compact that it will fit in the palm of your hand. It will even find watermarks on covers & postcards. Engineered to last a lifetime. Order today, only $32.99 (add $2.01 shipping & handling).

NO NONSENSE GUARANTEE
If you are not completely satisfied, return within 15 days for a full refund.

V53

Vidiforms Co. Inc., Showgard House
110 Brenner Drive, Congers, NY 10920
Send me_____ Roll-A-Tectors at $32.99 ea. +$2.01 to cover insurance, 1st class postage & handling. Total $35.00 ea.
Name _____
Address _____
_____
City _____
State _____ Zip _____
Measures 2"x4". Comes in a sturdy, rigid carry case.

start your U.S. Collection *with Scott Minuteman*

Scott's U.S. Minuteman stamp album features:

- The famous Scott Catalogue identification number for every stamp.
- Exciting stories of almost every stamp.
- Attractive vinyl binder.
- Supplemented annually.

*** A must for every collector of U.S. postage stamps. ***

Available at your local dealer or direct from:

 Scott Publishing Co.
P.O. Box 828, Sidney, OH 45365

Your Reliable & Knowledgeable Supplier for

UNITED STATES & UNITED NATIONS

(European & Worldwide also)
From Quality Classics to Modern Year sets!
We can help you with all your stamp needs.

FREE PRICE LISTS!
United States and United Nations.
Ask for your free list today and be sure
to mention your collecting interests
to receive our other price lists!

FAIR PRICES— PROMPT SERVICE!

Please specify your current collecting interests

SAVE 10% every month!

Ask about our Monthly Purchase Plan

CALL NOW! 1-800-9-4-STAMP
(1-800-947-8267)

Mention "Scott US Pocket Cat" when
replying to receive your free gift!

WE BUY—TOP PRICES PAID!
"For the Best in Quality & Price...."

HENRY GITNER PHILATELISTS, INC.

P.O. Box 3077
Middletown, NY 10940
(914) 343-5151
FAX (914) 343-0068

AHPS

SHOWGARD®

THE STAMP MOUNTING SPECIALISTS

Forty years of research, development, and manufacturing experience has unlocked the secrets necessary to produce the most nearly perfect way to display your stamps with safety and beauty, The Showgard Mount.

And because we're as serious about our stamp mounts as you are about your stamps, we offer the most complete line of quality stamp mounts, and accessories.

- The Showgard line of strip and cut style mounts in clear or black background is the standard for stamp mounts.

- Our exclusive "Accommodation Range" of special sizes in black background provides collectors with a way to mount hard to fit items.

- Our quality mount accessories help give your collection that "Gold Medal" look. Showgard Guillotines, Organizers, and the Hawid Glue Pen give collectors wide flexibility in custom mounting your collection.

AVAILABLE AT DEALERS EVERYWHERE.
SAMPLE ON REQUEST FROM...

Vidiforms Company, Inc.
Showgard House

110 Brenner Drive, Congers, NY 10920

Yours Free – Mystic's New U.S. Stamp Catalog

A free copy of America's best U.S. stamp catalog is waiting for you. Enjoy 104 pages of color photographs, valuable collecting tips, fascinating history, and more. Collectors agree, a catalog like this is worth its weight in gold, but we'll send yours Free!

Send today for Mystic's Free 104-page catalog and also receive other stamp offers on approval.

☑ **YES!** Send me the Free Mystic U.S. Stamp Catalog for only $1.00

Name _____

Street _____

City _____

State/Zip _____

**Mystic's Free U.S. Stamp Catalog
Dept. SC392, Camden NY 13316**

Don't forget to update these Scott Albums with yearly supplements

Scott Minuteman Album
Scott National Album
Scott American Album

Published in March every year.

Giant Mint Never-Hinged
Mexico Collection

- 117 Stamps plus 17 Souvenir Sheets!
- 40 Complete Sets!
- OVER $80.00 CATALOG VALUE!

- Includes Stamps dating back to 1923!
- Beautifully Mounted!
- Early Airmail and Special Delivery issues, popular topicals, and much more!

Order No. MC
Price $49.50

We accept VISA, American Express, Discover and MasterCard or check or money order. We will include our new 52-page catalog with your order. Worldwide, U.S., and Kennedy topicals available on approval.

Wilton Stamp Company, Inc.   Dept. PXG
15 Londonderry Road #10, Londonderry, NH 03053-3386

Try Us Now! Over 50% Off!
ALL DIFFERENT! ALL COLLECTIBLE!
More than 10 Fascinating Sets from all over the World!

Only $4.95

Over $10.00 Retail Value!

YES! Rush your Postage Stamps Sets offer and giant stamp catalog. Also send me other stamps on 14-day approval. I may purchase any or none, return balance, cancel service anytime. **$4.95 enclosed.**
PLEASE CHECK YOUR APPROVAL PREFERENCE(S):
___Worldwide___U.S.___John F. Kennedy Topicals

Name _____

Address _____

City _____ State _____ Zip _____

Wilton Stamp Company, Inc. Dept. PHG
15 Londonderry Rd., #10, Londonderry, NH 03053

Collect the Scott Way...with Scott's

U.S. Trust Territories Album

- Spaces for stamps of Palau, Micronesia, and Marshall Islands including booklet panes.
- Each stamp pictured and listed by Scott number.
- Supplements issued to keep your album up-to-date.
- Chemically neutralized paper protects your stamps for generations.
- Extra spaces and blank pages allow for future expansion.

Available from your local or direct from:

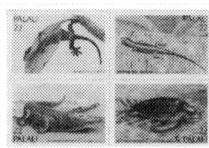

Scott Publishing Co.
P.O. Box 828, Sidney, OH 45365

U.S.A.
<u>BELOW</u>
<u>MARKET PRICES!</u>

**Used, Unused
Most Grades & Price Ranges**

Here is your opportunity to have the older
and scarcer stamps of our country at low,
reasonable prices. Issued prior to the year 1950
worth anywhere from
25¢ up to several hundred dollars each.
JUST SEND POSTAGE for complete price list.

Compare for PROOF OF LOWEST PRICES
before ordering and find out what
you have missed until you discovered us!!!

LOWELL H. DONALD CO.
P.O. Box 728, Rutland, Vermont 05702

FREE
UNITED STATES PRICE LIST

If you are a U.S. collector who likes a wide selection, competitive prices and efficient 24-hour service, you should be receiving our price list.

Our 16-page list contains a comprehensive offering of mint and used U.S. singles, mint plate blocks and strips, booklet panes, B-O-B, United Nations and a smattering of unusual items to dress up your collection.

We're ready and able to help you build the kind of collection you want!

Simply send a #10 SASE, and we'll fire off a copy of the current list in the next mail.

DALE
ENTERPRISES, INC.

P.O. Box 539-BK
Emmaus, PA 18049
Phone: 610-433-3303
FAX: 610-965-6089

AN OVERVIEW OF THE WORLD'S MOST POPULAR HOBBY

A fascinating hobby, an engrossing avocation and a universal pastime, stamp collecting is pursued by millions. Young and old, and from all walks of life, stamp collectors are involved in the indoor sport known as "the paper chase."

It was more than 150 years ago that Rowland Hill's far-reaching postal reforms became a reality and the world's first adhesive postage stamp, the Penny Black, was placed on sale at post offices in Great Britain. Not long after, a hobby was born that has continued to grow since.

Although there were only four stamp issued in England from 1840-47, the Penny Black, two types of the 2-penny blue and the 1-penny red, there were people who saved them. One story relates that a woman covered a wall in a room of her home with copies of the Penny Black.

As country after country began to issue postage stamps, the fraternity of stamp collectors flourished. Today, collectors number in the millions, while the number of stamp-issuing entities has exceeded 650.

The hobby of stamp collecting may take many forms. There are those people who collect the stamps of a single country. Others collect a single issue, such as the current U.S. Transportation coils. Others specialize in but a single stamp, with all its nuances and variations. Some collectors save one type of postage stamp, such as airmails, commemoratives or other types. Another type of collection would consist only of covers (envelopes) bearing a stamp with a postmark from the first day of that stamp's issue.

Most popular, however, is collecting by country, especially one's own country. This catalogue is designed to aid in forming just such a collection. It lists the postage stamps of the United States and is a simplified edition of information found in Volume I of the *Scott Standard Postage Stamp Catalogue.*

Catalogue Information

The number (1581) in the first column of the example below is the stamp's identifying Scott number. Each stamp issued by the United States has a unique Scott number. The letter-number combination in the second column (A984) indicates the design type and refers to the illustration with the same designation. Following in the same line are the denomination of the stamp, its color or other description along with the color of the paper (in italic type) if other than white, and the catalogue value both unused and used.

Scott Number	Illustration Design No.	Denomination	Color or Description	Color of the Stamp Paper	Unused Value	Used Value
1581	A984	1c	dark blue	*greenish*	15	15

About this edition

The Scott Catalogue values stamps on the basis of the cost of purchasing them individually. You will find packets, mixtures and collections where the unit cost of the material will be substantially less than the total catalogue value of the component stamps.

Catalogue value

Scott Catalogue value is a retail price; what you could expect to pay for a sound stamp in a grade of Fine to Very Fine. The value listed is a reference that reflects recent actual dealer selling prices.

Dealer retail price lists, public auction results, published prices in advertising and individual solicitation of retail prices from dealers, collectors and specialty organizations have been used in establishing the values found in this catalogue.

Use this catalogue as a guide in your own buying and selling. The actual price you pay for a stamp may be higher or lower than the catalogue value because of one or more of the following factors: the grade and condition of the actual stamp; the amount of personal service a dealer offers: increased interest in the country or topic represented by the stamp or set; whether an item is a "loss leader," part of a special sale, or is otherwise being sold for a short period of time at a lower price; or if at a public auction you are able to obtain an item inexpensively because of little interest in the item at that time.

Unused stamps are valued never-hinged beginning with Nos. 772, C18, E17, FA1, J88, O127, RW1 and all of Marshall Islands, Micronesia and Palau.

THE AMERICAN PHILATELIC SOCIETY

…Offers the Services You Need to Really Enjoy Stamp Collecting!

- 100-page magazine
- Sales Circuit Approvals
- Correspondence Courses
- Stamp Insurance
- Authentication Service
- Publications
- Stamp Dealer Directory
- Book Loans and Copy Service
- And Much, Much More!

PLEASE send illustrated membership brochure.

☐ for a sample magazine, enclose $1.

Name _____

Address _____

_____

**Send to: APS, Dept. TP
Box 8000, State College, PA 16803**

Grade

A stamp's grade and condition are crucial to its value. Values quoted in this catalogue are for stamps graded at Fine to Very Fine, and with no faults. Exceptions are noted in the text. The accompanying illustrations show an example of a Fine to Very Fine grade between the grades immediately below and above it: Fine and Very Fine.

FINE stamps have the design noticeably off-center on two sides. Imperforate stamps may have small margins and earlier issues may show the design touching one edge of the stamp. Used stamps may have heavier than usual cancellations.

FINE to VERY FINE stamps may be somewhat off-center on one side, or only slightly off-center on two sides. Imperforate stamps will have two margins at least normal size and the design will not touch the edge. *Early issues of a country may be printed in such a way that the design is naturally very close to the edges.* Used stamps will not have a cancellation that detracts from the design. This is the grade used to establish Scott Catalogue values.

VERY FINE stamps may be slightly off-center on one side, with the design well clear of the edge. Imperforate stamps will have three margins at least normal size. Used stamps will have light or otherwise neat cancellations.

It should be noted that many imperforate stamps are priced as pairs only, since it is an easy matter to trim perforations from a normal stamp.

FINE

Scott Catalogues value stamps in **FINE-VERY FINE** condition.

VERY FINE

Condition

The definitions given with the illustrations describe *grade,* which is centering and, for used stamps, cancellation. *Condition* refers to the soundness of the stamp; that is, faults, repairs and other factors influencing price.

Copies of a stamp that are of a lesser grade or condition trade at lower prices. Those of exceptional quality often command higher than catalogue prices.

Factors that can increase the value of a stamp include exceptionally wide margins, particularly fresh color and, in the case of older stamps, the presence of selvage (sheet margin).

Factors other than faults that decrease the value of a stamp include loss of gum or regumming, hinge remnants, foreign objects adhering to gum, natural inclusions, or straight edges.

Faults include a missing piece, tear, clipped perforation, pin or other hole, surface scuff, thin spot, crease, toning, oxidation or other form of color changeling, short or pulled perforation, stains or such man-made changes as reperforation or the chemical removal or lightening of a cancellation.

Scott Publishing Co. recognizes that there is no formal, enforced grading scheme for postage stamps, and that the final price you pay for a stamp or obtain for a stamp you are selling will be determined by individual agreement at the time of the transaction.

Forming a collection

Methods of collecting stamps are many and varied. A person may begin by attempting to gather a single specimen of every face-different stamp issued by a country. An extension of that approach is to include the different types of each stamp, such as perforation varieties, watermark varieties, different printings and color changes. The stamps may be collected on cover (envelope) complete with postal markings, thus showing postal rates, types of cancellations and other postal information.

Collections also may be limited to types of stamps. The stamps issued by most countries are divided into such categories as regular postage (made up of definitives and commemoratives), airmail stamps, special delivery stamps, postage due stamps and others. Any of those groups may provide the basis for a good collection.

Definitive stamps are those regular issues used on most mail sent out on a daily basis. they are normally issued in extended sets, sometimes over a period of years. The sets feature a rising series of face values that allows a mailer to meet any current postal rate. Definitive stamps may be printed in huge quantities and are often kept in service by the Postal Service for long periods of time.

Commemorative stamps meet another need. They are primarily issued to celebrate an important event, honor a famous person or promote a special project or cause. Such stamps are issued on a limited basis for a limited time. They are usually more colorful and are often of a larger size than definitives, making them of special interest to collectors.

Although few airmail stamps are currently issued by the United States, they continue to remain very popular among collectors. Just as with regular issues, airmail stamps are subject to several types of collecting. In addition to amassing the actual stamps, airmail enthusiasts pursue first-flight covers, airport dedication covers and even crash covers.

Not as popular, but still collected as units, are special delivery and postage due stamps. Special delivery stamps ensured speedier delivery of a letter once it reached its destination post office through normal postal means. Postage due stamps were used when a letter or parcel did not carry enough postage to pay for its delivery, subjecting the recipient to a fee to make up the difference. The United States no longer issues postage due stamps.

The resurgence in 1983 of Official Mail stamps-those used only by departments and office of the federal government-has also brought about a resurgence of interest in them by stamp collectors. Originally issued between 1873 and 1911, Official Mail stamps were obsolete until recently. To be legally used, they must be on cards, envelopes or parcels that bear the return address of a federal office or facility.

"Topical" collecting is becoming more and more popular. Here the paramount attraction to the collector is the subject depicted on the stamp. The topics or themes from which to choose are virtually unlimited, other than by your own imagination. Animals, flowers, music, ships, birds and famous people on stamps make interesting collections. The degree of specializations is limitless, leading to such topics as graduates of a specific college or university, types of aircraft or the work of a specific artist.

There are several ways to obtain topical information, one of which is through the "By Topic" section of the *Scott Stamp Monthly.* "By Topic" is a regular feature of the magazine that divides the stamps of the world into more than 100 topical areas.

The album

To be displayed at their best, stamps should be properly housed. A quality album not only achieves this, but gives protection from dirt, loss and damage. When choosing an album, consider these three points: Is it within your means, does it meet your special interests and is it the best you can afford?

The Scott *Pony Express* and *Minuteman* albums are ideal companions to this Catalogue. Scott also publishes the National Album series for United States stamps, for a more complete collection.

Looseleaf albums are recommended for all collectors beyond the novice level. Not only do looseleaf albums allow for expansion of a collection, but the pages may be removed for mounting stamps as well as for display. A special advantage of a loose-leaf album is that in many cases it may be kept current with supplements published annually on matching pages. All Scott albums noted are looseleaf and are supplemented annually.

Mounts and hinges

Mounts and hinges specially manufactured for collectors are used to affix stamps to album pages. Most stamp mounts are pre-gummed, clear plastic containers that hold a stamp safely and may be affixed to an album page with minimum effort. They are available in sizes to fit any stamp, block or even complete envelopes. Mounts are particularly important with unused stamps when there is a desire to not disturb the gum.

Although the mount is important, so is the venerable hinge. Innumerable stamps have been ruined beyond redemption by being glued to an album page. Hinges are inexpensive and effective. Use only peelable hinges. These may be removed from a stamp or album page without leaving an unsightly mark or causing damage to either.

Hinges are perfect for less-expensive stamps, used stamps and stamps that previously have been hinged. The use of stamp hinges is simple. Merely fold back, adhesive side out, about a quarter of the hinge (if it is not pre-folded). Lightly moisten the shorter side and affix it near the top of the back of the stamp. Then, holding the stamp with a pair of tongs, moisten the longer side of the hinge and place it (with stamp attached) in its proper place on the album page.

Stamp tongs

As previously noted, stamp tongs are a simple but important accessory and should always be used when handling a stamp. Fingers can easily damage or soil a stamp. Tongs cost little and will quickly pay for themselves. They come in a variety of styles. Beginners should start with tongs having a blunt or rounded tip. those with sharp ends may inadvertently cause damage to a stamp. With just a little practice you will find tongs easier to work with than using your fingers...and your stamps will be better for it.

Magnifying glass

A good magnifying glass for scrutinizing stamps in detail is another useful philatelic tool. It allows you to see variations in stamps that may otherwise be invisible to the naked eye. Also, a magnifying glass makes minute parts of a stamp design large enough to see well. Your first glass should be a least 5- to 10-power magnification, with edge-to-edge clarity. Stronger magnifications are available and may also be useful.

Perforation gauge and watermark detector

Although many stamps appear to be alike, they are not. Even though the design may be the same and the color identical, there are at least two other areas where differences occur, and where specialized devices are needed for such identification. These are perforation measurement and watermark detection. A ruler that measures in millimeters is also useful.

The perforation gauge, printed on plastic, cardboard or metal, contains a graded scale that enables you to measure the number of perforation "teeth" in two centimeters. To determine the perforation measurement, place the stamp on the gauge and move the former along the scale until the points on one entry of the scale align perfectly with the teeth of the stamp's perforations. A stamp may have different perforations horizontally and vertically.

Watermarks are a bit more difficult to detect. They are letters or designs impressed into the paper at the time of manufacture. A watermark may occasionally be seen by holding a stamp up to the light, but a watermark detector is often necessary. the simplest of the many types of detectors available consists of a small black tray (glass or hard plastic). The stamp is place face down in the tray and watermark detection fluid is poured over it. If there is a watermark, or a part of one, it should become visible when the stamp becomes soaked with the fluid.

There are a number of other liquids that over the years have been recommended for use to detect watermarks. The currently available fluids made specifically for that purpose are the safest-to the stamp and the collector. We do not recommend anything other than such watermark detection fluids for that use.

Benjamin
Franklin
A1
A3

George
Washington
A2
A4

Reproductions (found in Special Printings section). The letters R. W. H. & E. at the bottom of each stamp are less distinct on the reproductions than on the originals.

5c. On the originals the left side of the white shift frill touches the oval on a level with the top of the "F" of "Five." On the reproductions it touches the oval about on a level with the top of the figure "5."

10c. On the reproductions, line of coat at left points to right tip of "X" and line of coat at right points to center of "S" of CENTS. On the originals, line of coat points to "T" of TEN and between "T" and "S" of CENTS. On the reproductions the eyes have a sleepy look, the line of the mouth is straighter, and in the curl of hair near the left cheek is a strong black dot, while the originals have only a faint one.

Franklin
A5

A5

ONE CENT.

Type I. Has complete curved lines outside the labels with "U.S. Postage" and "One Cent." The scrolls below the lower label are turned under, forming little balls. The ornaments at top are substantially complete.

Type Ib. Same as I but balls below the bottom label are not so clear. The plume-like scrolls at bottom are not complete.

A6

Type Ia. Same as I at bottom but top ornaments and outer line at top are partly cut away.

A7

Type II. The little balls of the bottom scrolls and the bottoms of the lower plume ornaments are missing. The side ornaments are complete.

A8

Type III. The top and bottom curved lines outside the labels are broken in the middle. The side ornaments are complete.

Type IIIa. Similar to type III with the outer line broken at top or bottom but not both.

A9

Type IV. Similar to type II, but with the curved lines outside the labels recut at top or bottom or both.

Prices for types I and III are for stamps showing the marked characteristics plainly. Copies of type I showing the balls indistinctly and of type III with the lines only slightly broken, sell for much lower prices.

UNITED STATES

Scott No.	Illus. No.		Description	Unused Value	Used Value	//////
1847, Imperf.						
1	A1	5c	red brown, *bluish*	4,500.	425.00	
a.		5c	dark brown, *bluish*	4,500.	450.00	
b.		5c	orange brown, *bluish*.......	5,000.	525.00	
c.		5c	red orange, *bluish*............	10,000.	4,000.	
d.			Double impression		—	
2	A2	10c	black, *bluish*	20,000.	900.00	
a.			Diagonal half used as 5c on cover.......................		10,000.	
b.			Vert. half used as 5c on cover		35,000.	
c.			Horiz. half used as 5c on cover		—	
1875, Reproductions, Bluish Paper Without Gum, Imperf.						
3	A3	5c	red brown	700.00		
4	A4	10c	black	900.00		
1851-57, Imperf.						
5	A5	1c	blue, type I......................	200,000.	17,500.	
5A	A5	1c	blue, type Ib....................	8,500.	3,500.	
6	A6	1c	blue, type Ia....................	22,500.	6,000.	
b.			Type Ic	5,000.	1,200.	
7	A7	1c	blue, type II	575.00	110.00	
8	A8	1c	blue, type III	6,500.	1,500.	
8A	A8	1c	blue, type IIIa	2,500.	600.00	
9	A9	1c	blue, IV	425.00	90.00	
a.			Printed on both sides, reverse inverted............		—	
10	A10	3c	orange brown, type I	1,600.	40.00	
a.			Printed on both sides.......		—	

Washington
A10

Thomas Jefferson
A11

A13

Type II. The design is complete at the top. The outer line at the bottom is broken in the middle. The shells are partly cut away.

A10

THREE CENTS.

Type I. There is an outer frame line at top and bottom.

A14

Type III. The outer lines are broken above the top label and the "X" numerals. The outer line at the bottom and the shells are partly cut away, as in Type II.

A11

FIVE CENTS.

Type I. There are projections on all four sides.

A12

A15

Type IV. The outer lines have been recut at top or bottom or both.

Types I, II, III and IV have complete ornaments at the sides of the stamps and three pearls at each outer edge of the bottom panel.

A12

TEN CENTS.

Type I. The "shells" at the lower corners are practically complete. The outer line below the label is very nearly complete. The outer lines are broken above the middle of the top label and the "X" in each upper corner.

A16

Franklin
A20

ONE CENT.

Type V. Similar to type III of 1851-56 but with side ornaments partly cut away.

A21

THREE CENTS.

Type II. The outer frame line has been removed at top and bottom. The side frame lines were recut so as to be continuous from the top to the bottom of the plate.

Type IIa. The side frame lines extend only to the top and bottom of the stamp design.

A22

A22

FIVE CENTS.

Type II. The projections at top and bottom are partly cut away.

A23
(Two typical examples).

TEN CENTS.

Type V. The side ornaments are slightly cut away. Usually only one pearl remains at each end of the lower label but some copies show two or three pearls at the right side. At the bottom the outer line is complete and the shells nearly so. The outer lines at top are complete except over the right "X".

A17   **A18**

A19

TWELVE CENTS.

Plate I. Outer frame lines complete.
Plate III. Outer frame lines noticeably uneven or broken, sometimes partly missing.

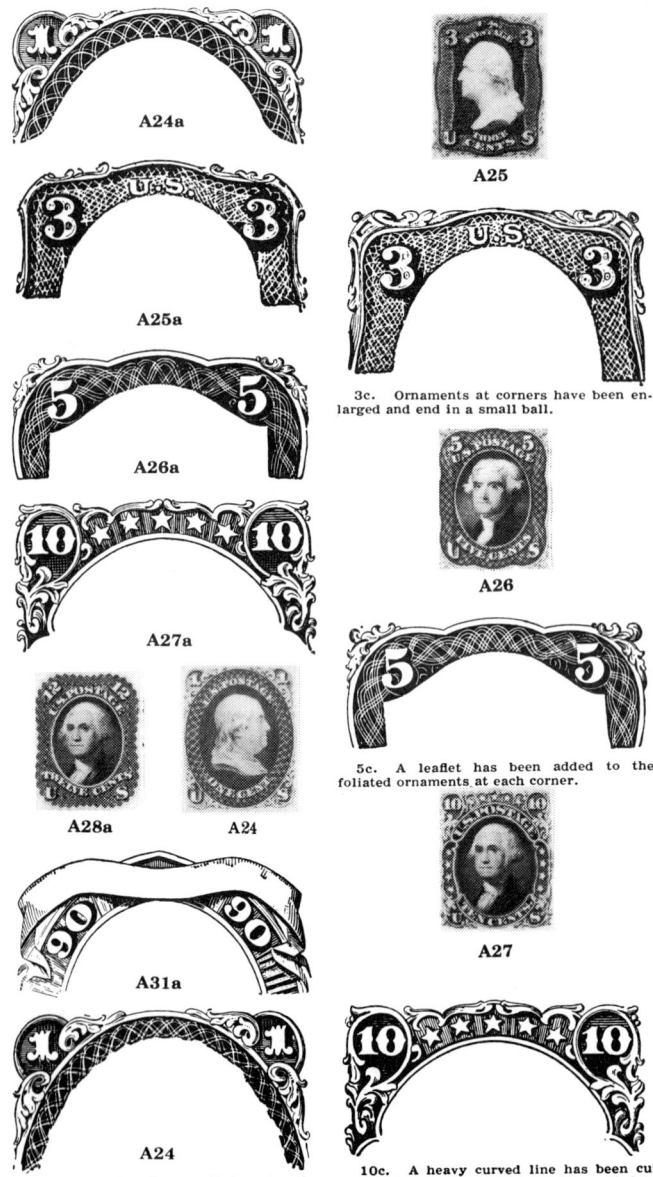

3c. Ornaments at corners have been enlarged and end in a small ball.

5c. A leaflet has been added to the foliated ornaments at each corner.

1c. A dash has been added under the tip of the ornament at right of the numeral in upper left corner.

10c. A heavy curved line has been cut below the stars and an outer line added to the ornaments above them.

Scott No.	Illus. No.	Description	Unused Value	Used Value	//////
11	A10	3c dull red, type I	130.00	7.00	
c.		Vert. half used as 1c on cover		5,000.	
d.		Diagonal half used as 1c on cover		5,000.	
e.		Double impression	5,000.	—	
12	A11	5c red brown, type I	11,000.	875.00	
13	A12	10c green, type I	9,000.	575.00	
14	A13	10c green, type II	2,100.	190.00	
15	A14	10c green, type III	2,100.	190.00	
16	A15	10c green, type IV	12,500.	1,100.	
17	A16	12c black	2,600.	225.00	
a.		Diagonal half used as 6c on cover		2,000.	
b.		Vert. half used as 6c on cover		8,500.	
c.		Printed on both sides		10,000.	

1857-61, Perf. 15½

Scott No.	Illus. No.	Description	Unused Value	Used Value	//////
18	A5	1c blue, type I	800.00	325.00	
19	A6	1c blue, type Ia	11,500.	3,250.	
b.		Type Ic	1,500.	800.00	
20	A7	1c blue, type II	450.00	150.00	
21	A8	1c blue, type III	5,000.	1,250.	
22	A8	1c blue, type IIIa	800.00	275.00	
b.		Horiz. pair, imperf. btwn.		5,000.	
23	A9	1c blue, type IV	2,750.	325.00	
24	A20	1c blue, type V	120.00	25.00	
b.		Laid paper		—	
25	A10	3c rose, type I	1,000.	30.00	
b.		Vert. pair, imperf. horiz.		6,750.	
26	A21	3c dull red, type II	40.00	3.00	
a.		3c dull red, type IIa	110.00	20.00	
b.		Horiz. pair, imperf. vert., type II	4,000.	—	
c.		Vert. pair, imperf. horiz., type II		—	
d.		Horiz. pair, imperf. between, type II		—	
e.		Double impression, type II		2,500.	
27	A11	5c brick red, type I	9,000.	600.00	
28	A11	5c red brown, type I	1,350.	250.00	
b.		bright red brown	1,850.	400.00	
28A	A11	5c Indian red, type I	12,000.	1,750.	
29	A11	5c brown, type I	950.00	200.00	
30	A22	5c orange brown, type II	800.00	1,000.	
30A	A22	5c brown, type II	525.00	185.00	
b.		Printed on both sides	3,750.	4,500.	
31	A12	10c green, type I	8,000.	500.00	

Scott No.	Illus. No.		Description	Unused Value	Used Value	/ / / / / /
32	A13	10c	green, type II	2,800.	165.00	
33	A14	10c	green, type III	2,800.	165.00	
34	A15	10c	green, type IV	*17,500.*	*1,400.*	
35	A23	10c	green, type V	200.00	50.00	
36	A16	12c	black, plate 1	400.00	95.00	
a.			Diagonal half used as 6c on cover (I)		17,500.	
b.		12c	black, plate 3	350.00	100.00	
c.			Horiz. pair, imperf. between (I)		12,500.	
37	A17	24c	gray lilac	675.00	200.00	
a.		24c	gray	675.00	200.00	
38	A18	30c	orange	850.00	300.00	
39	A19	90c	blue	1,150.	*5,000.*	

1875, Reprints, Without Gum, Perf. 12

40	A5	1c	bright blue	*500.00*		
41	A10	3c	scarlet	*2,000.*		
42	A22	5c	orange brown	*900.00*		
43	A12	10c	blue green	*1,750.*		
44	A16	12c	greenish black	*2,000.*		
45	A17	24c	black violet	*2,000.*		
46	A18	30c	yellow orange	*2,000.*		
47	A19	90c	deep blue	*3,250.*		

1861

62B	A27a	10c	dark green	*5,000.*	450.00	

1861-62

63	A24	1c	blue	140.00	15.00	
a.		1c	ultramarine	350.00	100.00	
b.		1c	dark blue	350.00	25.00	
c.			Laid paper	—	—	
d.			Vert. pair, imperf. horiz.		—	
e.			Printed on both sides	—	*2,500.*	
64	A25	3c	pink	4,500.	450.00	
a.		3c	pigeon blood pink	*10,000.*	*2,500.*	
b.		3c	rose pink	300.00	90.00	
65	A25	3c	rose	90.00	1.00	
b.			Laid paper	—	—	
d.			Vert. pair, imperf. horiz.	*3,500.*	750.00	
e.			Printed on both sides	*1,650.*	*1,000.*	
f.			Double impression		*6,000.*	
67	A26	5c	buff	*6,000.*	425.00	
a.		5c	brown yellow	*6,000.*	425.00	
b.		5c	olive yellow	*6,000.*	425.00	
68	A27	10c	yellow green	275.00	30.00	
a.		10c	dark green	290.00	31.00	
b.			Vert. pair, imperf. horiz.		*3,500.*	

Scott No.	Illus. No.	Description	Unused Value	Used Value	/ / / / / /
69	A28	12c black	550.00	55.00	
70	A29	24c red lilac............................	800.00	80.00	
a.		24c brown lilac........................	600.00	67.50	
b.		24c steel blue..........................	5,000.	300.00	
c.		24c violet, thin paper	6,500.	550.00	
d.		24c pale gray violet, thin paper	1,400.	350.00	
71	A30	30c orange...............................	625.00	70.00	
a.		Printed on both sides.......	—		
72	A31	90c blue..................................	1,450.	250.00	
a.		90c pale blue...........................	1,450.	250.00	
b.		90c dark blue..........................	1,600.	275.00	

1861-66

Scott No.	Illus. No.	Description	Unused Value	Used Value	
73	A32	2c black	175.00	22.50	
a.		Half used as 1c as part of 3c rate on cover, diagonal, vert. or horiz................		1,250.	
b.		Diagonal half used alone as 1c on cover...................	3,000.		
d.		Laid paper.........................	—	—	
e.		Printed on both sides.......		5,000.	
75	A26	5c red brown	2,000.	250.00	
76	A26	5c brown................................	500.00	70.00	
a.		5c dark brown	550.00	80.00	
b.		Laid paper.........................		—	
77	A33	15c black	650.00	70.00	
78	A29	24c lilac	400.00	50.00	
a.		24c grayish lilac	400.00	50.00	
b.		24c gray...................................	400.00	50.00	
c.		24c black violet.......................	17,500.	1,100.	
d.		Printed on both sides.......		3,500.	

1867, Perf. 12, Grill with points up
A. Grill covering the entire stamp

79	A25	3c rose	2,000.	550.00	
b.		Printed on both sides.......		—	
80	A26	5c brown................................	—	—	
a.		5c dark brown	—	—	
81	A30	30c orange...............................	—	—	

B. Grill about 18x15mm (22 by 18 points)

82	A25	3c rose		100,000.	

Grill with points down
C. Grill about 13x16mm (16 to 17 by 18 to 21 points)

83	A25	3c rose	3,000.	475.00	

A28

12c. Ovals and scrolls have been added to the corners.

A34   **A35**

A29   **A30**

A36   **A37**

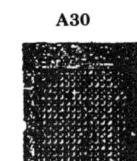

A31   Grill

A38   **A39**

A40   **A41**

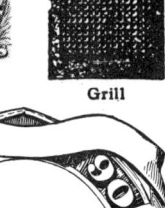

A31

90c. Parallel lines form an angle above the ribbon with "U. S. Postage"; between these lines a row of dashes has been added and a point of color to the apex of the lower pair.

A42   **A43**

A40

FIFTEEN CENTS. Type I. Picture unframed.

A40a

Type II. Picture framed.
Type III. Same as type I but without fringe of brown shading lines around central vignette.

A32   **A33**

Scott No.	Illus. No.	Description	Unused Value	Used Value	//////

D. Grill about 12x14mm (15 by 17 to 18 points)
84	A32	2c black	9,000.	1,450.	
85	A25	3c rose	3,000.	450.00	

Z. Grill about 11x14mm (13 to 14 by 17 to 18 points)
85A	A24	1c blue		—	
85B	A32	2c black	3,000.	400.00	
85C	A25	3c rose	5,000.	1,100.	
85D	A27	10c green		*45,000.*	
85E	A28	12c black	2,500.	575.00	
85F	A33	15c black		*100,000.*	

E. Grill about 11x13mm (14 by 15 to 17 points)
86	A24	1c blue	1,000.	275.00	
a.		1c dull blue	1,000.	275.00	
87	A32	2c black	450.00	70.00	
a.		Half used as 1c on cover, diagonal or vert.		*2,000.*	
88	A25	3c rose	350.00	10.00	
a.		3c lake red	400.00	12.50	
89	A27	10c green	2,000.	175.00	
90	A28	12c black	2,250.	200.00	
91	A33	15c black	5,000.	450.00	

F. Grill about 9x13mm (11 to 12 by 15 to 17 points)
92	A24	1c blue	450.00	100.00	
a.		1c pale blue	450.00	100.00	
93	A32	2c black	175.00	25.00	
a.		Half used as 1c as part of 3c rate on cover, diagonal or vert.		*1,250.*	
c.		Horiz. or diagonal half used alone as 1c on cover		*2,500.*	
94	A25	3c red	125.00	2.50	
a.		3c rose	125.00	2.50	
c.		Vert. pair, imperf. horiz.	*1,000.*		
d.		Printed on both sides	*1,100.*		
95	A26	5c brown	1,500.	275.00	
a.		5c dark brown	1,600.	270.00	
96	A27	10c yellow green	1,200.	110.00	
a.		10c dark green	1,200.	110.00	
97	A28	12c black	1,500.	125.00	
98	A33	15c black	1,500.	175.00	
99	A29	24c gray lilac	2,000.	425.00	
100	A30	30c orange	2,750.	400.00	
101	A31	90c blue	5,000.	800.00	

1875, Reprints, Without Gum, Perf. 12
102	A24	1c blue	*500.00*	*800.00*	

A44 A45 A48 A49

A44 A48

A45 A49

A46 A50

A46 A51

A47 A50

A47 A51

Scott No.	Illus. No.	Description	Unused Value	Used Value	/ / / / / /
103	A32	2c black	2,250.	4,000.	
104	A25	3c brown red	2,500.	4,250.	
105	A26	5c brown	1,850.	2,250.	
106	A27	10c green	2,000.	3,750.	
107	A28	12c black	2,750.	4,500.	
108	A33	15c black	2,750.	4,750.	
109	A29	24c deep violet	3,750.	6,000.	
110	A30	30c brownish orange	4,250.	6,000.	
111	A31	90c blue	5,250.	20,000.	

1869, Perf. 12
G. Grill measuring 9½x9mm

Scott No.	Illus. No.	Description	Unused Value	Used Value	
112	A34	1c buff	275.00	65.00	
b.		Without grill	750.00		
113	A35	2c brown	200.00	25.00	
b.		Without grill	600.00		
c.		Half used as 1c on cover, diagonal, vert. or horiz.		3,000.	
d.		Printed on both sides		—	
114	A36	3c ultramarine	175.00	7.00	
a.		Without grill	600.00	—	
b.		Vert. one third used as 1c on cover		—	
c.		Vert. two thirds used as 2c on cover		—	
d.		Double impression		3,500.	
115	A37	6c ultramarine	900.00	95.00	
b.		Vert. half used as 3c on cover		—	
116	A38	10c yellow	1,000.	85.00	
117	A39	12c green	950.00	95.00	
118	A40	15c brown & blue, Type I	2,400.	325.00	
a.		Without grill	4,000.		
119	A40a	15c brown & blue, type II	1,000.	150.00	
b.		Center inverted	220,000.	14,000.	
c.		Center double, one inverted	—	—	
120	A41	24c green & violet	4,000.	500.00	
a.		Without grill	6,500.		
b.		Center inverted	220,000.	15,000.	
121	A42	30c blue & carmine	2,400.	250.00	
a.		Without grill	3,750.		
b.		Flags inverted	165,000.	55,000.	
122	A43	90c carmine & black	5,000.	1,150.	
a.		Without grill	8,500.		

1875, Re-issues, Without Gum, Hard White Paper

Scott No.	Illus. No.	Description	Unused Value	Used Value	
123	A34	1c buff	325.00	225.00	
124	A35	2c brown	375.00	325.00	

A52

A46a

3c. The under part of the upper tail of the left ribbon is heavily shaded.

A53

A47a

6c. The first four vertical lines of the shading in the lower part of the left ribbon have been strengthened.

A54

A48a

7c. Two small semi-circles are drawn around the ends of the lines which outline the ball in the lower right hand corner.

A44a

1c. In pearl at left of numeral "1" is a small crescent.

A45a

2c. Under the scroll at the left of "U. S." there is a small diagonal line. This mark seldom shows clearly. The stamp, No. 157, can be distinguished by its color.

A49a

10c. There is a small semi-circle in the scroll at the right end of the upper label.

Scott No.	Illus. No.	Description	Unused Value	Used Value
125	A36	3c blue	3,000.	*10,000.*
126	A37	6c blue	850.00	550.00
127	A38	10c yellow	1,400.	1,200.
128	A39	12c green	1,500.	1,200.
129	A40	15c brown & blue, type III	1,300.	750.00
a.		Imperf. horiz., single	1,600.	—
130	A41	24c green & violet	1,250.	850.00
131	A42	30c blue & carmine	1,750.	1,500.
132	A43	90c carmine & black	4,000.	*4,250.*

1880, Soft Porous Paper
133	A34	1c buff	200.00	175.00
a.		1c brown orange	175.00	150.00

1870-71, Perf. 12, With Grill
134	A44	1c ultramarine	900.00	60.00
135	A45	2c red brown	525.00	37.50
a.		Diagonal half used as 1c on cover		—
136	A46	3c green	400.00	10.00
137	A47	6c carmine	2,100.	300.00
138	A48	7c vermilion	1,500.	275.00
139	A49	10c brown	1,800.	450.00
140	A50	12c dull violet	*13,000.*	2,000.
141	A51	15c orange	2,750.	750.00
142	A52	24c purple	—	*11,500.*
143	A53	30c black	5,750.	950.00
144	A54	90c carmine	7,500.	850.00

1870-71, Perf. 12, Without grill
145	A44	1c ultramarine	225.00	7.50
146	A45	2c red brown	140.00	5.00
a.		Half used as 1c on cover, diagonal or vert.		—
c.		Double impression	—	
147	A46	3c green	170.00	50
a.		Printed on both sides		*1,500.*
b.		Double impression		*1,000.*
148	A47	6c carmine	325.00	12.00
a.		Vert. half used as 3c on cover		—
b.		Double impression		*1,250.*
149	A48	7c vermilion	425.00	55.00
150	A49	10c brown	325.00	12.00
151	A50	12c dull violet	750.00	80.00
152	A51	15c bright orange	725.00	85.00
a.		Double impression		—
153	A52	24c purple	775.00	85.00
154	A53	30c black	1,500.	100.00
155	A54	90c carmine	1,700.	185.00

A50a

12c. The balls of the figure "2" are crescent shaped.

A51a

15c. In the lower part of the triangle in the upper left corner two lines have been made heavier forming a "V". This mark can be found on some of the Continental and American (1879) printings, but not all stamps show it.

Secret marks were added to the dies of the 24c, 30c and 90c but new plates were not made from them. The various printings of these stamps can be distinguished only by the shades and paper.

A55 **A56**

A44b

1c. The vertical lines in the upper part of the stamp have been so deepened that the background often appears to be solid. Lines of shading have been added to the upper arabesques.

A46b

3c. The shading at the sides of the central oval appears only about one-half the previous width. A short horizontal dash has been cut about 1mm. below the "TS" of "CENTS."

A47b

6c. On the original stamps four vertical lines can be counted from the edge of the panel to the outside of the stamp. On the re-engraved stamps there are but three lines in the same place.

A49b

10c. On the original stamps there are five vertical lines between the left side of the oval and the edge of the shield. There are only four lines on the re-engraved stamps. In the lower part of the latter, also, the horizontal lines of the background have been strengthened.

Scott No.	Illus. No.	Description	Unused Value	Used Value	//////
1873, Perf. 12					
156	A44a	1c ultramarine..................	120.00	1.75	
e.		With grill.....................	1,400.		
f.		Imperf., pair..................	—	500.00	
157	A45a	2c brown........................	250.00	10.00	
c.		With grill.....................	1,100.	600.00	
d.		Double impression...........	—	—	
e.		Vert. half used as 1c on cover		—	
158	A46a	3c green........................	75.00	15	
e.		With grill.....................	175.00		
h.		Horiz. pair, imperf. vert. .		—	
i.		Horiz. pair, imperf. btwn.		1,300.	
j.		Double impression...........		1,250.	
k.		Printed on both sides.......		—	
159	A47a	6c dull pink.....................	275.00	10.00	
b.		With grill.....................	1,000.		
160	A48a	7c orange vermilion............	600.00	57.50	
a.		With grill.....................	1,500.		
161	A49a	10c brown.......................	335.00	11.50	
c.		With grill.....................	2,000.		
d.		Horiz. pair, imperf. btwn.		2,500.	
162	A50a	12c black violet.................	900.00	67.50	
a.		With grill.....................	3,000.		
163	A51a	15c yellow orange..............	800.00	62.50	
a.		With grill.....................	3,000.		
164	A52	24c purple......................		—	
165	A53	30c gray black..................	925.00	65.00	
c.		With grill.....................	3,000.		
166	A54	90c rose carmine...............	1,800.	185.00	
1875, Re-issues, Without Gum, Hard White Paper, Perf. 12					
167	A44a	1c ultra...........................	7,500.		
168	A45a	2c dark brown................	3,500.		
169	A46a	3c blue green..................	9,500.		
170	A47a	6c dull rose.....................	8,500.	—	
171	A48a	7c reddish vermilion.........	2,250.		
172	A49a	10c pale brown.................	8,250.		
173	A50a	12c dark violet..................	3,000.		
174	A51a	15c bright orange..............	8,250.		
175	A52	24c dull purple..................	1,850.		
176	A53	30c greenish black.............	6,000.		
177	A54	90c violet carmine.............	7,500.		
Yellowish Wove Paper, Perf. 12					
178	A45a	2c vermilion....................	210.00	5.00	
b.		Half used as 1c on cover.		—	
c.		With grill.....................	300.00		
179	A55	5c blue..........................	260.00	9.00	
c.		With grill.....................	600.00		

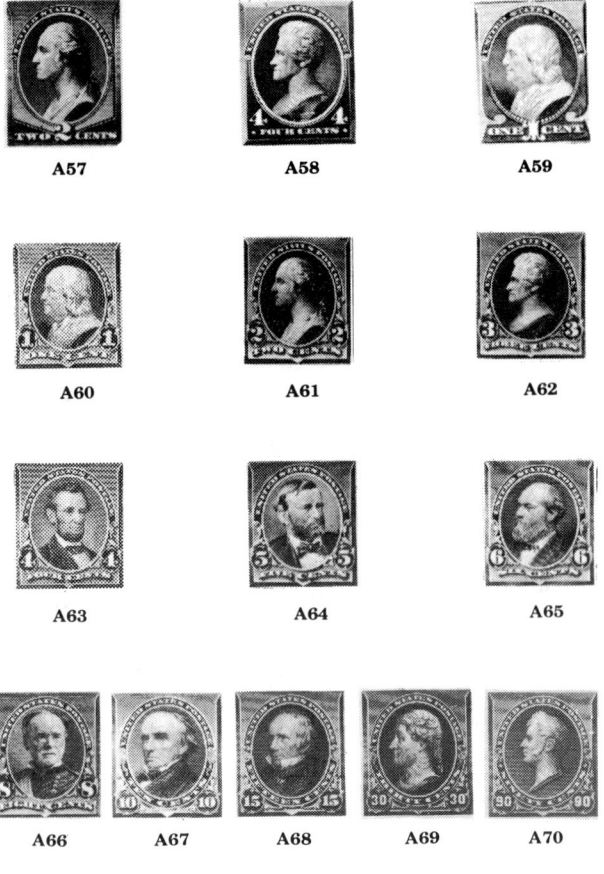

HOW TO USE THIS BOOK

The number in the first column is its Scott number or identifying number. The letter and number that come next (A41) indicate the design and refer to the illustration so designated. Following that is the denomination of the stamp and its color. Finally, the value, unused and used is shown.

Scott No.	Illus. No.		Description	Unused Value	Used Value	/ / / / / /
Re-issues, Without Gum, Hard White Paper, Perf. 12						
180	A45a	2c	carmine vermilion	*17,500.*		
181	A55	2c	bright blue	*27,500.*		
1879, Perf. 12, Soft Paper						
182	A44a	1c	dark ultra	175.00	1.25	
183	A45a	2c	vermilion	80.00	1.25	
a.			Double impression	—	500.00	
184	A46a	3c	green	60.00	15	
b.			Double impression		—	
185	A55	5c	blue	325.00	8.00	
186	A47a	6c	pink	600.00	13.00	
187	A49	10c	brown (without secret mark)	975.00	15.00	
188	A49a	10c	brown (with secret mark)	700.00	16.00	
189	A51a	15c	red orange	225.00	15.00	
190	A53	30c	full black	625.00	35.00	
191	A54	90c	carmine	1,300.	155.00	
1880, Special Printing, Without Gum, Soft Porous Paper, Perf. 12						
192	A44a	1c	dark ultra	*10,000.*		
193	A45a	2c	black brown	*6,000.*		
194	A46a	3c	blue green	*15,000.*		
195	A47a	6c	dull rose	*11,000.*		
196	A48a	7c	scarlet vermilion	*2,250.*		
197	A49a	10c	deep brown	*10,000.*		
198	A50a	12c	black purple	*3,500.*		
199	A51a	15c	orange	*11,000.*		
200	A52	24c	dark violet	*3,500.*		
201	A53	30c	greenish black	*8,500.*		
202	A54	90c	dull carmine	*9,000.*		
203	A45a	30c	scarlet vermilion	*18,000.*		
204	A55	90c	deep blue	*30,000.*		
1882, Perf. 12						
205	A56	5c	yellow brown	135.00	4.50	
Special Printing, Soft Porous Paper, Without Gum						
205C	A56	5c	gray brown	*20,000.*		
1881-82, Perf. 12						
206	A44b	1c	gray blue	40.00	40	
207	A46b	3c	blue green	45.00	15	
c.			Double impression		—	
208	A47b	6c	rose	250.00	45.00	
a.		6c	brown red	225.00	55.00	
209	A49b	10c	brown	90.00	2.50	
b.		10c	black brown	140.00	10.00	
c.			Double impression		—	

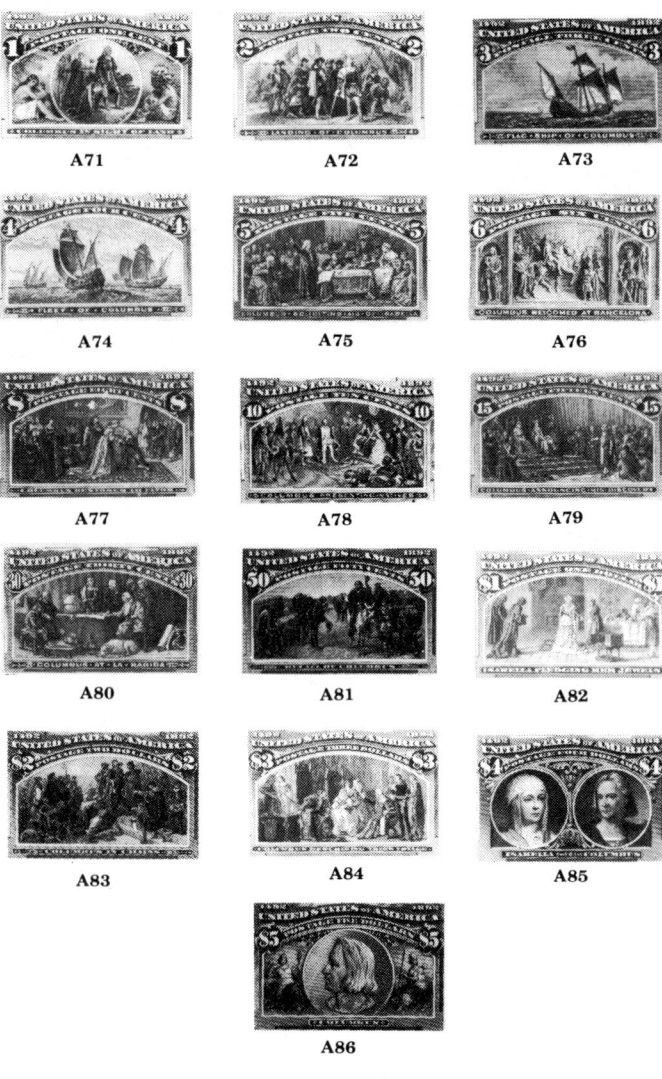

TWO CENTS.

Type I. The horizontal lines of the ground work run across the triangle and are of the same thickness within it as without.

Type II. The horizontal lines cross the triangle but are thinner within it than without.

Type III. The horizontal lines do not cross the double frame lines of the triangle. The lines within the triangle are thin, as in type II.

Scott No.	Illus. No.	Description	Unused Value	Used Value	/ / / / / /
1883, Perf. 12					
210	A57	2c red brown	37.50	15	☐☐☐☐☐
211	A58	4c blue green	160.00	8.00	☐☐☐☐☐

Special Printing, Soft Porous Paper, Without Gum

211B	A57	2c pale red brown	*600.00*	—	☐☐☐☐☐
c.		Horiz. pair, imperf. btwn.	*2,000.*	—	☐☐☐☐☐
211D	A58	4c deep blue green	*15,000.*		☐☐☐☐☐

1887, Perf. 12					
212	A59	1c ultramarine	65.00	65	☐☐☐☐☐
213	A57	2c green	25.00	15	☐☐☐☐☐
b.		Printed on both sides		—	☐☐☐☐☐
214	A46b	3c vermilion	50.00	37.50	☐☐☐☐☐
1888, Perf. 12					
215	A58	4c carmine	160.00	11.00	☐☐☐☐☐
216	A56	5c indigo	160.00	6.50	☐☐☐☐☐
217	A53	30c orange brown	360.00	75.00	☐☐☐☐☐
218	A54	90c purple	850.00	130.00	☐☐☐☐☐
1890-93, Perf. 12					
219	A60	1c dull blue	18.50	15	☐☐☐☐☐
219D	A61	2c lake	150.00	45	☐☐☐☐☐
220	A61	2c carmine	15.00	15	☐☐☐☐☐
a.		Cap on left "2"	35.00	1.00	☐☐☐☐☐
c.		Cap on both "2s"	125.00	8.00	☐☐☐☐☐
221	A62	3c purple	50.00	4.50	☐☐☐☐☐
222	A63	4c dark brown	50.00	1.50	☐☐☐☐☐
223	A64	5c chocolate	50.00	1.50	☐☐☐☐☐
224	A65	6c brown red	55.00	15.00	☐☐☐☐☐
225	A66	8c lilac	40.00	8.50	☐☐☐☐☐
226	A67	10c green	95.00	1.75	☐☐☐☐☐
227	A68	15c indigo	150.00	15.00	☐☐☐☐☐
228	A69	30c black	225.00	20.00	☐☐☐☐☐
229	A70	90c orange	350.00	95.00	☐☐☐☐☐
1893, Perf. 12					
230	A71	1c deep blue	21.00	25	☐☐☐☐☐
231	A72	2c brown violet	19.00	15	☐☐☐☐☐
232	A73	3c green	50.00	12.50	☐☐☐☐☐
233	A74	4c ultra	70.00	5.50	☐☐☐☐☐
a.		4c blue (error)	*10,000.*	*4,000*	☐☐☐☐☐
234	A75	5c chocolate	75.00	6.50	☐☐☐☐☐
235	A76	6c purple	70.00	18.00	☐☐☐☐☐
a.		6c red violet	70.00	18.00	☐☐☐☐☐
236	A77	8c magenta	60.00	8.00	☐☐☐☐☐
237	A78	10c black brown	115.00	5.50	☐☐☐☐☐

ONE DOLLAR.

Type I. The circles enclosing "$1" are broken where they meet the curved line below "One Dollar." The fifteen left vertical rows of impressions from plate 76 are Type I, the balance being Type II.

Type II. The circles are complete.

TEN CENTS

Type I. Tips of foliate ornaments do not impinge on white curved line below "TEN CENTS".

Type II. Tips of ornaments break curved line below "E" of "TEN" and "T" of "CENTS".

Scott No.	Illus. No.	Description	Unused Value	Used Value	//////
238	A79	15c dark green	190.00	50.00	
239	A80	30c orange brown	260.00	70.00	
240	A81	50c slate blue	450.00	120.00	
241	A82	$1 salmon	1,350.	525.00	
242	A83	$2 brown red	1,400.	450.00	
243	A84	$3 yellow green	2,000.	800.00	
a.		$3 olive green	2,000.	800.00	
244	A85	$4 crimson lake	2,600.	1,000.	
a.		$4 rose carmine	2,600.	1,000.	
245	A86	$5 black	3,000.	1,200.	

1894, Perf. 12, Unwatermarked

Scott No.	Illus. No.	Description	Unused Value	Used Value	
246	A87	1c ultramarine	16.00	2.00	
247	A87	1c blue	40.00	85	
248	A88	2c pink, type I	12.50	1.50	
249	A88	2c carmine lake, type I	77.50	1.00	
250	A88	2c carmine, type I	15.00	25	
a.		Vert. pair, imperf. horiz.	1,500.		
b.		Horiz. pair, imperf. btwn.	1,500.		
251	A88	2c carmine, type II	125.00	1.50	
252	A88	2c carmine, type III	70.00	2.00	
a.		Horiz. pair, imperf. vert.	1,350.		
b.		Horiz. pair, imperf. btwn.	1,500.		
253	A89	3c purple	52.50	4.25	
254	A90	4c dark brown	60.00	2.00	
255	A91	5c chocolate	50.00	2.50	
c.		Vert. pair, imperf. horiz.	1,350.		
256	A92	6c dull brown	90.00	12.00	
a.		Vert. pair, imperf. horiz.	850.00		
257	A93	8c violet brown	80.00	8.00	
258	A94	10c dark green	115.00	5.00	
259	A95	15c dark blue	185.00	30.00	
260	A96	50c orange	250.00	60.00	
261	A97	$1 black, type I	650.00	160.00	
261A	A97	$1 black, type II	1,650.	350.00	
262	A98	$2 bright blue	2,250.	400.00	
263	A99	$5 dark green	3,500.	750.00	

1895, Watermark 191, Perf. 12

Scott No.	Illus. No.	Description	Unused Value	Used Value	
264	A87	1c blue	3.50	15	
265	A88	2c carmine, type I	18.00	40	
266	A88	2c carmine, type II	15.00	1.75	
267	A88	2c carmine, type III	3.00	15	
268	A89	3c purple	22.50	65	
269	A90	4c dark brown	24.00	75	
270	A91	5c chocolate	22.50	1.20	
271	A92	6c dull brown	42.50	2.50	
a.		Wmkd. USIR	2,250.	350.00	

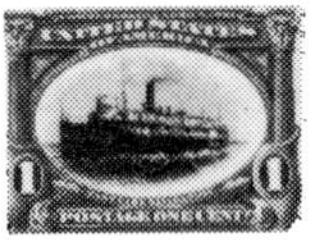
A109

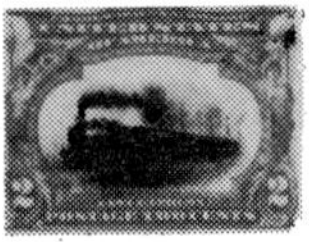
A110

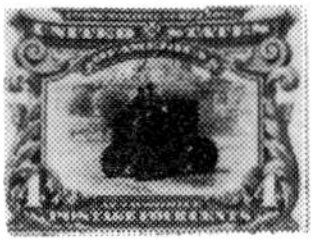
A111

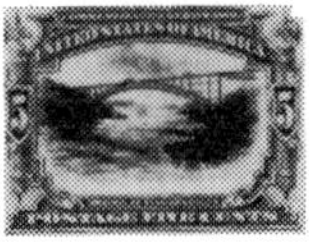
A112

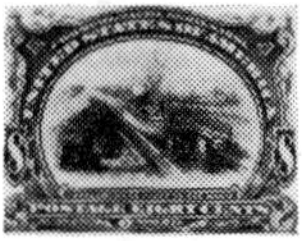
A113

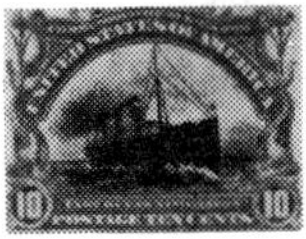
A114

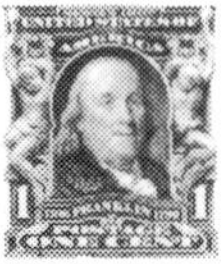
A115

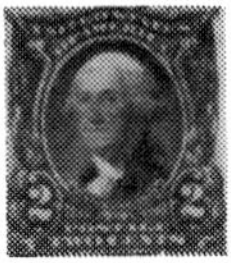
A116

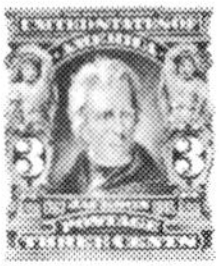
A117

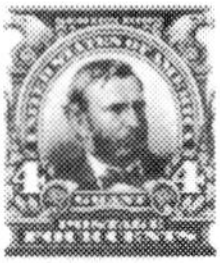
A118

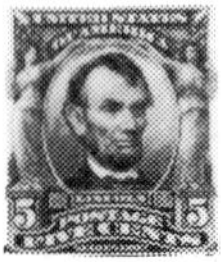
A119

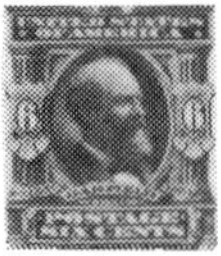
A120

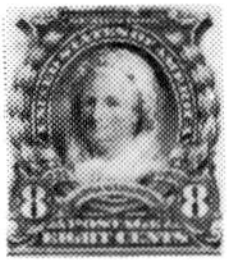
A121

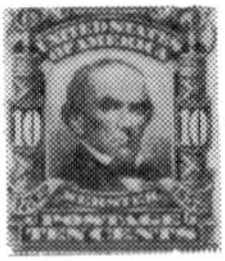
A122

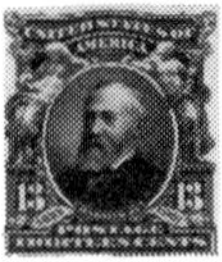
A123

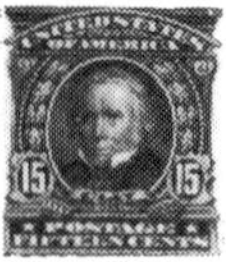
A124

A125

A126

A127

A128

A129

A130

A131

A132

A133

A134

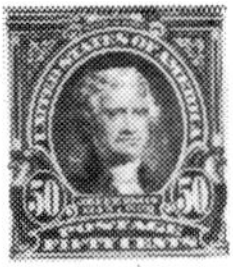

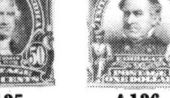

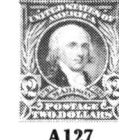

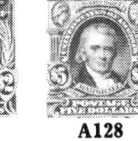

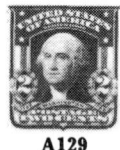

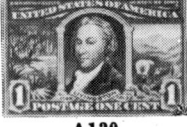

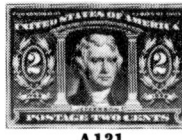

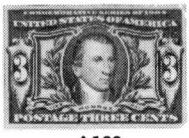

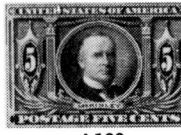

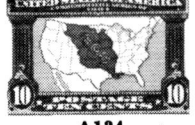

Scott No.	Illus. No.	Description	Unused Value	Used Value	/ / / / / /
272	A93	8c violet brown	35.00	65	
a.		Wmkd. USIR	1,750.	110.00	
273	A94	10c dark green	45.00	80	
274	A95	15c dark blue	125.00	5.50	
275	A96	50c orange	175.00	14.00	
a.		50c red orange	195.00	16.00	
276	A97	$1 black, type I	500.00	45.00	
276A	A97	$1 black, type II	1,000.	95.00	
277	A98	$2 bright blue	850.00	225.00	
a.		$2 dark blue	825.00	235.00	
278	A99	$5 dark green	1,750.	300.00	

1898, Watermark 191, Perf. 12

Scott No.	Illus. No.	Description	Unused Value	Used Value	
279	A87	1c deep green	6.00	15	
279B	A88	2c red, type III	5.50	15	
c.		2c rose carmine, type III	185.00	25.00	
d.		2c orange red, type III	6.50	15	
e.		Booklet pane of 6	300.00	—	
f.		2c deep red, type III	12.50	75	
280	A90	4c rose brown	20.00	45	
a.		4c lilac brown	20.00	45	
b.		4c orange brown	20.00	45	
281	A91	5c dark blue	22.50	40	
282	A92	6c lake	32.50	1.40	
a.		6c purple lake	35.00	1.65	
282C	A94	10c brown, type I	125.00	1.20	
283	A94	10c org brown, type II	75.00	1.00	
284	A95	15c olive green	100.00	4.50	
285	A100	1c dk yellow green	21.00	4.00	
286	A101	2c copper red	19.00	1.00	
287	A102	4c orange	110.00	16.00	
288	A103	5c dull blue	95.00	14.00	
289	A104	8c violet brown	140.00	30.00	
a.		Vert. pair, imperf. horiz.	*13,500.*		
290	A105	10c gray violet	135.00	18.00	
291	A106	50c sage green	400.00	150.00	
292	A107	$1 black	1,050.	400.00	
293	A108	$2 orange brown	1,700.	700.00	

1901, Watermark 191, Perf. 12

Scott No.	Illus. No.	Description	Unused Value	Used Value	
294	A109	1c green & black	16.00	2.50	
a.		Center inverted	*10,000.*	*5,500.*	
295	A110	2c carmine & black	15.00	75	
a.		Center inverted	*30,000.*	*13,500.*	
296	A111	4c deep red brown & black	75.00	12.50	
a.		Center inverted	*12,500.*		
297	A112	5c ultra & black	90.00	11.00	

start your U.S. Collection *with Scott Minuteman*

Scott's U.S. Minuteman stamp album features:

- The famous Scott Catalogue identification number for every stamp.
- Exciting stories of almost every stamp.
- Attractive vinyl binder.
- Supplemented annually.

“ A must for every collector of U.S. postage stamps. ”

Available at your local dealer or direct from:

SCOTT Scott Publishing Co.
P.O. Box 828, Sidney, OH 45365

Scott No.	Illus. No.	Description	Unused Value	Used Value	//////
298	A113	8c brown violet & black	100.00	45.00	
299	A114	10c yellow brown & black	160.00	20.00	

1902-03, Watermark 191, Perf. 12

300	A115	1c blue green	6.00	15	
b.		Booklet pane of 6	*400.00*	—	
301	A116	2c carmine	8.00	15	
c.		Booklet pane of 6	*375.00*	—	
302	A117	3c bright violet	30.00	2.00	
303	A118	4c brown	30.00	90	
304	A119	5c blue	35.00	1.10	
305	A120	6c claret	40.00	2.00	
306	A121	8c violet black	27.50	1.50	
307	A122	10c pale red brown	30.00	70	
308	A123	13c purple black	27.50	5.00	
309	A124	15c olive green	90.00	3.75	
310	A125	50c orange	285.00	17.50	
311	A126	$1 black	550.00	45.00	
312	A127	$2 dark blue	800.00	140.00	
313	A128	$5 dark green	2,250.	550.00	

1906-08, Imperf.

314	A115	1c blue green	20.00	15.00	
314A	A118	4c brown	*22,500.*	*15,000.*	
315	A119	5c blue	300.00	*350.00*	

1908, Coil Stamps, Perf. 12 Horizontally

316	A115	1c blue green, pair	*75,000.*	—	
317	A119	5c blue, pair	*6,000.*	—	

Perf. 12 Vertically

318	A115	1c blue green, pair	*5,500.*	—	

1903, Watermark 191, Perf. 12

319	A129	2c carmine (I)	4.00	15	
a.		2c lake (I)	—	—	
b.		2c carmine rose (I)	6.00	20	
c.		2c scarlet (I)	4.00	15	
d.		Vert. pair, imperf. horiz.	*2,000.*		
e.		Vert. pair, imperf. btwn.	*950.00*		
f.		2c lake (II)	5.00	20	
g.		Booklet pane of 6, car (I)	75.00	*125.00*	
h.		As "g" (II)	125.00		
i.		2c carmine (II)	17.50	—	
j.		2c carmine rose (II)	8.00	50	
k.		2c scarlet (II)	5.00	30	
m.		As "g," lake (I)	—		
n.		As "g," carmine rose (I)	100.00		
p.		As "g," scarlet (I)	110.00	125.00	
q.		As "g," lake (II)	130.00		

A135   **A136**   **A137**

Franklin   Washington   Washington   Franklin
A138   **A139**   **A140**   **A148**   **A141**

A142   **A143**

A144   **A145**   **A146**   **A147**

TYPE I

THREE CENTS.

Type I. The top line of the toga rope is weak and the rope shading lines are thin. The fifth line from the left is missing.

The line between the lips is thin.

Used on both flat plate and rotary press printings.

Scott No.	Illus. No.	Description	Unused Value	Used Value	/ / / / / /

1906, Imperf.

320	A129	2c carmine	17.50	11.00	
a.		2c lake (II)	50.00	40.00	
b.		2c scarlet	16.00	12.00	
c.		2c carmine rose	60.00	40.00	

1908, Coil Stamps, Perf. 12 Horizontally

321	A129	2c carmine, pair	*95,000.*	—	

Perf. 12 Vertically

322	A129	2c carmine, pair	*6,500.*	*5,000.*	

1904, Watermark 191, Perf. 12

323	A130	1c green	19.50	3.00	
324	A131	2c carmine	17.00	1.00	
a.		Vert. pair, imperf. horiz.	6,750.		
325	A132	3c violet	65.00	24.00	
326	A133	5c dark blue	67.50	15.00	
327	A134	10c red brown	130.00	21.00	

1907, Watermark 191, Perf. 12

328	A135	1c green	13.00	2.00	
329	A136	2c carmine	17.00	1.75	
330	A137	5c blue	72.50	16.00	

1908-09, Watermark 191, Perf. 12

331	A138	1c green	4.75	15	
a.		Booklet pane of 6	130.00	*90.00*	
332	A139	2c carmine	4.50	15	
a.		Booklet pane of 6	125.00	*90.00*	
333	A140	3c deep violet, type I	21.00	1.75	
334	A140	4c orange brown	25.00	55	
335	A140	5c blue	32.50	1.50	
336	A140	6c red orange	40.00	3.50	
337	A140	8c olive green	30.00	1.75	
338	A140	10c yellow	47.50	1.00	
339	A140	13c blue green	27.50	14.00	
340	A140	15c pale ultra	42.50	3.75	
341	A140	50c violet	190.00	10.00	
342	A140	$1 violet brown	350.00	50.00	

Imperf.

343	A138	1c green	5.50	4.00	
344	A139	2c carmine	7.50	2.50	
345	A140	3c deep violet, type I	14.00	17.50	
346	A140	4c orange brown	24.00	17.50	
347	A140	5c blue	42.50	30.00	

TYPE I

TWO CENTS.
Type I. There is one shading line in the first curve of the ribbon above the left "2" and one in the second curve of the ribbon above the right "2."

The button of the toga has a faint outline.

The top line of the toga rope, from the button to the front of the throat, is also very faint.

The shading lines at the face terminate in front of the ear with little or no joining, to form a lock of hair.

Used on both flat and rotary press printings.

TYPE II

TWO CENTS.
Type II. Shading lines in ribbons as on type I.

The toga button, rope, and shading lines are heavy.

The shading lines of the face at the lock of hair end in a strong vertical curved line.

Used on rotary press printings only.

TYPE III

TWO CENTS.
Type III. Two lines of shading in the curves of the ribbons.

Other characteristics similar to type II.

Used on rotary press printings only.

HOW TO USE THIS BOOK

The number in the first column is its Scott number or identifying number. The letter and number that come next (A41) indicate the design and refer to the illustration so designated. Following that is the denomination of the stamp and its color. Finally, the value, unused and used is shown.

Scott No.	Illus. No.	Description	Unused Value	Used Value	//////
1908-10, Coil Stamps, Perf. 12 Horizontally					
348	A138	1c green	21.00	10.00	
349	A139	2c carmine	37.50	6.00	
350	A140	4c orange brown	80.00	60.00	
351	A140	5c blue	90.00	90.00	
Perf. 12 Vertically					
352	A138	1c green	40.00	25.00	
353	A139	2c carmine	40.00	6.00	
354	A140	4c orange brown	100.00	45.00	
355	A140	5c blue	110.00	65.00	
356	A140	10c yellow	1,750.	750.00	
1909, Bluish paper, Perf. 12					
357	A138	1c green	80.00	65.00	
358	A139	2c carmine	75.00	55.00	
359	A140	3c deep violet, type I	1,500.	*1,300.*	
360	A140	4c orange brown	*13,500.*		
361	A140	5c blue	3,250.	*3,500.*	
362	A140	6c red orange	1,150.	850.00	
363	A140	8c olive green	*13,500.*		
364	A140	10c yellow	1,350.	1,000.	
365	A140	13c blue green	2,250.	*1,250.*	
366	A140	15c pale ultra	1,150.	800.00	
1909, Watermark 191, Perf. 12					
367	A141	2c carmine	4.25	1.40	
Imperf.					
368	A141	2c carmine	20.00	16.00	
Bluish paper					
369	A141	2c carmine	170.00	175.00	
Perf. 12					
370	A142	2c carmine	7.50	1.25	
Imperf.					
371	A142	2c carmine	27.50	20.00	
Perf. 12					
372	A143	2c carmine	10.00	3.25	
Imperf.					
373	A143	2c carmine	32.50	22.50	
1910-11, Watermark 190, Perf. 12					
374	A138	1c green	5.00	15	
a.		Booklet pane of 6	90.00	*75.00*	

TYPE Ia

TWO CENTS.

Type Ia. Design characteristics similar to type I except that all lines of design are stronger.

The toga button, toga rope and rope shading lines are heavy. The latter characteristics are those of type II, which, however, occur only on impressions from rotary plates.

Used only on flat plates 10208 and 10209.

TYPE II

THREE CENTS.

Type II. The top line of the toga rope is strong and the rope shading lines are heavy and complete.
The line between the lips is heavy.
Used on both flat plate and rotary press printings.

TYPE IV

TWO CENTS.

Type IV. Top line of toga rope is broken. Shading lines in toga button are so arranged that the curving of the first and last form "(ID".

Line of color in left "2" is very thin and usually broken.

Used on offset printings only.

Scott No.	Illus. No.	Description	Unused Value	Used Value
375	A139	2c carmine	5.00	15
a.		Booklet pane of 6	75.00	*60.00*
376	A140	3c deep violet, type I	11.50	1.00
377	A140	4c brown	20.00	30
378	A140	5c blue	17.50	30
379	A140	6c red orange	25.00	40
380	A140	8c olive green	75.00	8.50
381	A140	10c yellow	70.00	2.50
382	A140	15c pale ultra	190.00	11.50

1910, Imperf.

383	A138	1c green	2.25	2.00
384	A139	2c carmine	3.50	2.50

1910, Coil Stamps, Perf. 12 Horizontally

385	A138	1c green	18.00	10.00
386	A139	2c carmine	32.50	12.50

1910-11, Perf. 12 Vertically

387	A138	1c green	60.00	30.00
388	A139	2c carmine	550.00	200.00
389	A140	3c dp vio, type I	*15,000.*	*8,500.*

1910, Perf. 8½ Horizontally

390	A138	1c green	3.00	4.00
391	A139	2c carmine	20.00	6.75

1910-13, Perf. 8½ Vertically

392	A138	1c green	12.00	14.00
393	A139	2c carmine	24.00	5.50
394	A140	3c deep violet, type I	32.50	40.00
395	A140	4c brown	32.50	35.00
396	A140	5c blue	32.50	35.00

1913, Watermark 190, Perf. 12

397	A144	1c green	11.00	85
398	A145	2c carmine	12.50	30
399	A146	5c blue	52.50	6.50
400	A147	10c orange yellow	95.00	14.00
400A	A147	10c orange	175.00	10.50

1914-15, Perf. 10

401	A144	1c green	16.00	4.00
402	A145	2c carmine	55.00	1.00
403	A146	5c blue	120.00	11.00
404	A147	10c orange	825.00	42.50

TYPE V

TWO CENTS.

Type V. Top line of toga is complete.
Five vertical shading lines in toga button.
Line of color in left "2" is very thin and usually broken.
Shading dots on the nose and lip are as indicated on the diagram.
Used on offset printings only.

TYPE Va

TWO CENTS.

Type Va. Characteristics same as type V, except in shading dots of nose. Third row from bottom has 4 dots instead of 6. Overall height of type Va is 1/3 mm. less than type V.

Used on offset printings only.

TYPE VI

TWO CENTS.

Type VI. General characteristics same as type V, except that line of color in left "2" is very heavy.

Used on offset printings only.

HOW TO USE THIS BOOK

The number in the first column is its Scott number or identifying number. The letter and number that come next (A41) indicate the design and refer to the illustration so designated. Following that is the denomination of the stamp and its color. Finally, the value, unused and used is shown.

Scott No.	Illus. No.	Description	Unused Value	Used Value	/ / / / / /
1912-14, Watermark 190, Perf. 12					
405	A140	1c green	4.00	15	
a.		Vert. pair, imperf. horiz.	*650.00*	—	
b.		Booklet pane of 6	50.00	*25.00*	
406	A140	2c carmine, type I	3.75	15	
a.		Booklet pane of 6	50.00	*40.00*	
b.		Double impression	—		
407	A140	7c black	60.00	8.00	
1912, Imperf.					
408	A140	1c green	90	50	
409	A140	2c carmine, type I	1.00	50	
Coil Stamps, Perf. 8 ½ Horizontally					
410	A140	1c green	4.50	3.00	
411	A140	2c carmine, type I	6.00	2.50	
Coil Stamps, Perf. 8 ½ Vertically					
412	A140	1c green	15.00	3.75	
413	A140	2c carmine, type I	24.00	75	
1912-14, Watermark 190, Perf. 12					
414	A148	8c pale olive green	27.50	85	
415	A148	9c salmon red	35.00	9.50	
416	A148	10c orange yellow	30.00	25	
417	A148	12c claret brown	30.00	3.00	
418	A148	15c gray	55.00	2.00	
419	A148	20c ultra	125.00	9.00	
420	A148	30c orange red	90.00	10.00	
421	A148	50c violet	325.00	10.00	
1912, Watermark 191, Perf. 12					
422	A148	50c violet	175.00	9.50	
423	A148	$1 violet brown	400.00	40.00	
1914-15, Watermark 190, Perf. 10					
424	A140	1c green	1.60	15	
a.		Perf. 12x10	*600.00*	*500.00*	
b.		Perf. 10x12		250.00	
c.		Vert. pair, imperf. horiz.	*425.00*	*250.00*	
d.		Booklet pane of 6	3.00	75	
e.		Vert. pair, imperf. btwn. & at top	—		
425	A140	2c rose red, type I	1.50	15	
c.		Perf. 10x12	—	—	
d.		Perf. 12x10	—	*600.00*	
e.		Booklet pane of 6	9.00	3.00	
426	A140	3c deep violet, type I	10.00	90	

TYPE VII

TWO CENTS.

Type VII. Line of color in left "2" is invariably continuous, clearly defined, and heavier than in type V or Va, but not as heavy as in type VI.

Additional vertical row of dots has been added to the upper lip.

Numerous additional dots have been added to hair on top of head.

Used on offset printings only.

TYPE III

THREE CENTS.

Type III. The top line of the toga rope is strong but the fifth shading line is missing as in type I.

Center shading line of the toga button consists of two dashes with a central dot.

The "P" and "O" of "POSTAGE" are separated by a line of color.

The frame line at the bottom of the vignette is complete.

Used on offset printings only.

TYPE IV

THREE CENTS.

Type IV. Shading lines of toga rope are complete.

Second and fourth shading lines in toga button are broken in the middle and the third line is continuous with a dot in the center.

"P" and "O" of "POSTAGE" are joined.

Frame line at bottom of vignette is broken.

Used on offset printings only.

Scott No.	Illus. No.	Description	Unused Value	Used Value	/ / / / / /
427	A140	4c brown	26.00	30	☐☐☐☐☐
428	A140	5c blue	22.50	30	☐☐☐☐☐
a.		Perf. 12x10		1,000.	☐☐☐☐☐
429	A140	6c red orange	35.00	90	☐☐☐☐☐
430	A140	7c black	65.00	2.50	☐☐☐☐☐
431	A148	8c pale olive green	27.50	1.10	☐☐☐☐☐
432	A148	9c salmon red	37.50	5.00	☐☐☐☐☐
433	A148	10c orange yellow	35.00	20	☐☐☐☐☐
434	A148	11c dark green	16.00	5.50	☐☐☐☐☐
435	A148	12c claret brown	18.00	2.75	☐☐☐☐☐
a.		12c copper red	19.00	2.75	☐☐☐☐☐
437	A148	15c gray	87.50	4.50	☐☐☐☐☐
438	A148	20c ultra	165.00	2.50	☐☐☐☐☐
439	A148	30c orange red	190.00	10.00	☐☐☐☐☐
440	A148	50c violet	475.00	10.00	☐☐☐☐☐

1914, Coil Stamps, Perf. 10 Horizontally

441	A140	1c green	55	80	☐☐☐☐☐
442	A140	2c carmine, type I	6.00	4.50	☐☐☐☐☐

Perf. 10 Vertically

443	A140	1c green	15.00	4.00	☐☐☐☐☐
444	A140	2c carmine, type I	21.00	1.00	☐☐☐☐☐
445	A140	3c violet, type I	175.00	100.00	☐☐☐☐☐
446	A140	4c brown	90.00	30.00	☐☐☐☐☐
447	A140	5c blue	30.00	20.00	☐☐☐☐☐

1914-16, Coil Stamps, Perf. 10 Horizontally Rotary Press Printing

448	A140	1c green	4.25	2.25	☐☐☐☐☐
449	A140	2c red, type I	1,900.	300.00	☐☐☐☐☐
450	A140	2c carmine, type III	7.00	2.25	☐☐☐☐☐

1914-16, Coil Stamps, Perf. 10 Vertically

452	A140	1c green	7.50	1.40	☐☐☐☐☐
453	A140	2c carmine rose, type I	90.00	3.25	☐☐☐☐☐
454	A140	2c red, type II	72.50	7.50	☐☐☐☐☐
455	A140	2c carmine, type III	7.00	75	☐☐☐☐☐
456	A140	3c violet, type I	190.00	75.00	☐☐☐☐☐
457	A140	4c brown	19.00	15.00	☐☐☐☐☐
458	A140	5c blue	22.50	15.00	☐☐☐☐☐

1914, Imperf.

459	A140	2c car, type I	300.00	*750.00*	☐☐☐☐☐

1915, Watermark 191, Perf. 10

460	A148	$1 violet black	600.00	55.00	☐☐☐☐☐

1915, Watermark 190, Perf. 11

461	A140	2c pale carmine red, type I	75.00	*175.00*	☐☐☐☐☐

Scott No.	Illus. No.	Description	Unused Value	Used Value	//////
1916-17, Perf. 10, Unwatermarked					
462	A140	1c green	5.00	15	
a.		Booklet pane of 6	7.50	1.00	
463	A140	2c carmine, type I	3.25	15	
a.		Booklet pane of 6	62.50	20.00	
464	A140	3c violet, type I	57.50	8.00	
465	A140	4c orange brown	32.50	1.00	
466	A140	5c blue	57.50	1.00	
467	A140	5c car (error in plate of 2c, 17)	475.00	525.00	
468	A140	6c red orange	70.00	5.00	
469	A140	7c black	92.50	7.50	
470	A148	8c olive green	42.50	3.75	
471	A148	9c salmon red	45.00	9.50	
472	A148	10c orange yellow	85.00	75	
473	A148	11c dark green	25.00	11.00	
474	A148	12c claret brown	40.00	3.50	
475	A148	15c gray	135.00	7.00	
476	A148	20c light ultra	200.00	7.50	
476A	A148	30c orange red	*3,500.*	—	
477	A148	50c light violet	875.00	40.00	
478	A148	$1 violet black	600.00	11.00	
479	A127	$2 dark blue	290.00	30.00	
480	A128	$5 light green	225.00	32.50	
Imperf.					
481	A140	1c green	65	45	
482	A140	2c carmine, type I	1.25	1.00	
482A	A140	2c deep rose, type Ia		*7,500.*	
483	A140	3c violet, type I	9.50	6.50	
484	A140	3c violet, type II	7.00	3.00	
485	A140	5c car (error in plate of 2c)	*9,000.*		
1916-22, Coil Stamps, Perf. 10 Horizontally, Rotary Press Printing					
486	A140	1c green	65	20	
487	A140	2c carmine, type II	12.00	2.50	
488	A140	2c carmine, type III	2.00	1.35	
489	A140	3c violet, type I	4.00	1.00	
1916-22, Coil Stamps, Perf.10 Vertically					
490	A140	1c green	40	15	
491	A140	2c carmine, type II	1,500.	450.00	
492	A140	2c carmine, type III	6.50	15	
493	A140	3c violet, type I	13.50	2.00	
494	A140	3c violet, type II	7.50	1.00	
495	A140	4c orange brown	8.00	3.00	
496	A140	5c blue	2.75	90	
497	A148	10c orange yellow	16.00	9.00	

Scott No.	Illus. No.		Description	Unused Value	Used Value	/ / / / / /
Types of 1912-14 Issue						
1917-19, Perf. 11						
498	A140	1c	green	30	15	
a.			Vert. pair, imperf. horiz.	175.00		
b.			Horiz. pair, imperf. btwn.	75.00		
c.			Vert. pair, imperf. btwn.	450.00	—	
d.			Double impression	150.00		
e.			Booklet pane of 6	1.60	35	
f.			Booklet pane of 30	750.00		
499	A140	2c	rose, type I	35	15	
a.			Vert. pair, imperf. horiz.	150.00		
b.			Horiz. pair, imperf. vert.	200.00	100.00	
c.			Vert. pair, imperf. btwn.	500.00	225.00	
e.			Booklet pane of 6	2.75	50	
f.			Booklet pane of 30	15,000.		
g.			Double impression	125.00	—	
500	A140	2c	deep rose, type Ia	200.00	150.00	
501	A140	3c	light violet, type I	8.00	15	
b.			Booklet pane of 6	50.00	15.00	
c.			Vert. pair, imperf. horiz.	300.00		
d.			Double impression	200.00		
502	A140	3c	dark violet, type II	11.00	15	
b.			Booklet pane of 6	35.00	10.00	
c.			Vert. pair, imperf. horiz.	250.00	125.00	
d.			Double impression	200.00		
503	A140	4c	brown	7.50	15	
b.			Double impression	—		
504	A140	5c	blue	6.50	15	
a.			Horiz. pair, imperf. btwn.	2,500.	—	
505	A140	5c	rose (error in plate of 2c)	350.00	400.00	
506	A140	6c	red orange	10.00	20	
507	A140	7c	black	20.00	85	
508	A148	8c	olive bister	9.00	40	
b.			Vert. pair, imperf. btwn.	—	—	
509	A148	9c	salmon red	11.00	1.40	
510	A148	10c	orange yellow	13.00	15	
511	A148	11c	light green	7.00	2.00	
512	A148	12c	claret brown	7.00	30	
a.		12c	brown carmine	7.50	35	
513	A148	13c	apple green	8.50	4.75	
514	A148	15c	gray	30.00	80	
515	A148	20c	light ultra	37.50	20	
b.			Vert. pair, imperf. btwn.	325.00		
c.			Double impression	400.00		
516	A148	30c	orange red	30.00	60	
b.			Double impression	—		

Scott No.	Illus. No.	Description	Unused Value	Used Value	/ / / / / /
517	A148	50c red violet..........................	60.00	45	☐☐☐☐☐
b.		Vert. pair, imperf. btwn. & at bottom	1,750.	1,000.	☐☐☐☐☐
518	A148	$1 violet brown	45.00	1.20	☐☐☐☐☐
b.		$1 deep brown.....................	1,000.	600.00	☐☐☐☐☐

1917-19, Watermark 191
519	A139	2c carmine...........................	225.00	450.00	☐☐☐☐☐

1918, Perf. 11, Unwatermarked
523	A149	$2 orange red & black..........	600.00	200.00	☐☐☐☐☐
524	A149	$5 deep green & black	200.00	27.50	☐☐☐☐☐

1918-20, Perf. 11, Offset Printing
525	A140	1c gray green......................	1.50	35	☐☐☐☐☐
a.		1c dark green......................	1.65	75	☐☐☐☐☐
c.		Horiz. pair, imperf. btwn.	100.00		☐☐☐☐☐
d.		Double impression	15.00	15.00	☐☐☐☐☐
526	A140	2c carmine, type IV............	21.00	2.75	☐☐☐☐☐
527	A140	2c carmine, type V	11.50	60	☐☐☐☐☐
a.		Double impression	55.00	10.00	☐☐☐☐☐
b.		Vert. pair, imperf. horiz. .	600.00		☐☐☐☐☐
c.		Horiz. pair, imperf. vert. .	1,000.		☐☐☐☐☐
528	A140	2c carmine, type Va	6.00	15	☐☐☐☐☐
c.		Double impression	25.00		☐☐☐☐☐
g.		Vert. pair, imperf. btwn. .	1,000.		☐☐☐☐☐
528A	A140	2c carmine, type VI............	37.50	1.00	☐☐☐☐☐
d.		Double impression	150.00	—	☐☐☐☐☐
f.		Vert. pair, imperf. horiz. .	—		☐☐☐☐☐
h.		Vert. pair, imperf. btwn. .	1,000.		☐☐☐☐☐
528B	A140	2c carmine, type VII	14.00	30	☐☐☐☐☐
e.		Double impression	55.00		☐☐☐☐☐
529	A140	3c violet, type III................	2.25	15	☐☐☐☐☐
a.		Double impression	30.00	—	☐☐☐☐☐
b.		Printed on both sides.......	350.00		☐☐☐☐☐
530	A140	3c purple, type IV	1.00	15	☐☐☐☐☐
a.		Double impression	20.00	6.00	☐☐☐☐☐
b.		Printed on both sides.......	250.00		☐☐☐☐☐

Imperf.
531	A140	1c green...............................	7.00	7.00	☐☐☐☐☐
532	A140	2c carmine rose, type IV......	35.00	25.00	☐☐☐☐☐
533	A140	2c carmine, type V	175.00	75.00	☐☐☐☐☐
534	A140	2c carmine, type Va	9.00	6.00	☐☐☐☐☐
534A	A140	2c carmine, type VI............	32.50	20.00	☐☐☐☐☐
534B	A140	2c carmine, type VII	1,250.	700.00	☐☐☐☐☐
535	A140	3c violet, type IV	7.00	4.50	☐☐☐☐☐
a.		Double impression	100.00	—	☐☐☐☐☐

Scott No.	Illus. No.	Description	Unused Value	Used Value	//////

Perf. 12 ½

536	A140	1c gray green........................	11.00	14.00	
a.		Horiz. pair, imperf. vert..	500.00		

1919, Perf. 11, Flat Plate Printing

537	A150	3c violet..............................	7.50	2.75	
a.		3c deep red violet.................	350.00	50.00	
b.		3c light reddish violent	7.50	2.75	
c.		3c red violet........................	30.00	7.50	

1919, Perf. 11x10, Rotary Press Printings,
Size: 19 ½ to 20mm wide by 22 to 22 ¼mm high

538	A140	1c green..............................	7.50	6.00	
a.		Vert. pair, imperf. horiz..	50.00	100.00	
539	A140	2c carmine rose, type II	3,000.	3,000.	
540	A140	2c carmine rose, type III	7.50	6.00	
a.		Vert. pair, imperf. horiz..	50.00	100.00	
b.		Horiz. pair, imperf. vert..	550.00		
541	A140	3c violet, type II	22.50	20.00	

1920, Perf. 10x11, Size: 19mmx22 ½ -22 ¾mm

542	A140	1c green..............................	6.50	65	

1921, Perf. 10, Size: 19x22 ½mm

543	A140	1c green..............................	35	15	
a.		Horiz. pair, imperf. btwn.	550.00		

1922, Perf. 11, Size: 19x22 ½mm

544	A140	1c green..............................	12,500.	3,000.	

1921, Perf. 11, Size: 19 ½ -20x22mm

545	A140	1c green..............................	95.00	110.00	
546	A140	2c carmine rose, type III	60.00	110.00	

1920, Perf. 11

547	A149	$2 carmine & black..............	175.00	32.50	
548	A151	1c green..............................	3.50	1.65	
549	A152	2c carmine rose	5.50	1.25	
550	A153	5c deep blue	35.00	10.00	

1922-25, Perf. 11

551	A154	½c olive brown	15	15	
552	A155	1c deep green	1.25	15	
a.		Booket pane of 6	4.50	50	
553	A156	1 ½c yellow brown	2.25	15	
554	A157	2c carmine...........................	1.25	15	
a.		Horiz. pair, imperf. vert..	175.00		
b.		Vert. pair, imperf. horiz..	500.00		
c.		Booklet pane of 6	5.50	1.00	

A149 A150

A151 A152 A153

A154 A155 A156 A157

A158 A159 A160 A161

A162 A163 A164 A165

A166 A167 A168 A169

Scott No.	Illus. No.	Description	Unused Value	Used Value	//////
555	A158	3c violet	15.00	85	
556	A159	4c yellow brown	15.00	20	
a.		Vert. pair, imperf. horiz.	—		
557	A160	5c dark blue	15.00	15	
a.		Imperf., pair	1,500.		
b.		Horiz. pair, imperf. vert.	—		
558	A161	6c red orange	27.50	75	
559	A162	7c black	7.00	45	
560	A163	8c olive green	37.50	35	
561	A164	9c rose	12.00	90	
562	A165	10c orange	16.00	15	
a.		Vert. pair, imperf. horiz.	1,250.		
b.		Imperf., pair	1,250.		
563	A166	11c light blue	1.25	25	
d.		Imperf., pair		—	
564	A167	12c brown violet	5.50	15	
a.		Horiz. pair, imperf. vert.	1,000.		
b.		Imperf., pair			
565	A168	14c blue	3.50	65	
566	A169	15c gray	19.00	15	
567	A170	20c carmine rose	19.00	15	
a.		Horiz. pair, imperf. vert.	1,500.		
568	A171	25c yellow green	17.00	38	
b.		Vert. pair, imperf. horiz.	850.00		
569	A172	30c olive brown	30.00	30	
570	A173	50c lilac	50.00	15	
571	A174	$1 violet black	40.00	35	
572	A175	$2 deep blue	87.50	8.00	
573	A176	$5 carmine & blue	140.00	12.50	

1923-25, Imperf.

575	A155	1c green	7.00	4.00	
576	A156	1½c yellow brown	1.50	1.50	
577	A157	2c carmine	1.50	1.25	

Rotary Press Printings, Perf. 11x10, Size: 19 ¾ x 22 ¼ mm

578	A155	1c green	70.00	110.00	
579	A157	2c carmine	60.00	100.00	

Perf 10

581	A155	1c green	7.00	55	
582	A156	1½c brown	3.50	45	
583	A157	2c carmine	1.75	15	
a.		Booklet pane of 6	75.00	25.00	
584	A158	3c violet	19.00	1.75	
585	A159	4c yellow brown	11.50	30	
586	A160	5c blue	12.00	18	
a.		Horiz. pair, imperf. btwn.		—	

A170  A171  A172

A173  A174  A175

A176  A177

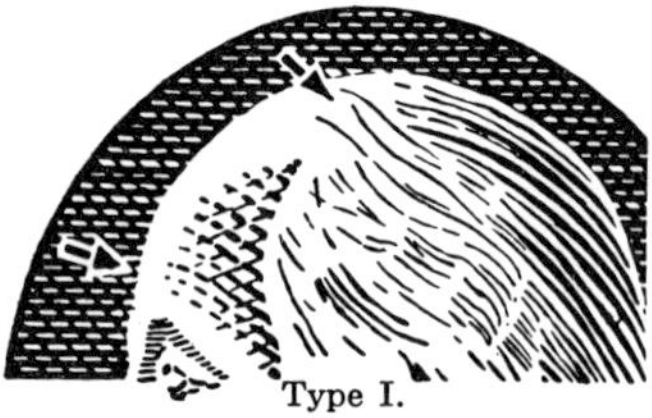

Type I.

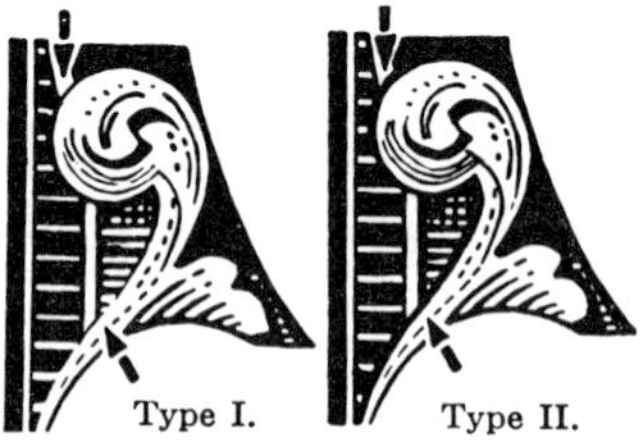

Type I.   Type II.

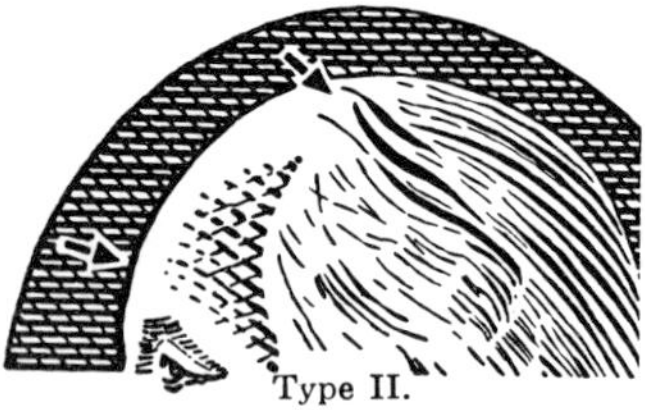

Type II.

Type I—No heavy hair lines at top center of head. Outline of left acanthus scroll generally faint at top and toward base at left side.
Type II—The heavy hair lines at top center of head; two being outstanding in the white area. Outline of left acanthus scroll very strong and clearly defined at top (under left edge of lettered panel) and at lower curve (above and to left of numeral oval). Type II is found only on Nos. 599A and 634A.

A178  A179  A180

Scott No.	Illus. No.	Description	Unused Value	Used Value	//////
587	A161	6c red orange	5.50	25	
588	A162	7c black	8.00	4.25	
589	A163	8c olive green	17.50	2.75	
590	A164	9c rose	3.75	1.90	
591	A165	10c orange	47.50	15	

Perf 11

594	A155	1c green	*15,000.*	4,000.	
595	A157	2c carmine	200.00	225.00	
596	A155	1c green		*27,500.*	

1923-29, Coil Stamps, Perf. 10 Vertically, Rotary Press Printing

597	A155	1c green	25	15	
598	A156	1½c brown	60	15	
599	A157	2c carmine, type I	30	15	
599A	A157	2c carmine, type II	100.00	9.50	
600	A158	3c violet	5.50	15	
601	A159	4c yellow brown	2.75	30	
602	A160	5c dark blue	1.25	15	
603	A165	10c orange	2.75	15	

Perf 10 Horizontally

604	A155	1c yellow green	20	15	
605	A156	1½c yellow brown	25	15	
606	A157	2c carmine	25	15	

1923, Perf. 11, Flat Plate Printing, Size: 19 ¼x22 ¼mm

610	A177	2c black	55	15	
a.		Horiz. pair, imperf. vert.	*1,100.*		

Imperf.

611	A177	2c black	6.50	4.25	

1923, Sept. 12, Perf. 10, Rotary Press Printing, Size: 19 ¼x22 ¾mm

612	A177	2c black	12.00	1.50	

1923, Perf. 11

613	A177	2c black		*15,000.*	

1924-26, Perf. 11

614	A178	1c dark green	2.50	3.00	
615	A179	2c carmine rose	5.00	2.00	
616	A180	5c dark blue	25.00	11.00	
617	A181	1c deep green	2.50	2.25	
618	A182	2c carmine rose	5.00	3.75	
619	A183	5c dark blue	24.00	12.50	
620	A184	2c carmine & black	3.50	2.75	
621	A185	5c dark blue & black	14.00	10.50	

A181

A182

A183

A184

A185

A186

A187

A188

A190

A189

A191

A192

A193

Scott No.	Illus. No.	Description	Unused Value	Used Value	//////
622	A186	13c green	12.00	40	
623	A187	17c black	13.00	20	

1926, Perf. 11
627	A188	2c carmine rose	2.75	40	
628	A189	5c gray lilac	5.50	2.75	
629	A190	2c carmine rose	1.75	1.50	
a.		Vert. pair, imperf. btwn.	—		
630	A190a	2c carmine rose, sheet of 25	350.00	375.00	

1926, Imperf., Rotary Press Printings
631	A156	1½c yellow brown	1.75	1.60	

1926-34, Perf. 11x10 1/2
632	A155	1c green	15	15	
a.		Booklet pane of 6	4.50	25	
b.		Vert. pair, imperf. btwn.	200.00	*125.00*	
633	A156	1½c yellow brown	1.60	15	
634	A157	2c carmine, type I	15	15	
b.		2c carmine lake	—	—	
c.		Horiz. pair, imperf. btwn.	2,000.		
d.		Booklet pane of 6	1.25	15	
634A	A157	2c carmine, type II	300.00	12.50	
635	A158	3c violet	35	15	
a.		3c bright violet	25	15	
636	A159	4c yellow brown	2.00	15	
637	A160	5c dark blue	1.90	15	
638	A161	6c red orange	2.00	15	
639	A162	7c black	2.00	15	
a.		Vert. pair, imperf. btwn.	150.00	80.00	
640	A163	8c olive green	2.00	15	
641	A164	9c orange red	2.00	15	
642	A165	10c orange	3.25	15	

1927, Perf. 11
643	A191	2c carmine rose	1.25	75	
644	A192	2c carmine rose	3.00	1.90	

1928, Perf. 11
645	A193	2c carmine rose	90	35	

1928, Perf. 11x10 ½, Rotary Press Printing
646	A157	2c carmine	95	95	
647	A157	2c carmine	3.75	3.75	
648	A160	5c dark blue	11.00	11.00	

1928, Perf. 11
649	A194	2c carmine rose	1.00	75	
650	A195	5c blue	4.50	3.00	

No. 634 Overprinted	**MOLLY PITCHER**	Nos. 634 and 637 Overprinted	**HAWAII 1778 - 1928**
SCOTT 646		SCOTT 647-648	

A194

A195

A196

A197

A198

A199

A200

A201

A202

A203

A204

A205

HOW TO USE THIS BOOK

The number in the first column is its Scott number or identifying number. The letter and number that come next (A41) indicate the design and refer to the illustration so designated. Following that is the denomination of the stamp and its color. Finally, the value, unused and used is shown.

Scott No.	Illus. No.	Description	Unused Value	Used Value	/ / / / / /
1929, Perf. 11					
651	A196	2c carmine & black............	55	40	
1929, May 25, Perf. 11x10 ½, Rotary Press Printing					
653	A154	½c olive brown....................	15	15	
1929, Perf. 11					
654	A197	2c carmine rose...................	60	60	
Perf. 11x10 ½, Rotary Press Printing					
655	A197	2c carmine rose...................	55	15	
Coil Stamp (Rotary Press), Perf. 10 Vertically					
656	A197	2c carmine rose...................	11.50	1.25	
1929, Perf. 11					
657	A198	2c carmine rose...................	60	50	
1929, Perf. 11x10 ½, Rotary Press Printing, Overprinted					
658	A155	1c green...............................	1.50	1.35	
a.		Vert. pair, one without ovpt.	*300.00*		
659	A156	1½c brown.............................	2.25	1.90	
a.		Vert. pair, one without ovpt.	*325.00*		
660	A157	2c carmine...........................	2.75	75	
661	A158	3c violet...............................	12.50	10.00	
a.		Vert. pair, one without ovpt.	*400.00*		
662	A159	4c yellow brown	12.50	6.00	
a.		Vert. pair, one without ovpt.	*400.00*		
663	A160	5c deep blue	9.00	6.50	
664	A161	6c red orange......................	19.00	12.00	
665	A162	7c black	18.00	18.00	
a.		Vert. pair, one without ovpt.	*400.00*		
666	A163	8c olive green......................	60.00	50.00	
667	A164	9c light rose.........................	9.00	7.50	
668	A165	10c orange yel	15.00	8.00	
669	A155	1c green...............................	2.25	1.50	
a.		Vert. pair, one without ovpt.	*275.00*		
670	A156	1½c brown.............................	2.00	1.65	
671	A157	2c carmine...........................	2.00	85	
672	A158	3c violet...............................	8.50	7.50	
a.		Vert. pair, one without ovpt.	*400.00*		
673	A159	4c yellow brown	13.00	9.50	
674	A160	5c deep blue	11.00	9.50	
675	A161	6c red orange......................	27.50	15.00	
676	A162	7c black	15.00	11.50	
677	A163	8c olive green......................	20.00	16.00	
678	A164	9c light rose.........................	24.00	18.00	
a.		Vert. pair, one without ovpt.	*600.00*		
679	A165	10c orange yellow..................	70.00	14.00	

A206　　**A207**　　**A208**　　**A209**

A210　　**A211**　　**A212**　　**A213**

A214　　**A215**　　**A216**　　**A217**

A218　　**A219**　　**A220**　　**A221**

A222　　**A223**　　**A224**　　**A225**

A226　　**A227**　　**A228**

Scott No.	Illus. No.	Description	Unused Value	Used Value	/ / / / / /

1929, Perf. 11

| 680 | A199 | 2c carmine rose | 65 | 65 | |
| 681 | A200 | 2c carmine rose | 50 | 50 | |

1930, Perf. 11

| 682 | A201 | 2c carmine rose | 50 | 38 | |
| 683 | A202 | 2c carmine rose | 1.00 | 90 | |

1930, Perf. 11x10½, Rotary Press Printing

| 684 | A203 | 1½c brown | 25 | 15 | |
| 685 | A204 | 4c brown | 75 | 15 | |

Coil Stamps, Perf. 10 Vertically

| 686 | A203 | 1½c brown | 1.50 | 15 | |
| 687 | A204 | 4c brown | 2.75 | 38 | |

1930, Perf. 11

688	A205	2c carmine rose	85	75	
689	A206	2c carmine rose	45	45	
a.		Imperf., pair	*2,500.*		

1931, Perf. 11

| 690 | A207 | 2c carmine rose | 20 | 15 | |

1931, Perf. 11x10½, Rotary Press Printing

692	A166	11c light blue	2.00	15	
693	A167	12c brown violet	4.00	15	
694	A186	13c yellow green	1.75	15	
695	A168	14c dark blue	2.75	22	
696	A169	15c gray	6.50	15	

Perf 10½x11

697	A187	17c black	3.50	15	
698	A170	20c carmine rose	7.75	15	
699	A171	25c blue green	7.25	15	
700	A172	30c brown	11.50	15	
701	A173	50c lilac	35.00	15	

1931, Perf. 11, Flat Plate

702	A208	2c black & red	15	15	
703	A209	2c carmine rose & black	35	25	
a.		2c lake & black	4.00	65	
b.		2c dark lake & black	*350.00*		
c.		Horiz. pair, imperf. vert.	*4,000.*		

1932, Perf. 11x10½, Rotary Press Printings

| 704 | A210 | ½c olive brown | 15 | 15 | |
| 705 | A211 | 1c green | 15 | 15 | |

A229

A230   **A231**   **A232**

A233   **A235**

A234

A236

A237   **A238**

Scott No.	Illus. No.	Description	Unused Value	Used Value	/ / / / /
706	A212	1½c brown....................	32	15	☐☐☐☐☐
707	A213	2c carmine rose............	15	15	☐☐☐☐☐
708	A214	3c deep violet...............	40	15	☐☐☐☐☐
709	A215	4c light brown..............	22	15	☐☐☐☐☐
710	A216	5c blue...........................	1.40	15	☐☐☐☐☐
711	A217	6c red orange................	2.75	15	☐☐☐☐☐
712	A218	7c black.........................	22	15	☐☐☐☐☐
713	A219	8c olive bister...............	2.50	50	☐☐☐☐☐
714	A220	9c pale red.....................	2.00	15	☐☐☐☐☐
715	A221	10c orange yellow........	8.50	15	☐☐☐☐☐

Perf. 11

716	A222	2c carmine rose............	35	16	☐☐☐☐☐

Perf. 11x10 ½, Rotary Press Printing

717	A223	2c carmine rose............	15	15	☐☐☐☐☐

Perf. 11x10 ½

718	A224	3c violet.........................	1.25	15	☐☐☐☐☐
719	A225	5c blue...........................	2.00	20	☐☐☐☐☐
720	A226	3c deep violet...............	15	15	☐☐☐☐☐
b.		Booklet pane of 6..........	27.50	*5.00*	☐☐☐☐☐
c.		Vert. pair, imperf. btwn..	300.00	250.00	☐☐☐☐☐

Coil Stamps, Perf. 10 Vertically, Rotary Press Printing

721	A226	3c deep violet...............	2.25	15	☐☐☐☐☐

Perf. 10 Horizontally

722	A226	3c deep violet...............	1.25	30	☐☐☐☐☐

Perf. 10 Vertically

723	A161	6c deep orange.............	8.50	25	☐☐☐☐☐

1932-33, Perf. 11

724	A227	3c violet.........................	25	15	☐☐☐☐☐
a.		Vert. pair, imperf. horiz..	—		☐☐☐☐☐
725	A228	3c violet.........................	30	24	☐☐☐☐☐
726	A229	3c violet.........................	25	18	☐☐☐☐☐

1933, Perf. 10 ½x11, Rotary Press Printing

727	A230	3c violet.........................	15	15	☐☐☐☐☐
728	A231	1c yellow green............	15	15	☐☐☐☐☐
729	A232	3c violet.........................	15	15	☐☐☐☐☐

1933, Imperf., Flat Plate Printing

730 &		Sheet of 25....................	24.00	24.00	☐☐☐☐☐
a.	A231	1c deep yellow green...	65	35	☐☐☐☐☐
731 &		Sheet of 25....................	22.50	22.50	☐☐☐☐☐
a.	A232	3c deep violet...............	50	35	☐☐☐☐☐

A240

A239

A241

A242

A243

A244

A245

A246

A247

A249

A250

A248

A252

A253

Scott No.	Illus. No.	Description	Unused Value	Used Value	/ / / / / /
732	A233	3c violet	15	15	
733	A234	3c dark blue	40	48	
734	A235	5c blue	50	22	
a.		Horiz. pair, imperf. vert.	*2,000.*		

1934, Imperf.

735		Sheet of 6	12.50	10.00	
a.	A234	3c dark blue	2.00	1.65	
736	A236	3c carmine rose	15	15	

Perf. 11x10 ½

737	A237	3c deep violet	15	15	

Perf. 11

738	A237	3c deep violet	15	15	
739	A238	3c deep violet	15	15	
a.		Vert. pair, imperf. horiz.	250.00		
b.		Horiz. pair, imperf. vert.	325.00		
740	A239	1c green	15	15	
a.		Vert. pair, imperf. horiz., with gum	*450.00*		
741	A240	2c red	15	15	
a.		Vert. pair, imperf. horiz., with gum	*300.00*		
b.		Horiz. pair, imperf. vert., with gum	*300.00*		
742	A241	3c deep violet	15	15	
a.		Vert. pair, imperf. horiz., with gum	*350.00*		
743	A242	4c brown	35	32	
a.		Vert. pair, imperf. horiz., with gum	*500.00*		
744	A243	5c blue	60	55	
a.		Horiz. pair, imperf. vert., with gum	*400.00*		
745	A244	6c dark blue	1.00	75	
746	A245	7c black	55	65	
a.		Horiz. pair, imperf. vert., with gum	*550.00*		
747	A246	8c sage green	1.40	1.65	
748	A247	9c red orange	1.50	55	
749	A248	10c gray black	2.75	90	

Imperf.

750		Sheet of 6	27.50	25.00	
a.	A241	3c deep violet	3.25	3.00	
751		Sheet of 6	12.00	12.00	
a.	A239	1c green	1.35	1.50	

SUBSCRIBE TO SCOTT STAMP MONTHLY MAGAZINE

INCLUDING THE SCOTT CATALOGUE UPDATE SECTION

LIVELY, ENGAGING ARTICLES

THAT CAPTURE

THE SPECIAL FASCINATION

STAMPS HOLD,

PLUS THE LATEST

INFORMATION ON NEW ISSUES,

INCLUDING SCOTT NUMBERS.

ONE YEAR, 12 ISSUES – $16.95

TWO YEARS, 24 ISSUES – $28.95

CALL TODAY...
1-800-488-5351

OR WRITE TODAY TO: SCOTT PUBLISHING CO., P.O. BOX 828, SIDNEY, OH 45365

Scott No.	Illus. No.		Description	Unused Value	Used Value	//////
1935, Perf. 10 ½x11, Rotary Press Printing						
752	A230	3c	violet	15	15	☐☐☐☐☐
Perf. 11, Flat Plate Printing						
753	A234	3c	dark blue	40	40	☐☐☐☐☐
Imperf.						
754	A237	3c	deep violet	50	50	☐☐☐☐☐
755	A238	3c	deep violet	50	50	☐☐☐☐☐
756	A239	1c	green	20	20	☐☐☐☐☐
757	A240	2c	red	22	22	☐☐☐☐☐
758	A241	3c	deep violet	45	40	☐☐☐☐☐
759	A242	4c	brown	90	90	☐☐☐☐☐
760	A243	5c	blue	1.40	1.25	☐☐☐☐☐
761	A244	6c	dark blue	2.25	2.00	☐☐☐☐☐
762	A245	7c	black	1.40	1.25	☐☐☐☐☐
763	A246	8c	sage green	1.50	1.40	☐☐☐☐☐
764	A247	9c	red orange	1.75	1.50	☐☐☐☐☐
765	A248	10c	gray black	3.50	3.00	☐☐☐☐☐
766			Pane of 25	24.00	24.00	☐☐☐☐☐
a.	A231	1c	yellow green	65	55	☐☐☐☐☐
767			Pane of 25	22.50	22.50	☐☐☐☐☐
a.	A232	3c	violet	50	35	☐☐☐☐☐
768			Pane of 6	18.00	12.50	☐☐☐☐☐
a.	A234	3c	dark blue	2.50	2.00	☐☐☐☐☐
769			Pane of 6	12.00	9.00	☐☐☐☐☐
a.	A239	1c	green	1.75	1.50	☐☐☐☐☐
770			Pane of 6	27.50	22.50	☐☐☐☐☐
a.	A241	3c	deep violet	3.00	3.00	☐☐☐☐☐
771	APSD1	16c	dark blue	2.00	2.00	☐☐☐☐☐
1935, Perf. 11x10 ½, 11						
772	A249	3c	violet	15	15	☐☐☐☐☐
773	A250	3c	purple	15	15	☐☐☐☐☐
774	A251	3c	purple	15	15	☐☐☐☐☐
775	A252	3c	purple	15	15	☐☐☐☐☐
1936						
776	A253	3c	purple	15	15	☐☐☐☐☐
777	A254	3c	purple	15	15	☐☐☐☐☐
778	A254a		Sheet of 4	1.75	1.75	☐☐☐☐☐
a.	A249	3c	violet	40	30	☐☐☐☐☐
b.	A250	3c	violet	40	30	☐☐☐☐☐
c.	A252	3c	violet	40	30	☐☐☐☐☐
d.	A253	3c	violet	40	30	☐☐☐☐☐
782	A255	3c	purple	15	15	☐☐☐☐☐
783	A256	3c	purple	15	15	☐☐☐☐☐
784	A257	3c	dark violet	15	15	☐☐☐☐☐

A251

A255

A254

A256

A257

A258

A259

A260

A261

A262

A263

A264

A265

A266

A267

A268

A269

A269a

A270

A272

A273

A274

A275

A271

A277

A276

A278

Thomas Jefferson	James Madison	White House	James Monroe
A279	**A280**	**A281**	**A282**

John Q. Adams	Andrew Jackson	Martin Van Buren	William H. Harrison
A283	**A284**	**A285**	**A286**

John Tyler	James K. Polk	Zachary Taylor	Millard Fillmore
A287	**A288**	**A289**	**A290**

Franklin Pierce	James Buchanan	Abraham Lincoln	Andrew Johnson
A291	**A292**	**A293**	**A294**

Ulysses S. Grant	Rutherford B. Hayes	James A. Garfield	Chester A. Arthur
A295	**A296**	**A297**	**A298**

Grover Cleveland	Benjamin Harrison	William McKinley	Theodore Roosevelt
A299	**A300**	**A301**	**A302**

Scott No.	Illus. No.	Description	Unused Value	Used Value	/ / / / / /
1936-37					
785	A258	1c green	15	15	
786	A259	2c carmine	15	15	
787	A260	3c purple	15	15	
788	A261	4c gray	30	15	
789	A262	5c ultra	60	15	
790	A263	1c green	15	15	
791	A264	2c carmine	15	15	
792	A265	3c purple	15	15	
793	A266	4c gray	30	15	
794	A267	5c ultra	60	15	
1937					
795	A268	3c red violet	15	15	
796	A269	5c gray blue	20	18	
797	A269a	10c blue green	60	40	
798	A270	3c bright red violet	15	15	
799	A271	3c violet	15	15	
800	A272	3c violet	15	15	
801	A273	3c bright violet	15	15	
802	A274	3c light violet	15	15	
1938-54, Perf. 11x10 ½, 11					
803	A275	½c deep orange	15	15	
804	A276	1c green	15	15	
b.		Booklet pane of 6	1.50	*20*	
805	A277	1 ½c bister brown	15	15	
b.		Horiz. pair, imperf. btwn.	150.00	25.00	
806	A278	2c rose carmine	15	15	
b.		Booklet pane of 6	3.50	*50*	
807	A279	3c deep violet	15	15	
a.		Booklet pane of 6	6.50	*50*	
b.		Horiz. pair, imperf. btwn.	650.00	—	
c.		Imperf., pair	*2,500.*		
808	A280	4c red violet	80	15	
809	A281	4 ½c dark gray	15	15	
810	A282	5c bright blue	22	15	
811	A283	6c red orange	25	15	
812	A284	7c sepia	28	15	
813	A285	8c olive green	30	15	
814	A286	9c rose pink	38	15	
815	A287	10c brown red	28	15	
816	A288	11c ultra	65	15	
817	A289	12c bright violet	1.00	15	
818	A290	13c blue green	1.25	15	
819	A291	14c blue	90	15	
820	A292	15c blue gray	50	15	
821	A293	16c black	90	25	

William
Howard Taft
A303

Woodrow
Wilson
A304

Warren G.
Harding
A305

Calvin
Coolidge
A306

A308

A307

A309

A311

A310

A312

A314

A313

A315

A316

A317

Scott No.	Illus. No.	Description	Unused Value	Used Value	/ / / / / /
822	A294	17c rose red	85	15	
823	A295	18c brown carmine	1.50	15	
824	A296	19c bright violet	1.25	35	
825	A297	20c brt blue green	70	15	
826	A298	21c dull blue	1.25	15	
827	A299	22c vermilion	1.00	40	
828	A300	24c gray black	3.50	18	
829	A301	25c deep red lilac	80	15	
830	A302	30c deep ultra	4.50	15	
831	A303	50c light red violet	7.00	15	
832	A304	$1 purple & black	7.00	15	
a.		Vert. pair, imperf. horiz.	*1,750.*		
b.		Wmkd. USIR	300.00	70.00	
c.		$1 red violet & black	6.00	15	
d.		As "c," vert. pair, imperf. horiz.	*1,000.*		
e.		Vert. pair, imperf. btwn.	*2,500.*		
f.		As "c," vert. pair, imperf. btwn.	*7,000.*		
833	A305	$2 yellow green & black	21.00	3.75	
834	A306	$5 carmine & black	95.00	3.00	
a.		$5 red brown & black	*2,000.*	*1,250.*	

1938

Scott No.	Illus. No.	Description	Unused Value	Used Value	/ / / / / /
835	A307	3c deep violet	22	15	
836	A308	3c red violet	15	15	
837	A309	3c bright violet	15	15	
838	A310	3c violet	15	15	

1939, Coil Stamps, Perf. 10 Vertically

Scott No.	Illus. No.	Description	Unused Value	Used Value	/ / / / / /
839	A276	1c green	20	15	
840	A277	1½c bister brown	24	15	
841	A278	2c rose carmine	24	15	
842	A279	3c deep violet	42	15	
843	A280	4c red violet	6.00	35	
844	A281	4½c dark gray	50	35	
845	A282	5c bright blue	4.50	30	
846	A283	6c red orange	1.10	15	
847	A287	10c brown red	10.00	40	

Perf. 10 Horizontally

Scott No.	Illus. No.	Description	Unused Value	Used Value	/ / / / / /
848	A276	1c green	55	15	
849	A277	1½c bister brown	1.10	30	
850	A278	2c rose carmine	2.00	40	
851	A279	3c deep violet	1.90	35	

1939

Scott No.	Illus. No.	Description	Unused Value	Used Value	/ / / / / /
852	A311	3c bright purple	15	15	
853	A312	3c deep purple	15	15	
854	A313	3c bright red violet	40	15	

Washington
Irving
A318

James Fenimore
Cooper
A319

Ralph Waldo
Emerson
A320

Louisa May
Alcott
A321

Samuel L. Clemens (Mark Twain)
A322

Henry W.
Longfellow
A323

John Greenleaf
Whittier
A324

James Russell
Lowell
A325

Walt
Whitman
A326

James Whitcomb Riley
A327

Horace Mann
A328

Mark Hopkins
A329

Charles W.
Eliot
A330

Frances E.
Willard
A331

Booker T. Washington
A332

Scott No.	Illus. No.	Description	Unused Value	Used Value	/ / / / / /
855	A314	3c violet	1.25	15	
856	A315	3c deep red violet	18	15	
857	A316	3c violet	15	15	
858	A317	3c rose violet	15	15	
1940					
859	A318	1c bright blue green	15	15	
860	A319	2c rose carmine	15	15	
861	A320	3c bright red violet	15	15	
862	A321	5c ultra	28	20	
863	A322	10c dark brown	1.50	1.35	
864	A323	1c bright blue green	15	15	
865	A324	2c rose carmine	15	15	
866	A325	3c bright red violet	15	15	
867	A326	5c ultra	32	18	
868	A327	10c dark brown	1.65	1.40	
869	A328	1c bright blue green	15	15	
870	A329	2c rose carmine	15	15	
871	A330	3c bright red violet	15	15	
872	A331	5c ultra	38	25	
873	A332	10c dark brown	1.10	1.25	
874	A333	1c bright blue green	15	15	
875	A334	2c rose carmine	15	15	
876	A335	3c bright red violet	15	15	
877	A336	5c ultra	25	15	
878	A337	10c dark brown	1.00	95	
879	A338	1c bright blue green	15	15	
880	A339	2c rose carmine	15	15	
881	A340	3c bright red violet	15	15	
882	A341	5c ultra	40	22	
883	A342	10c dark brown	3.50	1.35	
884	A343	1c bright blue green	15	15	
885	A344	2c rose carmine	15	15	
886	A345	3c bright red violet	15	15	
887	A346	5c ultra	48	22	
888	A347	10c dark brown	1.75	1.40	
889	A348	1c bright blue green	15	15	
890	A349	2c rose carmine	15	15	
891	A350	3c bright red violet	25	15	
892	A351	5c ultra	1.00	32	
893	A352	10c dark brown	10.00	2.25	
894	A353	3c henna brown	25	15	
895	A354	3c light violet	20	15	
896	A355	3c bright violet	15	15	
897	A356	3c brown violet	15	15	
898	A357	3c violet	15	15	
899	A358	1c bright blue green	15	15	
a.		Vert. pair, imperf. btwn.	*500.00*	—	
b.		Horiz. pair, imperf. btwn.	40.00	—	

John James
Audubon
A333

Dr. Crawford
W. Long
A334

Luther Burbank
A335

Dr. Walter Reed
A336

Jane Addams
A337

Stephen Collins
Foster
A338

John Philip
Sousa
A339

Victor
Herbert
A340

Edward
MacDowell
A341

Ethelbert Nevin
A342

Gilbert Charles
Stuart
A343

James A. McNeill
Whistler
A344

Augustus
Saint-Gaudens
A345

Daniel Chester
French
A346

Frederic Remington— A347

Scott No.	Illus. No.	Description	Unused Value	Used Value	/ / / / / /
900	A359	2c rose carmine	15	15	
a.		Horiz. pair, imperf. btwn.	40.00	—	
901	A360	3c bright violet	15	15	
a.		Horiz. pair, imperf. btwn.	30.00	—	
902	A361	3c deep violet	16	15	

1941

903	A362	3c light violet	15	15	

1942

904	A363	3c violet	15	15	
905	A364	3c violet	15	15	
b.		3c purple	*20.00*	*8.00*	
906	A365	5c bright blue	22	16	

1943

907	A366	2c rose carmine	15	15	
908	A367	1c bright blue green	15	15	

1943-44

909	A368	5c Poland	18	15	
910	A368	5c Czechoslovakia	18	15	
911	A368	5c Norway	15	15	
912	A368	5c Luxembourg	15	15	
913	A368	5c Netherlands	15	15	
914	A368	5c Belgium	15	15	
915	A368	5c France	15	15	
916	A368	5c Greece	38	25	
917	A368	5c Yugoslavia	28	15	
918	A368	5c Albania	18	15	
919	A368	5c Austria	18	15	
920	A368	5c Denmark	18	15	
921	A368	5c Korea	15	15	

1944

922	A369	3c violet	22	15	
923	A370	3c violet	15	15	
924	A371	3c bright red violet	15	15	
925	A372	3c deep violet	15	15	
926	A373	3c deep violet	15	15	

1945

927	A374	3c bright red violet	15	15	
928	A375	5c ultramarine	15	15	
929	A376	3c yellow green	15	15	

1945-46

930	A377	1c blue green	15	15	

Eli Whitney
A348

Samuel F. B. Morse
A349

Cyrus Hall McCormick
A350

Elias Howe
A351

A353

A352

A355

A356

A354

A361

A358

A357

A359

A362

A360

A363

A364

A366

A367

A365

A368

A369

A370

A371

A372

A373

A374

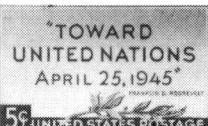
A375

A377

A376

A378

A379

A380

A381

A382

A383

A384 A385 A386 A387

A388 A389 A390

A391 A392 A393

A394 A399 A395

A396 A397 A398

A401 A400 A402

Scott No.	Illus. No.	Description	Unused Value	Used Value	/ / / / / /
931	A378	2c carmine rose	15	15	
932	A379	3c purple	15	15	
933	A380	5c bright blue	15	15	

1945

934	A381	3c olive	15	15	
935	A382	3c blue	15	15	
936	A383	3c bright blue green	15	15	
937	A384	3c purple	15	15	
938	A385	3c dark blue	15	15	

1946

939	A386	3c blue green	15	15	
940	A387	3c dark violet	15	15	
941	A388	3c dark violet	15	15	
942	A389	3c deep blue	15	15	
943	A390	3c violet brown	15	15	
944	A391	3c brown violet	15	15	

1947

945	A392	3c bright red violet	15	15	
946	A393	3c purple	15	15	
947	A394	3c deep blue	15	15	
948	A395	Sheet of 2	60	45	
a.	A1	5c blue	25	20	
b.	A2	10c brown orange	30	25	
949	A396	3c brown violet	15	15	
950	A397	3c dark violet	15	15	
951	A398	3c blue green	15	15	
952	A399	3c bright green	15	15	

1948

953	A400	3c bright red violet	15	15	
954	A401	3c dark violet	15	15	
955	A402	3c brown violet	15	15	
956	A403	3c gray black	15	15	
957	A404	3c dark violet	15	15	
958	A405	5c deep blue	15	15	
959	A406	3c dark violet	15	15	
960	A407	3c bright red violet	15	15	
961	A408	3c blue	15	15	
962	A409	3c rose pink	15	15	
963	A410	3c deep blue	15	15	
964	A411	3c brown red	15	15	
965	A412	3c bright red violet	15	15	
966	A413	3c blue	15	15	
a.		Vert. pair, imperf btwn.	*500.00*		
967	A414	3c rose pink	15	15	

A403 **A404** **A405**

A406 **A407** **A408**

A409 **A410** **A411**

A412 **A413**

A414 **A415**

A416

A417 **A418**

A419 **A420** **A421**

Scott No.	Illus. No.	Description	Unused Value	Used Value	/ / / / / /
968	A415	3c sepia	15	15	☐☐☐☐☐
969	A416	3c orange yellow	15	15	☐☐☐☐☐
970	A417	3c violet	15	15	☐☐☐☐☐
971	A418	3c bright rose carmine	15	15	☐☐☐☐☐
972	A419	3c dark brown	15	15	☐☐☐☐☐
973	A420	3c violet brown	15	15	☐☐☐☐☐
974	A421	3c blue green	15	15	☐☐☐☐☐
975	A422	3c bright red violet	15	15	☐☐☐☐☐
976	A423	3c henna brown	15	15	☐☐☐☐☐
977	A424	3c rose pink	15	15	☐☐☐☐☐
978	A425	3c bright blue	15	15	☐☐☐☐☐
979	A426	3c carmine	15	15	☐☐☐☐☐
980	A427	3c bright red violet	15	15	☐☐☐☐☐

1949

Scott No.	Illus. No.	Description	Unused Value	Used Value	
981	A428	3c blue green	15	15	☐☐☐☐☐
982	A429	3c ultramarine	15	15	☐☐☐☐☐
983	A430	3c green	15	15	☐☐☐☐☐
984	A431	3c aquamarine	15	15	☐☐☐☐☐
985	A432	3c bright rose carmine	15	15	☐☐☐☐☐
986	A433	3c bright red violet	15	15	☐☐☐☐☐

1950

Scott No.	Illus. No.	Description	Unused Value	Used Value	
987	A434	3c yellow green	15	15	☐☐☐☐☐
988	A435	3c bright red violet	15	15	☐☐☐☐☐
989	A436	3c bright blue	15	15	☐☐☐☐☐
990	A437	3c deep green	15	15	☐☐☐☐☐
991	A438	3c light violet	15	15	☐☐☐☐☐
992	A439	3c bright red violet	15	15	☐☐☐☐☐
993	A440	3c violet brown	15	15	☐☐☐☐☐
994	A441	3c violet	15	15	☐☐☐☐☐
995	A442	3c sepia	15	15	☐☐☐☐☐
996	A443	3c bright blue	15	15	
997	A444	3c yellow orange	15	15	

1951

Scott No.	Illus. No.	Description	Unused Value	Used Value	
998	A445	3c gray	15	15	☐☐☐☐☐
999	A446	3c light olive green	15	15	☐☐☐☐☐
1000	A447	3c blue	15	15	☐☐☐☐☐
1001	A448	3c blue violet	15	15	☐☐☐☐☐
1002	A449	3c violet brown	15	15	☐☐☐☐☐
1003	A450	3c violet	15	15	☐☐☐☐☐

1952

Scott No.	Illus. No.	Description	Unused Value	Used Value	
1004	A451	3c carmine rose	15	15	☐☐☐☐☐
1005	A452	3c blue green	15	15	☐☐☐☐☐
1006	A453	3c bright blue	15	15	☐☐☐☐☐
1007	A454	3c deep blue	15	15	☐☐☐☐☐

A422

A423

A424

A425

A426

A427

A428

A429

A430

A432

A433

A431

A434

A435

A436

Scott No.	Illus. No.		Description	Unused Value	Used Value	/ / / / / /
1008	A455	3c	deep violet	15	15	
1009	A456	3c	blue green	15	15	
1010	A457	3c	bright blue	15	15	
1011	A458	3c	blue green	15	15	
1012	A459	3c	violet blue	15	15	
1013	A460	3c	deep blue	15	15	
1014	A461	3c	violet	15	15	
1015	A462	3c	violet	15	15	
1016	A463	3c	deep blue & carmine	15	15	

1953

1017	A464	3c	bright blue	15	15	
1018	A465	3c	chocolate	15	15	
1019	A466	3c	green	15	15	
1020	A467	3c	violet brown	15	15	
1021	A468	5c	green	15	15	
1022	A469	3c	rose violet	15	15	
1023	A470	3c	yellow green	15	15	
1024	A471	3c	deep blue	15	15	
1025	A472	3c	violet	15	15	
1026	A473	3c	blue violet	15	15	
1027	A474	3c	bright red violet	15	15	
1028	A475	3c	copper brown	15	15	

1954

1029	A476	3c	blue	15	15	

1954-68, Perf. 11x10 ½, 10 ½x11, 11

1030	A477	½c	red orange	15	15	
1031	A478	1c	dark green	15	15	
1031A	A478a	1¼c	turquoise	15	15	
1032	A479	1½c	brown carmine	15	15	
1033	A480	2c	carmine rose	15	15	
1034	A481	2½c	gray blue	15	15	
1035	A482	3c	deep violet	15	15	
a.			Booklet pane of 6	4.00	*50*	
b.			Tagged	25	25	
c.			Vert. pair, imperf.	*1,500.*		
d.			Horiz. pair, imperf. btwn.	—		
g.			As "a," vert. imperf. btwn.	*5,000.*		
1036	A483	4c	red violet	15	15	
a.			Booklet pane of 6	2.25	*50*	
b.			Tagged	48	40	
d.			As "a," vert. imperf. horiz.	—		
1037	A484	4½c	blue green	15	15	
1038	A485	5c	deep blue	15	15	
1039	A486	6c	carmine	25	15	
1040	A487	7c	rose carmine	20	15	

A437 A438 A439

A440 A441 A442

A443 A444 A445

A446 A447 A448

A449 A450 A451

A452 A453

A454

A455

A456

A457

A458

A459

A460

A461

A462

A463

A464

A465

A466

A467

A468

A469

A470

A471

A472

A473

A474

A475

A476

A477

A478

A478a

A479

A480

A481

A482

A483

A484

A485

A486

A487

A488

A489

A489a

A490

A491

Scott No.	Illus. No.	Description	Unused Value	Used Value	//////
Perf. 11, Flat Plate or Rotary Press Printing					
1041	A488	8c dark violet blue & carmine	24	15	
a.		Double impression of carmine	*650.00*		
1042	A489	8c dark vio bl & car rose	20	15	
1042A	A489a	8c brown..................	22	15	
1043	A490	9c rose lilac	28	15	
1044	A491	10c rose lake	22	15	
b.		Tagged......................	2.00	1.00	
1044A	A491a	11c carmine & dark violet blue	28	15	
c.		Tagged......................	2.00	1.60	
1045	A492	12c red..............................	32	15	
a.		Tagged......................	45	15	
1046	A493	15c rose lake	90	15	
a.		Tagged......................	1.00	35	
1047	A494	20c ultra............................	45	15	
1048	A495	25c green.......................	1.40	15	
1049	A496	30c black........................	90	15	
1050	A497	40c brown red	1.90	15	
1051	A498	50c bright purple.............	1.50	15	
1052	A499	$1 purple........................	5.00	15	
1053	A500	$5 black	75.00	6.75	
1954-73, Perf. 10 Vertically, Horizontally					
1054	A478	1c dark green.................	18	15	
b.		Imperf., pair......................	*2,000.*	—	
1054A	A478a	1¼c turquoise......................	15	15	
1055	A480	2c rose carmine.............	15	15	
a.		Tagged......................	15	15	
b.		Imperf., pair (Bureau precanceled)...		450.00	
c.		As "a," imperf. pair.........	*525.00*		
1056	A481	2½c gray blue.....................	25	25	
1057	A482	3c deep violet................	15	15	
a.		Imperf., pair......................	*1,350.*	—	
b.		Tagged......................	50	50	
1058	A483	4c red violet.................	15	15	
a.		Imperf., pair......................	90.00	70.00	
1059	A484	4½c blue green..................	1.50	1.20	
1059A	A495	25c green............................	50	30	
b.		Tagged......................	55	20	
c.		Imperf., pair......................	*40.00*		
1954					
1060	A507	3c violet.......................	15	15	
1061	A508	3c brown orange	15	15	
1062	A509	3c violet brown	15	15	
1063	A510	3c violet brown	15	15	

A491a

A492

A493

A494

A495

A496 A497

A498 A499 A500

A507 A509 A508

A510

A511

A512

A513

A514

A516

A515

A517

A520

A518

A519

A521

Souvenir Sheet.

A523

A522

A524

A525

A526

A527

A528

A529

A530

A531

A532

A534

A533

A535

A537

A536

A538

A539

A540

A541

A542

A543

A544

Scott No.	Illus. No.		Description	Unused Value	Used Value	/ / / / / /
1955						
1064	A511	3c	violet brown	15	15	
1065	A512	3c	green	15	15	
1066	A513	8c	deep blue	16	15	
1067	A514	3c	purple	15	15	
1068	A515	3c	green	15	15	
1069	A516	3c	blue	15	15	
1070	A517	3c	deep blue	15	15	
1071	A518	3c	light brown	15	15	
1072	A519	3c	rose carmine	15	15	
1956						
1073	A520	3c	bright carmine	15	15	
1074	A521	3c	deep blue	15	15	
1075	A522		Sheet of 2	2.25	2.00	
a.	A482	3c	deep violet	90	80	
b.	A488	8c	dark violet blue & carmine	1.25	1.00	
1076	A523	3c	deep violet	15	15	
1077	A524	3c	rose lake	15	15	
1078	A525	3c	brown	15	15	
1079	A526	3c	blue green	15	15	
1080	A527	3c	dark blue green	15	15	
1081	A528	3c	black brown	15	15	
1082	A529	3c	deep blue	15	15	
1083	A530	3c	black, *orange*	15	15	
1084	A531	3c	violet	15	15	
1085	A532	3c	dark blue	15	15	
1957						
1086	A533	3c	rose red	15	15	
1087	A534	3c	red lilac	15	15	
1088	A535	3c	dark blue	15	15	
1089	A536	3c	red lilac	15	15	
1090	A537	3c	bright ultra	15	15	
1091	A538	3c	blue green	15	15	
1092	A539	3c	dark blue	15	15	
1093	A540	3c	rose lake	15	15	
1094	A541	4c	dark blue & deep carmine	15	15	
1095	A542	3c	deep violet	15	15	
1096	A543	8c	carmine, ultra & ocher	16	15	
1097	A544	3c	rose lake	15	15	
1098	A545	3c	blue, ocher & green	15	15	
1099	A546	3c	black	15	15	
1958						
1100	A547	3c	green	15	15	
1104	A551	3c	deep claret	15	15	
1105	A552	3c	purple	15	15	

A545

A546

A547

A551

A552

A553

A554

A555

A556

A557

A558

A559

A561

A560

A562

A564

A563

84

Scott No.	Illus. No.	Description	Unused Value	Used Value	/ / / / / /
1106	A553	3c green	15	15	
1107	A554	3c black & red orange	15	15	
1108	A555	3c light green	15	15	
1109	A556	3c bright greenish blue	15	15	
1110	A557	4c olive bister	15	15	
1111	A557	8c carmine, ultra & ocher	16	15	
1112	A558	4c reddish purple	15	15	

1958-59

1113	A559	1c green	15	15	
1114	A560	3c purple	15	15	
1115	A561	4c sepia	15	15	
1116	A562	4c dark blue	15	15	

1958

1117	A563	4c green	15	15	
1118	A563	8c carmine, ultra & ocher	16	15	
1119	A564	4c black	15	15	
1120	A565	4c crimson rose	15	15	
1121	A566	4c dark carmine rose	15	15	
1122	A567	4c green, yellow & brown	15	15	
1123	A568	4c blue	15	15	

1959

1124	A569	4c blue green	15	15	
1125	A570	4c blue	15	15	
a.		Horiz. pair, imperf. btwn.	1,250.		
1126	A570	8c carmine, ultra & ocher	16	15	
1127	A571	4c blue	15	15	
1128	A572	4c brt greenish blue	15	15	
1129	A573	8c rose lake	16	15	
1130	A574	4c black	15	15	
1131	A575	4c red & dark blue	15	15	
1132	A576	4c ocher, dark blue & deep carmine	15	15	
1133	A577	4c blue, green & ocher	15	15	
1134	A578	4c brown	15	15	
1135	A579	4c green	15	15	
1136	A580	4c gray	15	15	
1137	A580	8c carmine, ultra & ocher	16	15	
1138	A581	4c rose lake	15	15	
a.		Vert. pair, imperf. btwn.	400.00		
b.		Vert. pair, imperf. horiz.	275.00		

1960-61

1139	A582	4c dark violet blue & carmine	15	15	
1140	A583	4c olive bister & green	15	15	
1141	A584	4c gray & vermilion	15	15	
1142	A585	4c carmine & dark blue	15	15	

A565

A566

A568

A567

A569

A570

A572

A571

A573

A574

A578

A575

A577

A576

A580

A579

A581

Scott No.	Illus. No.	Description	Unused Value	Used Value	/ / / / / /
1143	A586	4c magenta & green............	15	15	
1144	A587	4c green & brown	15	15	

1960

1145	A588	4c red, dark blue & dark bister	15	15	
1146	A589	4c dull blue............................	15	15	
1147	A590	4c blue...................................	15	15	
a.		Vert. pair, imperf. btwn. .	3,250.		
1148	A590	8c carmine, ultra & ocher	16	15	
a.		Horiz. pair, imperf. btwn.	—		
1149	A591	4c gray black........................	15	15	
1150	A592	4c dark blue, brown orange & green	15	15	
1151	A593	4c blue...................................	15	15	
a.		Vert. pair, imperf. btwn. .	150.00		
1152	A594	4c deep violet	15	15	
1153	A595	4c dark blue & red	15	15	
1154	A596	4c sepia.................................	15	15	
1155	A597	4c dark blue..........................	15	15	
1156	A598	4c green	15	15	
1157	A599	4c green & rose red..............	15	15	
1158	A600	4c blue & pink......................	15	15	
1159	A601	4c blue...................................	15	15	
1160	A601	8c carmine, ultra & ocher	16	15	
1161	A602	4c dull violet	15	15	
1162	A603	4c dark blue..........................	15	15	
1163	A604	4c indigo, slate & rose red ...	15	15	
1164	A605	4c dark blue & carmine	15	15	
1165	A606	4c blue...................................	15	15	
1166	A606	8c carmine, ultra & ocher	16	15	
1167	A607	4c dark blue & bright red.....	15	15	
1168	A608	4c green	15	15	
1169	A608	8c carmine, ultra & ocher	16	15	
1170	A609	4c dull violet	15	15	
1171	A610	4c deep claret	15	15	
1172	A611	4c dull violet	15	15	
1173	A612	4c deep violet	18	15	

1961

1174	A613	4c red orange.......................	15	15	
1175	A613	8c carmine, ultra & ocher	16	15	
1176	A614	4c blue, slate & brown orange	15	15	
1177	A615	4c dull violet	15	15	

1961-65

1178	A616	4c light green........................	16	15	
1179	A617	4c black, *peach blossom*	15	15	
1180	A618	5c gray & blue......................	15	15	
1181	A619	5c dark red & black..............	15	15	

A582

A583

A584

A589

A585

A586

A587

A588

A590

A591

A592

A593

A594

A595

A596

A597

  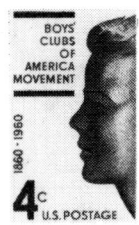 

A598   A599   A600   A604

A608   A603   A601

  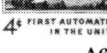

A613   A605   A606

A602   A609   A610   A611

A612   A607   A614

89

A616

A615

A617

A618

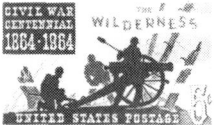
A619

A621

A622

A620

A623

A624

A625

A626

A627

A628

A629

A631

A630

Scott No.	Illus. No.	Description	Unused Value	Used Value	/ / / / / /
1182	A620	5c Prus blue & black............	25	15	
a.		Horiz. pair, imperf. vert. .	4,500.		

1961

1183	A621	4c brown, dark red & green, *yellow*	15	15	
1184	A622	4c blue green......................	15	15	
1185	A623	4c blue...............................	15	15	
1186	A624	4c ultra, *grayish*	15	15	
1187	A625	4c multicolored	15	15	
1188	A626	4c blue...............................	15	15	
1189	A627	4c brown............................	15	15	
1190	A628	4c blue, green, orange & black	15	15	

1962

1191	A629	4c light blue, maroon & bister	15	15	
1192	A630	4c carmine, violet blue & green	15	15	
1193	A631	4c dark blue & yellow	15	15	
1194	A632	4c blue & bister..................	15	15	
1195	A633	4c black, *buff*......................	15	15	
1196	A634	4c red & dark blue	15	15	
1197	A635	4c blue, dark slate grn & red	15	15	
1198	A636	4c slate...............................	15	15	
1199	A637	4c rose red..........................	15	15	
1200	A638	4c violet.............................	15	15	
1201	A639	4c black, *yellow bister*	15	15	
1202	A640	4c dark blue & red brown....	15	15	
1203	A641	4c black, brown & yellow ...	15	15	
1204	A641	4c blk, brown & yel (yellow inverted)..........	15	15	
1205	A642	4c green & red.....................	15	15	
1206	A643	4c blue green & black..........	15	15	
1207	A644	4c multicolored	15	15	
a.		Horiz. pair, imperf. btwn. and at right...................	6,750.		

1963-66

1208	A645	5c blue & red......................	15	15	
a.		Tagged............................	16	15	
b.		Horiz. pair, imperf. btwn.	1,500.		

1962-66, Perf. 11x10 ½

1209	A646	1c green...............................	15	15	
a.		Tagged............................	15	15	
1213	A650	5c dark blue gray.................	15	15	
a.		Booklet pane 5 + label	2.75	*1.50*	
b.		Tagged............................	50	22	
c.		As "a," tagged	1.75	*1.50*	

A633

A632

A637

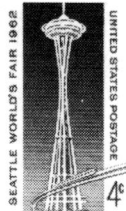
A634

A636

A640

A638

A639

A635

A642   A645

A663

A646   A650

A644

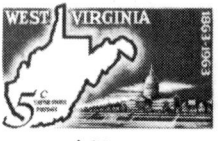
A643

A641

A662   A664   A665

Scott No.	Illus. No.	Description	Unused Value	Used Value	//////

Coil stamps, Perf. 10 Vertically

Scott No.	Illus. No.	Description	Unused Value	Used Value
1225	A646	1c green	15	15
a.		Tagged	15	15
1229	A650	5c dark blue gray	1.00	15
a.		Tagged	1.25	15
b.		Imperf., pair	*375.00*	

1963

Scott No.	Illus. No.	Description	Unused Value	Used Value
1230	A662	5c dark carmine & brown	15	15
1231	A663	5c green, buff & red	15	15
1232	A664	5c green, red & blk	15	15
1233	A665	5c dark blue, black & red	15	15
1234	A666	5c ultra & green	15	15
1235	A667	5c blue green	15	15
1236	A668	5c bright purple	15	15
1237	A669	5c Prussian blue & black	15	15
1238	A670	5c gray, dark blue & red	15	15
1239	A671	5c bluish black & red	15	15
1240	A672	5c dark blue, bluish black & red	15	15
a.		Tagged	65	40
1241	A673	5c dark blue & multi	15	15

1964

Scott No.	Illus. No.	Description	Unused Value	Used Value
1242	A674	5c black	15	15
1243	A675	5c indigo, red brown & olive	15	15
1244	A676	5c blue green	15	15
1245	A677	5c brown, grn, yel grn & olive	15	15
1246	A678	5c blue gray	15	15
1247	A679	5c bright ultra	15	15
1248	A680	5c red, yellow & blue	15	15
1249	A681	5c dark blue & red	15	15
1250	A682	5c black brown, *tan*	15	15
1251	A683	5c green	15	15
1252	A684	5c red, black & blue	15	15
a.		Blue omitted	*1,250.*	
1253	A685	5c multicolored	15	15
1254	A686	5c green, carmine & black	35	15
a.		Tagged	75	50
1255	A687	5c carmine, green & black	35	15
a.		Tagged	75	50
1256	A688	5c carmine, green & black	35	15
a.		Tagged	75	50
1257	A689	5c black, green & carmine	35	15
a.		Tagged	75	50
b.		Block of 4, #1254-1257	1.50	1.25
c.		Block of 4, #1254a-1257a	4.25	2.00
1258	A690	5c blue green	15	15
1259	A691	5c ultra, black & dull red	15	15
1260	A692	5c red lilac	15	15

A666

A667

A668

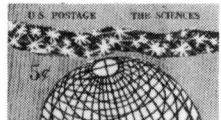
A669

A671

A675

A670

A676

A680

A672

A678

A679

A673

A677

A674

A681

A682

Scott No.	Illus. No.	Description	Unused Value	Used Value	/ / / / / /
1965					
1261	A693	5c deep carmine, violet blue & gray	15	15	
1262	A694	5c maroon & black..............	15	15	
1263	A695	5c black, purple & red orange	15	15	
1264	A696	5c black	15	15	
1265	A697	5c black, yellow ocher & red lilac	15	15	
1266	A698	5c dull blue & black..............	15	15	
1267	A699	5c red, black & dark blue.....	15	15	
1268	A700	5c maroon, *tan*	15	15	
1269	A701	5c rose red............................	15	15	
1270	A702	5c black & blue.....................	15	15	
1271	A703	5c red, yellow & black..........	15	15	
a.		Yellow omitted................	550.00		
1272	A704	5c emerald, black & red.......	15	15	
1273	A705	5c black, brown & olive	15	15	
1274	A706	11c black, carmine & bister...	32	16	
1275	A707	5c pale blue, blk, car & vio blue	15	15	
1276	A708	5c car, dk olive grn & bister	15	15	
a.		Tagged............................	75	25	
1965-78, Perf. 11x10 ½, 10 ½x11					
1278	A710	1c green, tagged...................	15	15	
a.		Booklet pane of 8............	1.00	*25*	
b.		Booklet pane of 4 + 2 labels	75	*20*	
c.		Untagged (Bureau precanceled)		15	
1279	A711	1 ¼c light green.......................	15	15	
1280	A712	2c dark blue gray, tagged.....	15	15	
a.		Booklet pane of 5 + label	1.20	*40*	
b.		Untagged (Bureau precanceled)		15	
c.		Booklet pane of 6	1.00	*35*	
1281	A713	3c violet, tagged...................	15	15	
a.		Untagged (Bureau precanceled)		15	
1282	A714	4c black	15	15	
a.		Tagged............................	15	15	
1283	A715	5c blue..................................	15	15	
a.		Tagged............................	15	15	
1283B	A715a	5c blue, tagged	15	15	
d.		Untagged (Bureau precanceled)		15	
1284	A716	6c gray brown	15	15	
a.		Tagged............................	15	15	
b.		Booklet pane of 8............	1.50	*50*	
c.		Booklet pane of 5 + label	1.25	*50*	
1285	A717	8c violet................................	20	15	
a.		Tagged............................	16	15	
1286	A718	10c lilac, tagged	20	15	
b.		Untagged (Bureau precanceled)		20	
1286A	A718a	12c black, tagged	25	15	
c.		Untagged (Bureau precanceled)		25	

A684

A683

A685

A686

A687

A688

A689

A690

A691

A692

A696

A694

A695

A697

A693

A698

Scott No.	Illus. No.		Description	Unused Value	Used Value	/ / / / / /
1287	A719	13c	brown, tagged..................	25	15	
a.			Untagged (Bureau precanceled)		25	
1288	A720	15c	rose claret, tagged	30	15	
a.			Untagged (Bureau precanceled)		30	
d.			Type II................	55	15	

Perf. 10

1288B	A720	15c	dk rose cl (from bklt. pane)	28	15	
c.			Booklet pane of 8.............	2.75	*1.25*	
e.			As "c," vert. imperf. btwn.	—		

Perf. 11x10 ½, 10 ½x11

1289	A721	20c	deep olive...............	42	15	
a.			Tagged........................	40	15	
1290	A722	25c	rose lake	55	15	
a.			Tagged........................	55	15	
b.		25c	maroon...........................	—		
1291	A723	30c	red lilac........................	65	15	
a.			Tagged........................	60	15	
1292	A724	40c	blue black	85	15	
a.			Tagged........................	75	15	
1293	A725	50c	rose magenta	1.00	15	
a.			Tagged........................	85	15	
1294	A726	$1	dull purple	2.50	15	
a.			Tagged........................	2.00	15	
1295	A727	$5	gray black.....................	12.50	2.00	
a.			Tagged........................	8.50	2.00	

1966-81, Coil stamps, Tagged, Perf. 10 Horizontally

1297	A713	3c	violet............................	15	15	
a.			Imperf., pair..................	*30.00*		
b.			Untagged (Bureau precanceled)		15	
c.			As "b," imperf. pair.........		6.00	
1298	A716	6c	gray brown	15	15	
a.			Imperf., pair..................	*2,000.*		

Perf. 10 Vertically

1299	A710	1c	green.............................	15	15	
a.			Untagged (Bureau precanceled)		15	
b.			Imperf., pair..................	*30.00*	—	
1303	A714	4c	black	15	15	
a.			Untagged (Bureau precanceled)		15	
b.			Imperf., pair..................	*800.00*		
1304	A715	5c	blue..............................	15	15	
a.			Untagged (Bureau precanceled)		15	
b.			Imperf., pair..................	*150.00*		
e.			As "a," imperf. pair.........		*450.00*	
1304C	A715a	5c	blue..............................	15	15	
d.			Imperf., pair..................	—		

A700

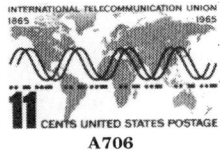
A706

A701

A703

A702

A704

A705

A707

A699

A708

A710

A711

A712

A713

A714

A715

A715a
Redrawn

A716

A717

Scott No.	Illus. No.		Description	Unused Value	Used Value	//////
1305	A727a	6c	gray brown	15	15	
a.			Imperf., pair	70.00		
b.			Untagged (Bureau precanceled)		20	
1305E	A720	15c	rose claret	25	15	
f.			Untagged (Bureau precanceled)		30	
g.			Imperf., pair	25.00		
h.			Pair, imperf. between	200.00		
i.			Type II	35	15	
j.			Imperf., pair, type II	70.00		
1305C	A726	$1	dull purple	1.50	20	
d.			Imperf., pair	2,250.		

1966

Scott No.	Illus. No.		Description	Unused Value	Used Value	//////
1306	A728	5c	blk, crimson & dark blue	15	15	
1307	A729	5c	orange brown & black	15	15	
1308	A730	5c	yellow, ocher & violet blue	15	15	
1309	A731	5c	multicolored	20	15	
1310	A732	5c	multicolored	15	15	
1311	A733	5c	multicolored	15	15	
1312	A734	5c	carmine, dark & light blue	15	15	
1313	A735	5c	red	15	15	
1314	A736	5c	yellow, black & green	15	15	
a.			Tagged	30	25	
1315	A737	5c	black, bister, red & ultra	15	15	
a.			Tagged	30	20	
b.			Black & bister (engr.) omitted	—		
1316	A738	5c	black, pink & blue	15	15	
a.			Tagged	30	20	
1317	A739	5c	green, red & black	15	15	
a.			Tagged	30	20	
1318	A740	5c	emerald, pink & black	15	15	
a.			Tagged	30	20	
1319	A741	5c	ver, yellow, blue & green	15	15	
a.			Tagged	30	20	
1320	A742	5c	red, dark & light blue, black	15	15	
a.			Tagged	30	20	
b.			Red, dark blue & black omitted	4,750.		
c.			Dark blue (engr.) omitted	8,000.		
1321	A743	5c	multicolored	15	15	
a.			Tagged	30	20	
1322	A744	5c	multicolored	15	15	
a.			Tagged	30	25	

1967

Scott No.	Illus. No.		Description	Unused Value	Used Value	//////
1323	A745	5c	multicolored	15	15	
1324	A746	5c	multicolored	15	15	
1325	A747	5c	multicolored	15	15	
1326	A748	5c	blue, red & black	15	15	

A718

A718a

A719

A720

A721

A723

A722

A724

A725

A726

A727

A727a

A730

A732

A731

A728

A729

A734

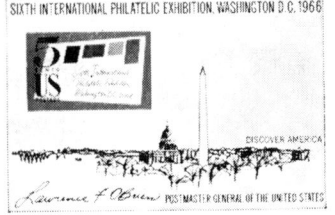
A733

A735

Scott No.	Illus. No.		Description	Unused Value	Used Value	//////
1327	A749	5c	red, black & green............	15	15	
1328	A750	5c	dk red brown, lemon & yel	15	15	
1329	A751	5c	red, blue, black & carmine	15	15	
1330	A752	5c	green, black & yellow.....	15	15	
a.			Vert. pair, imperf. btwn. .	6,000.		
b.			Green (engr.) omitted......	—		
c.			Black & green (engr.) omitted	—		
d.			Yellow & green (litho.) omitted	—		
1331	A753	5c	multicolored	55	15	
a.			Pair, #1331-1332.............	1.25	1.25	
1332	A754	5c	multicolored	55	15	
1333	A755	5c	dark & light blue, black ..	15	15	
1333	A755	5c	dark blue, light blue & black	15	15	
1334	A756	5c	blue.................................	15	15	
1335	A757	5c	gold & multicolored........	15	15	
1336	A758	5c	multicolored	15	15	
1337	A759	5c	brt grnsh blue, green & red brown	15	15	

1968-71, Perf. 11

1338	A760	6c	dark blue, red & green	15	15	
k.			Vert. pair, imperf. btwn. .	500.00		

Coil stamp, Perf. 10 Vertically

1338A	A760	6c	dark blue, red & green	15	15	
b.			Imperf., pair.....................	450.00		

Perf. 11x10 ½

1338D	A760	6c	dark blue, red & green	15	15	
e.			Horiz. pair, imperf. btwn.	100.00		
1338F	A760	8c	multicolored	16	15	
i.			Vert. pair, imperf.............	40.00		
j.			Horiz. pair, imperf. btwn.	40.00		
p.			Slate green omitted	—		

Coil stamp, Perf. 10 Vertically

1338G	A760	8c	multicolored	18	15	
h.			Imperf., pair.....................	55.00		

1968

1339	A761	6c	multicolored	15	15	
1340	A762	6c	blue, rose red & white.....	15	15	
a.			White omitted..................	1,400.		
1341	A763	$1	sepia, dk blue, ocher & brn red	2.65	1.25	
1342	A764	6c	ultra & orange red	15	15	
1343	A765	6c	chalky blue, black & red .	15	15	
1344	A766	6c	black, yellow & orange...	15	15	

A737

A736

A739

A738

A741

A743

A745

A740

A747

A744

A742

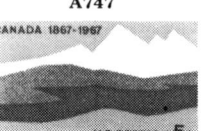
A746

A749

A748

A751

A750

A752

Scott No.	Illus. No.	Description	Unused Value	Used Value
1345	A767	6c dark blue..................	50	25
1346	A768	6c dark blue & red	35	25
1347	A769	6c dark blue & olive green ..	30	25
1348	A770	6c dark blue & red	30	25
1349	A771	6c dark blue, yellow & red ..	30	25
1350	A772	6c dark blue & red	30	25
1351	A773	6c dark bl, olive grn & red...	30	25
1352	A774	6c dark blue & red	30	25
1353	A775	6c dark blue, yellow & red ..	30	25
1354	A776	6c dark blue, red & yellow ..	30	25
a.		Strip of 10, #1345-1354..	3.25	3.00
1355	A777	6c multicolored..................	16	15
a.		Ocher (Walt Disney, 6c, etc.) omitted..........................	700.00	—
b.		Vert. pair, imperf. horiz. .	750.00	
c.		Imperf., pair.....................	600.00	
d.		Black omitted..................	2,100.	
e.		Horiz. pair, imperf. btwn. .	4,750.	
f.		Blue omitted....................	2,100.	
1356	A778	6c black, apple green & org brn	15	15
1357	A779	6c yel, dp yel, maroon & blk	15	15
1358	A780	6c bright blue, dk blue & blk	15	15
1359	A781	6c light gray brown & blk brn	15	15
1360	A782	6c brown..............................	15	15
1361	A783	6c multicolored..................	15	15
1362	A784	6c black & multi	15	15
a.		Vert. pair, imperf. btwn. .	550.00	
b.		Red & dark blue omitted.	1,400.	
1363	A785	6c multicolored..................	15	15
a.		Untagged	15	15
b.		Imperf., pair, tagged........	250.00	
c.		Light yellow omitted.......	120.00	
d.		Imperf., pair, untagged....	325.00	
1364	A786	6c black & multi	16	15

1969

Scott No.	Illus. No.	Description	Unused Value	Used Value
1365	A787	6c multicolored..................	40	15
1366	A788	6c multicolored..................	40	15
1367	A789	6c multicolored..................	40	15
1368	A790	6c multicolored..................	40	15
a.		Block of 4, #1365-1368..	1.85	1.50
1369	A791	6c red, blue & black.............	15	15
1370	A792	6c multicolored..................	15	15
a.		Horiz. pair, imperf. btwn.	225.00	
b.		Black and Prus blue omitted	1,000.	
1371	A793	6c black, blue & ocher........	15	15
1372	A794	6c multicolored..................	15	15
1373	A795	6c multicolored..................	15	15

A753

A754

A755

A757

A756

A758

A759

A760

A764

A761

A763

A762

A765

A769

A766

Scott No.	Illus. No.		Description	Unused Value	Used Value	/ / / / / /
1374	A796	6c	multicolored	15	15	
1375	A797	6c	multicolored	15	15	
1376	A798	6c	multicolored	75	15	
1377	A799	6c	multicolored	75	15	
1378	A800	6c	multicolored	75	15	
1379	A801	6c	multicolored	75	15	
a.			Block of 4, #1376-1379	3.00	3.00	
1380	A802	6c	green	15	15	
1381	A803	6c	yellow, red, black & green	55	15	
a.			Black (1869-1969, United States, 6c, Professional Baseball) omitted	1,100.		
1382	A804	6c	red & green	15	15	
1383	A805	6c	blue, black & red	15	15	
1384	A806	6c	dark green & multi	15	15	
			Precanceled	50	15	
b.			Imperf., pair	1,250.		
c.			Light green omitted	25.00		
d.			Lt grn, red & yellow omitted	1,000.	—	
e.			Yellow omitted	—		
g.			Red & yellow omitted	—		
1385	A807	6c	multicolored	15	15	
1386	A808	6c	multicolored	15	15	

1970

Scott No.	Illus. No.		Description	Unused Value	Used Value	
1387	A809	6c	multicolored	15	15	
1388	A810	6c	multicolored	15	15	
1389	A811	6c	multicolored	15	15	
1390	A812	6c	multicolored	15	15	
a.			Block of 4, #1387-1390	50	50	
1391	A813	6c	black & multi	15	15	
1392	A814	6c	black, *light brown*	15	15	

1970-74, Tagged, Perf. 11x10 ½, 10 ½x11, 11 (#1394)

1393	A815	6c	dark blue gray	15	15	
a.			Booklet pane of 8	1.25	*50*	
b.			Booklet pane of 5 + label	1.25	*50*	
c.			Untagged (Bureau precanceled)		15	
1393D	A816	7c	bright blue	15	15	
e.			Untagged (Bureau precanceled)		15	
1394	A815a	8c	black, red & blue gray	16	15	
1395	A815	8c	deep claret	18	15	
a.			Booklet pane of 8	1.80	*1.25*	
b.			Booklet pane of 6	1.25	*75*	
c.			Booklet pane of 4 + 2 labels	1.65	*50*	
d.			Booklet pane of 7 + label	1.75	*1.00*	
1396	A817	8c	multi	15	15	
1397	A817a	14c	gray brown	25	15	
a.			Untagged (Bureau precanceled)		25	

Scott No.	Illus. No.		Description	Unused Value	Used Value
1398	A818	16c	brown..............................	28	15
a.			Untagged (Bureau precanceled)		35
1399	A818a	18c	violet...............................	32	15
1400	A818b	21c	green...............................	32	15

Coil stamps, Perf. 10 Vertically

Scott No.	Illus. No.		Description	Unused Value	Used Value
1401	A815	6c	dark blue gray.................	15	15
a.			Untagged (Bureau precanceled)		15
b.			Imperf., pair....................	1,500.	
1402	A815	8c	deep claret	15	15
a.			Imperf., pair....................	45.00	
b.			Untagged (Bureau precanceled)		15
c.			Pair, imperf. btwn.	6,250.	

1970

Scott No.	Illus. No.		Description	Unused Value	Used Value
1405	A819	6c	black & olive bister........	15	15
1406	A820	6c	blue..................................	15	15
1407	A821	6c	bister, black & red..........	15	15
1408	A822	6c	gray..................................	15	15
1409	A823	6c	yellow & multi	15	15
1410	A824	6c	multicolored	22	15
1411	A825	6c	multicolored	22	15
1412	A826	6c	multicolored	22	15
1413	A827	6c	multicolored	22	15
a.			Block of 4, #1410-1413..	1.00	1.00
1414	A828	6c	multicolored	15	15
a.			Precanceled	15	15
b.			Black omitted.................	650.00	
c.			As "a," blue omitted........	1,500.	
1415	A829	6c	multicolored	40	15
a.			Precanceled	90	15
b.			Black omitted.................	2,500.	
1416	A830	6c	multicolored	40	15
a.			Precanceled	90	15
b.			Black omitted.................	2,500.	
c.			Imperf., pair (#1416, 1418)		4,000.
1417	A831	6c	multicolored	40	15
a.			Precanceled	90	15
b.			Black omitted.................	2,500.	
1418	A832	6c	multicolored	40	15
a.			Precanceled	90	15
b.			Block of 4, #1415-1418..	1.90	1.75
c.			As "b," precanceled	3.75	3.50
d.			Black omitted.................	2,500.	
1419	A833	6c	black, vermilion & ultra..	15	15
1420	A834	6c	black, org, yel, brn, mag & blue............................	15	15
a.			Orange & yellow omitted....................	1,200.	

A787

A788

A789

A790

A795

A791

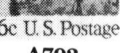
A792

A793

A796 **A794**

A797

A798

A799

A800

A801

Scott No.	Illus. No.	Description	Unused Value	Used Value	/ / / / / /
1421	A835	6c multicolored....................	15	15	
a.		Pair, #1421-1422.............	25	25	
1422	A836	6c dark blue, black & red.....	15	15	

1971

1423	A837	6c multicolored....................	15	15	
1424	A838	6c black, red & dark blue.....	15	15	
1425	A839	6c light blue, scarlet & indigo	15	15	
1426	A840	8c multicolored....................	15	15	
1427	A841	8c multicolored....................	16	15	
1428	A842	8c multicolored....................	16	15	
1429	A843	8c multicolored....................	16	15	
1430	A844	8c multicolored....................	16	15	
a.		Block of 4, #1427-1430..	65	65	
b.		As "a," lt grn & dk grn omitted from #1427-1428	3,500.		
c.		As "a," red omitted from #1427, 1429-1430	9,000.		
1431	A845	8c red & dark blue	16	15	
1432	A846	8c red, blue, gray & black....	16	15	
a.		Gray & black omitted	650.00		
b.		Gray ("U.S. Postage 8c") omitted........................	1,100.		
1433	A847	8c multicolored....................	15	15	
1434	A848	8c blkac, blue, yellow & red	15	15	
a.		Pair, #1434-1435.............	30	25	
b.		As "a," blue & red (litho.) omitted.........................	1,500.		
1435	A849	8c black, blue, yellow & red	15	15	
1436	A850	8c multi, *greenish*	15	15	
a.		Black & olive (engr.) omitted	950.00		
b.		Pale rose omitted.............	7,500.		
1437	A851	8c multicolored....................	15	15	
1438	A852	8c blue, deep blue & black ..	15	15	
1439	A853	8c multicolored....................	15	15	
a.		Black omitted..................	4,500.		
1440	A854	8c black brown & ocher.......	16	15	
1441	A855	8c black brown & ocher.......	16	15	
1442	A856	8c black brown & ocher.......	16	15	
1443	A857	8c black brown & ocher.......	16	15	
a.		Block of 4, #1440-1443 ..	65	65	
b.		As "a," black brown omitted	2,400.		
c.		As "a," ocher omitted......	—		
1444	A858	8c gold & multi	15	15	
a.		Gold omitted	600.00		
1445	A859	8c multicolored....................	15	15	

A802

A803

A807

A806

A805

A804

A808

A809

A810

A811

A812

A813

A814

EISENHOWER·USA
Dot between "R"
and "U"

A815

EISENHOWER USA
No dot between
"R" and "U"

A815a

A816

A817

A817a

A818

A818a

A818b

A820

A819

A821

A822

A823

A824

A825

A826

A827

A828

A829 A830

A831

A832

A835 A836

A833

A838

A834 A837

A839 A840

Scott No.	Illus. No.		Description	Unused Value	Used Value	/ / / / / /
1972						
1446	A860	8c	black, brown & light blue	15	15	
1447	A861	8c	dark blue, light blue & red	15	15	
1448	A862	2c	black & multi	15	15	
1449	A863	2c	black & multi	15	15	
1450	A864	2c	black & multi	15	15	
1451	A865	2c	black & multi	15	15	
a.			Block of 4, #1448-1451 ..	20	20	
b.			As "a," black (litho.) omitted	2,750.		
1452	A866	6c	black & multi	15	15	
1453	A867	8c	black, blue, brown & multi	15	15	
1454	A868	15c	black & multi	30	18	
1455	A869	8c	black & multi	15	15	
a.			Yellow omitted................	—		
b.			Dark brown & olive omitted	—		
c.			Dark brown omitted........	—		
1456	A870	8c	deep brown....................	16	15	
1457	A871	8c	deep brown....................	16	15	
1458	A872	8c	deep brown....................	16	15	
1459	A873	8c	deep brown....................	16	15	
a.			Block of 4, #1456-1459 ..	65	65	
1460	A874	6c	multicolored	15	15	
1461	A875	8c	multicolored	15	15	
1462	A876	15c	multicolored	28	18	
1463	A877	8c	yellow & black................	15	15	
1464	A878	8c	multicolored	16	15	
1465	A879	8c	multicolored	16	15	
1466	A880	8c	multicolored	16	15	
1467	A881	8c	multicolored	16	15	
a.			Block of 4, #1464-1467 ..	65	65	
b.			As "a," brown omitted	3,750.		
c.			As "a," green & blue omitted	—		
d.			As "a," red & brown omitted	4,250.		
1468	A882	8c	multicolored	15	15	
1469	A883	8c	yellow, orange & dark brown	15	15	
1470	A884	8c	black & multi	15	15	
a.			Horiz. pair, imperf. btwn.	4,500.		
b.			Red & black (engr.) omitted	2,000.		
c.			Yellow & tan (litho.) omitted	1,850.		
1471	A885	8c	multicolored	15	15	
a.			Pink omitted....................	250.00		
b.			Black omitted..................	4,000.		
1472	A886	8c	multicolored	15	15	
1473	A887	8c	black & multi	15	15	
a.			Blue & orange omitted....	1,000.		
b.			Blue omitted....................	2,000.		
c.			Orange omitted................	2,000.		

113

A841

A842

A843

A844

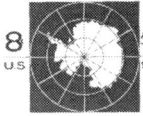
A845

A847

A846

A848

A849

A850

A851

A852

A853

Scott No.	Illus. No.	Description	Unused Value	Used Value	/ / / / / /
1474	A888	8c dark blue green, black & brown	15	15	
a.		Black (litho.) omitted......	1,000.		
1973					
1475	A889	8c red, emerald & violet blue	15	15	
1476	A890	8c ultra, greenish black & red	15	15	
1477	A891	8c black, vermilion & ultra..	15	15	
1478	A892	8c multicolored	15	15	
1479	A893	8c multicolored	15	15	
1480	A894	8c black & multi	15	15	
1481	A895	8c black & multi	15	15	
1482	A896	8c black & multi	15	15	
1483	A897	8c black & multi	15	15	
a.		Block of 4, #1480-1483..	65	45	
b.		As "a," black (engr.) omitted	1,650.		
c.		As "a," black (litho.) omitted	1,250.		
1484	A898	8c deep green & multi	15	15	
a.		Vert. pair, imperf. horiz..	250.00		
1485	A899	8c Prussian blue & multi	15	15	
a.		Vert. pair, imperf. horiz..	250.00		
1486	A900	8c yellow brown & multi......	15	15	
1487	A901	8c deep brown & multi	15	15	
a.		Vert. pair, imperf. horiz..	300.00		
1488	A902	8c black & orange................	15	15	
a.		Orange omitted................	1,100.		
b.		Black (engraved) omitted	1,500.		
1489	A903	8c multicolored	15	15	
1490	A904	8c multicolored	15	15	
1491	A905	8c multicolored	15	15	
1492	A906	8c multicolored	15	15	
1493	A907	8c multicolored	15	15	
1494	A908	8c multicolored	15	15	
1495	A909	8c multicolored	15	15	
1496	A910	8c multicolored	15	15	
1497	A911	8c multicolored	15	15	
1498	A912	8c multicolored	15	15	
a.		Strip of 10, #1489-1498..	1.50	1.00	
1499	A913	8c carmine rose, black & blue	15	15	
1500	A914	6c lilac & multi	15	15	
1501	A915	8c tan & multi	15	15	
a.		Black (inscriptions & U.S. 8c) omitted	650.00		
b.		Tan (background) & lilac omitted..................	1,000.		
1502	A916	15c gray green & multi	28	15	
a.		Black (inscriptions & "U.S. 15c") omitted	1,500.		
1503	A917	15c black & multicolored	15	15	
a.		Horiz. pair, imperf. vert..	300.00		

A854

A855

A856

A857

A862   A863

A858

A864

A865

A860

A859

A867

A861

A866

A868

Scott No.	Illus. No.	Description	Unused Value	Used Value	/ / / / / /
1973-74					
1504	A918	8c multicolored	15	15	
a.		Green & red brown omitted	1,150.		
b.		Vert. pair, imperf. between	—		
1505	A919	10c multicolored	18	15	
1506	A920	10c multicolored	18	15	
a.		Black & blue (engr.) omitted	750.00		
1973					
1507	A921	8c tan & multi	15	15	
1508	A922	8c green & multi	15	15	
a.		Vert. pair, imperf. btwn. .	500.00		
1973-74, Tagged, Perf. 11x10 ½					
1509	A923	10c red & blue......................	18	15	
a.		Horiz. pair, imperf. btwn.	50.00	—	
b.		Blue omitted....................	160.00		
c.		Vert. pair, imperf............	1,150.		
d.		Horiz. pair, imperf. vert. .	—		
1510	A924	10c blue	18	15	
a.		Untagged (Bureau precanceled)		18	
b.		Booklet pane of 5 + label	1.50	30	
c.		Booklet pane of 8............	1.65	30	
d.		Booklet pane of 6............	4.50	30	
e.		Vert. pair, imperf. horiz. .	300.00		
f.		Vert. pair, imperf. btwn. .	—		
1511	A925	10c multicolored	22	15	
a.		Yellow omitted................	50.00		
Coil Stamps, Perf. 10 Vertically					
1518	A926	6.3c brick red	15	15	
a.		Untagged (Bureau precanceled)		15	
b.		Imperf., pair....................	200.00		
c.		As "a," imperf. pair.........		110.00	
1519	A923	10c red & blue......................	18	15	
a.		Imperf., pair....................	30.00		
1520	A924	10c blue	18	15	
a.		Untagged (Bureau precanceled)		25	
b.		Imperf., pair....................	40.00		
1974					
1525	A928	10c red & dark blue	16	15	
1526	A929	10c black	16	15	
1527	A930	10c multicolored	18	15	
1528	A931	10c yellow & multi	18	15	
a.		Blue ("Horse Racing") omitted.........................	900.00		
b.		Red ("U.S. postage 10 cents") omitted........	—		

A869

A870

A871

A872

A873

A874

A875

A876

A877

A878

A879

A880

A881

A883

A882

A884

A885

A887

A886

A888

A889

A890

A891

A892

A893

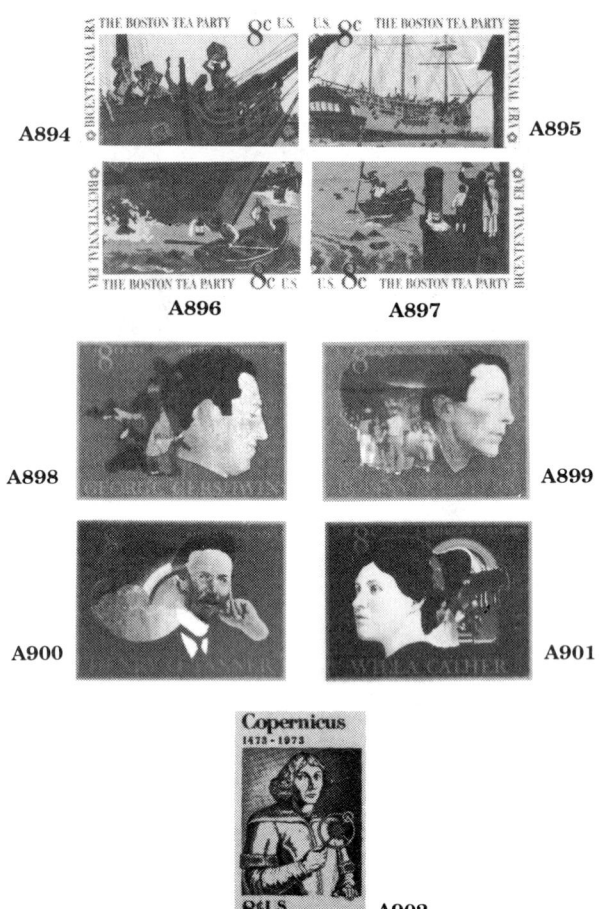

HOW TO USE THIS BOOK

The number in the first column is its Scott number or identifying number. The letter and number that come next (A41) indicate the design and refer to the illustration so designated. Following that is the denomination of the stamp and its color. Finally, the value, unused and used is shown.

Scott No.	Illus. No.		Description	Unused Value	Used Value	/ / / / / /
1529	A932	10c	multicolored	18	15	
a.			Vert. pair, imperf. btwn.	—		
1530	A933	10c	multicolored	20	15	
1531	A934	10c	multicolored	20	15	
1532	A935	10c	multicolored	20	15	
1533	A936	10c	multicolored	20	15	
1534	A937	10c	multicolored	20	15	
1535	A938	10c	multicolored	20	15	
1536	A939	10c	multicolored	20	15	
1537	A940	10c	multicolored	20	15	
a.			Block or strip of 8, #1530-1537	1.60	1.50	
b.			As "a" (block), imperf. vert.	7,500.		
1538	A941	10c	light blue & multi	16	15	
a.			Light blue & yellow omitted	—		
1539	A942	10c	light blue & multi	16	15	
a.			Light blue omitted	—		
b.			Black & purple omitted	—		
1540	A943	10c	light blue & multi	16	15	
a.			Light blue & yellow omitted	—		
1541	A944	10c	light blue & multi	16	15	
a.			Block or strip of 4, #1538-1541	75	80	
b.			As "a," lt bl & yel omitted	2,000.		
c.			Light blue omitted	—		
d.			Black & red omitted	—		
1542	A945	10c	green & multi	16	15	
a.			Dull black (litho.) omitted	800.00		
b.			Grn (engr. & litho.), blk (engr. & litho.), blue omitted	3,250.		
c.			Green (engr.) omitted	—		
d.			Green (engr.), black (litho.) omitted	—		
1543	A946	10c	dark blue & red	18	15	
1544	A947	10c	gray, dark blue & red	18	15	
1545	A948	10c	gray, dark blue & red	18	15	
1546	A949	10c	red & dark blue	18	15	
a.			Block of 4, #1543-1546	75	75	
1547	A950	10c	multicolored	18	15	
a.			Blue & orange omitted	800.00		
b.			Orange & green omitted	800.00		
c.			Green omitted	900.00		
1548	A951	10c	dk blue, black, org & yellow	16	15	
1549	A952	10c	brown red & dark brown	16	15	
1550	A953	10c	multicolored	16	15	
1551	A954	10c	multicolored	16	15	
a.			Buff omitted	—		
1552	A955	10c	multicolored	16	15	

A903　　A904　　A905　　A906

A907　　A908　　A909　　A910

A911　　A912

A913

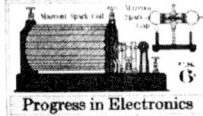 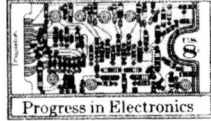 

A914　　A915　　A916

Scott No.	Illus. No.		Description	Unused Value	Used Value	/ / / / / /
1975						
1553	A956	10c	multicolored	18	15	
1554	A957	10c	multicolored	18	15	
a.			Imperf., pair	1,250.		
1555	A958	10c	multicolored	16	15	
a.			Brown (engr.) omitted	600.00		
1556	A959	10c	violet blue, yellow & red	16	15	
a.			Red (litho.) omitted	1,650.		
b.			Blue (engr.) omitted	800.00		
1557	A960	10c	blk, red, ultra & bister	16	15	
a.			Red omitted	650.00		
b.			Ultra & bister omitted	1,800.		
1558	A961	10c	multicolored	18	15	
1559	A962	8c	multicolored	15	15	
a.			Back inscription omitted.	300.00		
1560	A963	10c	multicolored	18	15	
a.			Back inscription omitted.	350.00		
1561	A964	10c	multicolored	18	15	
a.			Back inscription omitted.	300.00		
b.			Red omitted	250.00		
1562	A965	18c	multicolored	35	20	
1563	A966	10c	multicolored	18	15	
a.			Vert. pair, imperf. horiz.	400.00		
1564	A967	10c	multicolored	18	15	
1565	A968	10c	multicolored	18	15	
1566	A969	10c	multicolored	18	15	
1567	A970	10c	multicolored	18	15	
1568	A971	10c	multicolored	18	15	
a.			Block of 4, #1565-1568	75	75	
1569	A972	10c	multicolored	18	15	
a.			Pair, #1569-1570	36	25	
b.			As "a", vert. pair, imperf. horiz.	2,000.		
1570	A973	10c	multicolored	18	15	
1571	A974	10c	blue, orange & dark blue	16	15	
1572	A975	10c	multicolored	18	15	
1573	A976	10c	multicolored	18	15	
1574	A977	10c	multicolored	18	15	
1575	A978	10c	multicolored	18	15	
a.			Block of 4, #1572-1575	75	80	
b.			As "a," red (10c) omitted	—		
1576	A979	10c	green, Prus blue & rose brown	18	15	
1577	A980	10c	multicolored	18	15	
a.			Pair, #1577-1578	36	20	
b.			As "a," brown & blue (litho.) omitted	1,250.		
c.			As "a," brown, blue & yellow (litho.) omitted	2,500.		
1578	A981	10c	multicolored	18	15	

A917

A918

A919

A920

A921

A922

A923

A924

A925

A926

A928

A929

A930

A931

A932

A933

A934

A935

A936

A937

A938

A939

A940

A946

A947

A948

A949

A945

A951

A950

Retarded Children Can Be Helped

A952

A953

A954

A955

Benjamin West
American artist
10 cents U.S. postage

A956

A958

Paul Laurence Dunbar
American poet
10 cents U.S. postage

A957

A959

A960

Sybil Ludington — Youthful Heroine

A962

Salem Poor — Gallant Soldier

A963

Haym Salomon — Financial Hero

A964

Peter Francisco — Fighter Extraordinary

A965

A961

A966

A967

A968

A969

A970

A971

A972

A973

Scott No.	Illus. No.		Description	Unused Value	Used Value
1579	A982	(10c)	multicolored	18	15
a.			Imperf., pair..................	110.00	
1580	A983	(10c)	multicolored	18	15
a.			Imperf., pair..................	120.00	
b.			Perf. 10 ½x11	60	15

1973-81, Perf. 11x10 ½

1581	A984	1c	dark blue, *greenish*..........	15	15
a.			Untagged (Bureau precanceled)		15
1582	A985	2c	red brown, *greenish*	15	15
a.			Untagged (Bureau precanceled)		15
b.			Cream paper....................	15	15
1584	A987	3c	olive, *greenish*.................	15	15
a.			Untagged (Bureau precanceled)		15
1585	A988	4c	rose magenta, *cream*	15	15
a.			Untagged (Bureau precanceled)		1.25
1590	A994	9c	slate green......................	50	20
a.			Perf. 10	20.00	10.00
1591	A994	9c	slate green, *gray*	16	15
a.			Untagged (Bureau precanceled)		18
1592	A995	10c	violet, *gray*	18	15
a.			Untagged (Bureau precanceled)		25
1593	A996	11c	orange, *gray*	20	15
1594	A997	12c	brown red, *beige*..............	22	15
1595	A998	13c	brown..............................	25	15
a.			Booklet pane of 6............	1.90	*50*
b.			Booklet pane of 7 + label	1.75	*50*
c.			Booklet pane of 8............	2.00	*50*
d.			Booklet pane of 5 + label	1.40	*50*
e.			Vert. pair, imperf between	—	

Perf. 11

1596	A999	13c	multicolored	22	15
a.			Imperf., pair...................	*50.00*	—
b.			Yellow omitted................	*200.00*	
1597	A1001	15c	gray, dark blue & red	28	15
a.			Vert. pair, imperf............	*17.50*	
b.			Gray omitted	*250.00*	
c.			Vert. strip of 3, imperf. btwn. & at top or bottom........	—	

Perf. 11x10 ½

1598	A1001	15c	gray, dark blue & red	30	15
a.			Booklet pane of 8............	3.50	*60*
1599	A1002	16c	blue................................	34	15
1603	A1003	24c	red, *blue*.........................	45	15
1604	A1004	28c	brown, *blue*.....................	55	15
1605	A1005	29c	blue, *blue*........................	55	15
1606	A1006	30c	green, *blue*......................	55	15

A974

A979

A975

A976

A977

A978

A980

A981

A982

A983

 A984
 A985
 A987
 A988

 A994
 A995
 A996
 A997
 A998

 A999
 A1001
 A1002
 A1003

 A1004
 A1005
 A1006
 A1007

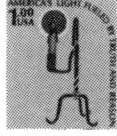 A1008
 A1009
 A1010

 A1011
 A1012
 A1013

 A1014
 A1015
 A1016

 A1019
 A1020
 A1021

 A1022

HOW TO USE THIS BOOK
The number in the first column is its Scott number or identifying number. The letter and number that come next (A41) indicate the design and refer to the illustration so designated. Following that is the denomination of the stamp and its color. Finally, the value, unused and used is shown.

Scott No.	Illus. No.		Description	Unused Value	Used Value	/ / / / / /

Perf. 11

1608	A1007	50c	tan, black & orange	85	15	
a.			Black omitted	325.00		
b.			Vert. pair, imperf. horiz.	—		
1610	A1008	$1	tan, brown, orange & yellow	2.00	20	
a.			Brown (engraved) omitted	300.00		
b.			Tan, orange & yellow omitted	300.00		
c.			Brown inverted	15,000.		
1611	A1009	$2	tan, dark grn, org & yel	3.50	45	
1612	A1010	$5	tan, red brown, yel & org	8.00	1.50	

Coil stamp, Perf. 10 Vertically

1613	A1011	3.1c	brown, *yellow*	15	15	
a.			Untagged (Bureau precanceled)		50	
b.			Imperf., pair	1,350.		
1614	A1012	7.7c	brown, *bright yellow*	18	15	
a.			Untagged (Bureau precanceled)		35	
b.			As "a," imperf., pair	1,400.		
1615	A1013	7.9c	carmine, *yellow*	15	15	
a.			Untagged (Bureau precanceled)		20	
b.			Imperf., pair	650.00		
1615C	A1014	8.4c	dark blue, *yellow*	22	15	
d.			Untagged (Bureau precanceled)		16	
e.			As "d," pair, imperf. between		50.00	
f.			As "d," imperf., pair		15.00	
1616	A994	9c	slate green, *gray*	20	15	
a.			Imperf., pair	125.00		
b.			Untagged (Bureau precanceled)		28	
c.			As "b," imperf., pair		600.00	
1617	A995	10c	violet, *gray*	20	15	
a.			Untagged (Bureau precanceled)		25	
b.			Imperf., pair	60.00		
1618	A998	13c	brown	25	15	
a.			Untagged (Bureau precanceled)		45	
b.			Imperf., pair	25.00		
g.			Pair, imperf. between	—		
h.			As "a," imperf., pair	—	—	
1618C	A1001	15c	gray, dark blue & red	40	15	
d.			Imperf., pair	20.00		
e.			Pair, imperf. between	150.00		
f.			Gray omitted	40.00		
1619	A1002	16c	blue	32	15	
a.			Huck press printing	50	15	

State Flags A1023-A1072

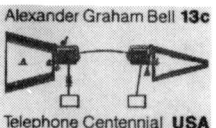

A1073

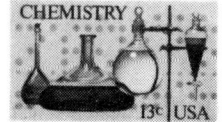

A1074

A1075

Scott No.	Illus. No.		Description	Unused Value	Used Value	/ / / / / /
1975-77, Perf. 11x10 ½						
1622	A1018	13c	dark blue & red	24	15	
a.			Horiz. pair, imperf. btwn.	50.00		
b.			Vert. pair, imperf............	1,250.		
c.			Perf. 11	65	15	
d.			As "c," vert. pair, imperf.	150.00		
e.			Horiz. pair, imperf. vert. .	—		
1623	A1016	13c	blue & red.......................	22	15	
a.			Booklet pane of 8, #1590, 7 #1623........................	2.50	60	
b.			Perf. 10	1.00	1.00	
c.			Booklet pane of 8, #1590a + 7 #1623b............................	30.00	—	
d.			Se-tenant pair, #1590 & 1623	75	—	
e.			Se-tenant pair, #1590a & 1623b	20.00	—	
Coil stamp, Perf. 10 Vertically						
1625	A1015	13c	dark blue & red	30	15	
a.			Imperf., pair....................	22.50		
1976						
1629	A1019	13c	multicolored	20	15	
1630	A1020	13c	multicolored	20	15	
1631	A1021	13c	multicolored	20	15	
a.			Strip of 3, #1629-1631	60	60	
b.			As "a," imperf.	1,200.		
c.			Vert. pair, imperf.............	900.00		
1632	A1022	13c	dark blue, red & ultra	20	15	
1633	A1023	13c	Delaware	25	20	
1634	A1024	13c	Pennsylvania	25	20	
1635	A1025	13c	New Jersey	25	20	
1636	A1026	13c	Georgia.............................	25	20	
1637	A1027	13c	Connecticut	25	20	
1638	A1028	13c	Massachusetts	25	20	
1639	A1029	13c	Maryland..........................	25	20	
1640	A1030	13c	South Carolina	25	20	
1641	A1031	13c	New Hampshire	25	20	
1642	A1032	13c	Virginia............................	25	20	
1643	A1033	13c	New York........................	25	20	
1644	A1034	13c	North Carolina	25	20	
1645	A1035	13c	Rhode Island	25	20	
1646	A1036	13c	Vermont...........................	25	20	
1647	A1037	13c	Kentucky	25	20	
1648	A1038	13c	Tennessee	25	20	
1649	A1039	13c	Ohio.................................	25	20	
1650	A1040	13c	Louisiana.........................	25	20	
1651	A1041	13c	Indiana.............................	25	20	
1652	A1042	13c	Mississippi	25	20	

Surrender of Cornwallis at Yorktown, by John Trumbull— **A1076**

Declaration of Independence, by John Trumbull— **A1077**

Scott No.	Illus. No.		Description	Unused Value	Used Value	/ / / / / /
1653	A1043	13c	Illinois	25	20	
1654	A1044	13c	Alabama	25	20	
1655	A1045	13c	Maine	25	20	
1656	A1046	13c	Missouri	25	20	
1657	A1047	13c	Arkansas	25	20	
1658	A1048	13c	Michigan	25	20	
1659	A1049	13c	Florida	25	20	
1660	A1050	13c	Texas	25	20	
1661	A1051	13c	Iowa	25	20	
1662	A1052	13c	Wisconsin	25	20	
1663	A1053	13c	California	25	20	
1664	A1054	13c	Minnesota	25	20	
1665	A1055	13c	Oregon	25	20	
1666	A1056	13c	Kansas	25	20	
1667	A1057	13c	West Virginia	25	20	
1668	A1058	13c	Nevada	25	20	
1669	A1059	13c	Nebraska	25	20	
1670	A1060	13c	Colorado	25	20	
1671	A1061	13c	North Dakota	25	20	
1672	A1062	13c	South Dakota	25	20	
1673	A1063	13c	Montana	25	20	
1674	A1064	13c	Washington	25	20	
1675	A1065	13c	Idaho	25	20	
1676	A1066	13c	Wyoming	25	20	
1677	A1067	13c	Utah	25	20	
1678	A1068	13c	Oklahoma	25	20	
1679	A1069	13c	New Mexico	25	20	
1680	A1070	13c	Arizona	25	20	
1681	A1071	13c	Alaska	25	20	
1682	A1072	13c	Hawaii	25	20	
a.			Pane of 50	13.00	—	
1683	A1073	13c	black, purple & red, *tan*	22	15	
1684	A1074	13c	blue & multi	22	15	
1685	A1075	13c	multicolored	22	15	
1686	A1076		Sheet of 5	3.25	—	
a.-e.		13c	multi, any single	45	40	
f.			USA 13c omitted on b, c & d, imperf., untagged	—	*1,500.*	
g.			USA 13c omitted on a & e	*450.00*	—	
h.			Imperf., untagged		*1,750.*	
i.			USA 13c omitted on b, c & d	*450.00*		
j.			USA 13c double on b	—		
k.			USA 13c omitted on c & d	—		
l.			USA 13c omitted on e	*500.00*		
m.			USA 13c omitted, imperf., untagged	—	—	

**Washington Crossing the Delaware, by
Emanuel Leutze/Eastman Johnson—** **A1078**

**Washington Reviewing Army at Valley Forge,
by William T. Trego—** **A1079**

A1080

Scott No.	Illus. No.		Description	Unused Value	Used Value	/ / / / / /
1687	A1077		Sheet of 5..........................	4.25	—	
a.-e.		18c	multi, any single...............	55	55	
f.			Design & marginal inscriptions omitted......	4,750.		
g.			USA 18c omitted on a & c	800.00		
h.			USA 18c omitted on b, d & e	500.00		
i.			USA 18c omitted on d	500.00	500.00	
j.			Black omitted in design ..	1,200.		
k.			USA 18c omitted, imperf., untagged	2,250.		
m.			USA 18c omitted on b & e	500.00		
n.			USA 18c omitted on b & d	—		
1688	A1078		Sheet of 5..........................	5.25	—	
a.-e.		24c	multi, any single...............	70	70	
f.			USA 24c omitted, imperf., untagged	2,850.		
g.			USA 24c omitted on d & e	—	450.00	
h.			Design & marginal inscriptions omitted......	2,250.		
i.			USA 24c omitted on a, b & c	500.00	—	
j.			Imperf., untagged.............	2,500.		
k.			USA 24c of d & e inverted			
1689	A1079		Sheet of 5..........................	6.25	—	
a.-e.		31c	multi, any single...............	85	85	
f.			USA 31c omitted, imperf., untagged	2,100.		
g.			USA 31c omitted on a & c	—		
h.			USA 31c omitted on b, d & e	—	—	
i.			USA 31c omitted on e.....	500.00		
j.			Black omitted in design ..	1,350.		
k.			Imperf., untagged.............		2,000.	
l.			USA 31c omitted on b & d	—		
m.			USA 31c omitted on a, c & e	—		
n.			As "m," imperf., untagged	—		
p.			As "h," imperf., untagged		2,500.	
q.			As "g," imperf., untagged	2,500.		
1690	A1080	13c	ultra & multi....................	20	15	
a.			Light blue omitted............	350.00		
1691	A1081	13c	multicolored	20	15	
1692	A1082	13c	multicolored	20	15	
1693	A1083	13c	multicolored	20	15	
1694	A1084	13c	multicolored	20	15	
a.			Strip of 4, #1691-1694	85	75	
1695	A1085	13c	multicolored	28	15	
1696	A1086	13c	multicolored	28	15	
1697	A1087	13c	multicolored	28	15	

JULY 4,1776; JULY 4,1776; JULY 4,1776; JULY 4,1776;
Declaration of Independence, by John Trumbull

A1081　　　　A1082　　　　A1083　　　　A1084

A1085　　　A1086　　　A1089

A1087　　　A1088

A1091

A1092　　　　A1093　　　　A1094

A1090

Scott No.	Illus. No.		Description	Unused Value	Used Value	/ / / / / /
1698	A1088	13c	multicolored	28	15	
a.			Block of 4, #1695-1698 ..	1.15	85	
b.			As "a," imperf.	750.00		
1699	A1089	13c	multicolored	22	15	
a.			Horiz. pair, imperf. vert. .	400.00		
1700	A1090	13c	black & gray	22	15	
1701	A1091	13c	multicolored	22	15	
a.			Imperf., pair	100.00		
1702	A1092	13c	multicolored	22	15	
a.			Imperf., pair	110.00		
1703	A1092	13c	multicolored	24	15	
a.			Imperf., pair	125.00		
b.			Vert. pair, imperf. btwn. .	—		

1977

Scott No.	Illus. No.		Description	Unused Value	Used Value	/ / / / / /
1704	A1093	13c	multicolored	22	15	
a.			Horiz. pair, imperf. vert. .	450.00		
1705	A1094	13c	black & multi	22	15	
1706	A1095	13c	multicolored	22	15	
1707	A1096	13c	multicolored	22	15	
1708	A1097	13c	multicolored	22	15	
1709	A1098	13c	multicolored	22	15	
a.			Block or strip of 4	90	60	
b.			As "a," imperf. vert.	2,500.		
1710	A1099	13c	multicolored	22	15	
a.			Imperf., pair	1,150.		
1711	A1100	13c	multicolored	22	15	
a.			Horiz. pair, imperf. btwn.	500.00		
b.			Horiz. pair, imperf. vert. .	900.00		
1712	A1101	13c	tan & multi	22	15	
1713	A1102	13c	tan & multi	22	15	
1714	A1103	13c	tan & multi	22	15	
1715	A1104	13c	tan & multi	22	15	
a.			Block of 4, #1712-1715 ..	90	60	
b.			As "a," imperf. horiz.	—		
1716	A1105	13c	blue, black & red	22	15	
1717	A1106	13c	multicolored	22	15	
1718	A1107	13c	multicolored	22	15	
1719	A1108	13c	multicolored	22	15	
1720	A1109	13c	multicolored	22	15	
a.			Block of 4, #1717-1720 ..	90	80	
1721	A1110	13c	blue	22	15	
1722	A1111	13c	multicolored	22	15	
1723	A1112	13c	multicolored	22	15	
a.			Pair, #1723-1724	45	40	
1724	A1113	13c	multicolored	22	15	
1725	A1114	13c	black & multi	22	15	
1726	A1115	13c	red & brown, *cream*	22	15	

Zia Museum of New Mexico
Pueblo Art USA 13c
A1095

San Ildefonso Denver Art Museum
Pueblo Art USA 13c
A1096

Hopi Heard Museum Phoenix
Pueblo Art USA 13c
A1097

Acoma School of American Research
Pueblo Art USA 13c
A1098

A1099

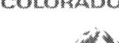

A1100

US Bicentennial 13c
A1105

Swallowtail
USA 13c *Papilio oregonius*
A1101

Checkerspot
USA 13c *Euphydryas phaeton*
A1102

Dogface
USA 13c *Colias eurydice*
A1103

Orange-Tip
USA 13c *Anthocaris midea*
A1104

A1106

A1107

A1108

A1109

A1110

A1112

A1111

A1114

A1113

A1115

A1116

A1117

A1118

A1120

A1119

Scott No.	Illus. No.		Description	Unused Value	Used Value	/ / / / / /
1727	A1116	13c	multicolored	22	15	
1728	A1117	13c	multicolored	22	15	
1729	A1118	13c	multicolored	22	15	
a.			Imperf., pair	75.00		
1730	A1119	13c	multicolored	22	15	
a.			Imperf., pair	275.00		

1978

1731	A1120	13c	black & brown	22	15	
1732	A1121	13c	dark blue	22	15	
a.			Pair, #1732-1733	50	30	
b.			As "a," imperf. between..	4,500.		
1733	A1122	13c	green	22	15	
a.			Vert. pair, imperf. horiz.	—		

1978-80

1734	A1123	13c	brown & blue green, *bister*	24	15	
a.			Horiz. pair, imperf. vert.	300.00		
1735	A1124	(15c)	orange	24	15	
a.			Imperf., vert. pair	80.00		
b.			Vert. pair, imperf. horiz.	300.00		
1736	A1124	(15c)	orange	25	15	
a.			Booklet pane of 8	2.25	*60*	
1737	A1126	15c	multicolored	25	15	
a.			Booklet pane of 8	2.25	*60*	
b.			As "a," imperf.	—		
1738	A1127	15c	sepia, *yellow*	30	15	
1739	A1128	15c	sepia, *yellow*	30	15	
1740	A1129	15c	sepia, *yellow*	30	15	
1741	A1130	15c	sepia, *yellow*	30	15	
1742	A1131	15c	sepia, *yellow*	30	15	
a.			Bklt. pane, 2 each #1738-1742	3.60	*60*	
b.			Strip of 5, #1738-1742	1.50	—	

Coil stamp, Perf. 10 Vertically

1743	A1124	(15c)	orange	25	15	
a.			Imperf., pair	90.00		

1978

1744	A1133	13c	multicolored	22	15	
1745	A1134	13c	multicolored	22	15	
1746	A1135	13c	multicolored	22	15	
1747	A1136	13c	multicolored	22	15	
1748	A1137	13c	multicolored	22	15	
a.			Block of 4, #1745-1748	90	60	
1749	A1138	13c	multicolored	22	15	
1750	A1139	13c	multicolored	22	15	

A1143 **A1146** **A1144**

A1149 **A1150** **A1145**

A1151 **A1152** **A1147**

A1153   **A1154**

A1155   **A1156**

Scott No.	Illus. No.	Description	Unused Value	Used Value	/ / / / / /
1751	A1140	13c multicolored	22	15	
1752	A1141	13c multicolored	22	15	
a.		Block of 4, #1749-1752	90	60	
1753	A1142	13c blue, black & red	22	15	
1754	A1143	13c brown	24	15	
1755	A1144	13c multicolored	24	15	
1756	A1145	15c multicolored	26	15	
1757	A1146	Block of 8	1.65	1.65	
a.		13c Cardinal	20	15	
b.		13c Mallard	20	15	
c.		13c Canada goose	20	15	
d.		13c Blue jay	20	15	
e.		13c Moose	20	15	
f.		13c Chipmunk	20	15	
g.		13c Red fox	20	15	
h.		13c Raccoon	20	15	
i.		Yel, grn, red, brn, bl, blk (litho.) omitted	5,000.		
1758	A1147	15c multicolored	26	15	
1759	A1148	15c multicolored	26	15	
1760	A1149	15c multicolored	26	15	
1761	A1150	15c multicolored	26	15	
1762	A1151	15c multicolored	26	15	
1763	A1152	15c multicolored	26	15	
a.		Block of 4, #1760-1763	1.05	85	
1764	A1153	15c multicolored	26	15	
1765	A1154	15c multicolored	26	15	
1766	A1155	15c multicolored	26	15	
1767	A1156	15c multicolored	26	15	
a.		Block of 4, #1764-1767	1.05	85	
b.		As "a," imperf. horiz.	12,500.		
1768	A1157	15c blue & multi	26	15	
a.		Imperf., pair	90.00		
1769	A1158	15c red & multi	26	15	
a.		Imperf., pair	100.00		
b.		Vert. pair, imperf. horiz.	1,750.		

1979

1770	A1159	15c blue	26	15	
1771	A1160	15c multicolored	26	15	
a.		Imperf., pair	—		
1772	A1161	15c orange red	26	15	
1773	A1162	15c dark blue	26	15	
1774	A1163	15c chocolate	28	15	
1775	A1164	15c multicolored	28	15	
1776	A1165	15c multicolored	28	15	
1777	A1166	15c multicolored	28	15	

A1148

A1157

A1158

A1159

A1161

A1160

A1162

A1163

A1164

A1165

A1166

A1167

Scott No.	Illus. No.		Description	Unused Value	Used Value	/ / / / / /
1778	A1167	15c	multicolored	28	15	
a.			Block of 4, #1775-1778 ..	1.15	85	
b.			As "a," imperf. horiz.	3,750.		
1779	A1168	15c	black & brick red	28	15	
1780	A1169	15c	black & brick red	28	15	
1781	A1170	15c	black & brick red	28	15	
1782	A1171	15c	black & brick red	28	15	
a.			Block of 4, #1779-1782 ..	1.15	85	
1783	A1172	15c	multicolored	28	15	
1784	A1173	15c	multicolored	28	15	
1785	A1174	15c	multicolored	28	15	
1786	A1175	15c	multicolored	28	15	
a.			Block of 4, #1783-1786 ..	1.15	85	
b.			As "a," imperf.	600.00		
1787	A1176	15c	multicolored	28	15	
a.			Imperf., pair....................	400.00		
1788	A1177	15c	multicolored	28	15	
1789	A1178	15c	multicolored	28	15	
a.			Perf. 11	30	15	
b.			Perf. 12	2,000.	1,000.	
c.			Vert. pair, imperf. horiz. .	200.00		
d.			As "a," vert. pair, imperf horiz.	150.00		

1979-80

1790	A1179	10c	multicolored	20	20	
1791	A1180	15c	multicolored	28	15	
1792	A1181	15c	multicolored	28	15	
1793	A1182	15c	multicolored	28	15	
1794	A1183	15c	multicolored	28	15	
a.			Block of 4, #1791-1794 ..	1.15	85	
b.			As "a," imperf.	1,400.		
1795	A1184	15c	multicolored	32	15	
a.			Perf. 11	1.05	—	
1796	A1185	15c	multicolored	32	15	
a.			Perf. 11	1.05	—	
1797	A1186	15c	multicolored	32	15	
a.			Perf. 11	1.05	—	
1798	A1187	15c	multicolored	32	15	
a.			Perf. 11	1.05	—	
b.			Block of 4, #1795-1798 ..	1.30	1.00	
c.			Block of 4, #1795a-1798a	4.25	—	

1979

1799	A1188	15c	multicolored	28	15	
a.			Imperf., pair....................	100.00		
b.			Vert. pair, imperf. horiz. .	700.00		
c.			Vert. pair, imperf. btwn. .	2,750.		

A1168

 A1169

A1170 A1171

A1172 A1173

A1174 A1175

A1176 A1177

A1178

A1179

A1180

A1181

A1182

A1183

A1184

A1185

A1186

A1187

A1188

A1191

A1189

A1190

A1192

A1193

A1194

A1195

A1196

A1197

A1199

A1209

A1208

A1210

A1211

A1212

A1213

Scott No.	Illus. No.		Description	Unused Value	Used Value
1800	A1189	15c	multicolored	28	15
a.			Green & yellow omitted.	600.00	
b.			Green, yellow & tan omitted	650.00	
1801	A1190	15c	multicolored	28	15
a.			Imperf., pair	250.00	
1802	A1191	15c	multicolored	28	15

1980

1803	A1192	15c	multicolored	28	15
1804	A1193	15c	multicolored	28	15
a.			Horiz. pair, imperf. vert.	800.00	
1805	A1194	15c	multicolored	28	15
1806	A1195	15c	claret & multi	28	15
1807	A1196	15c	multicolored	28	15
1808	A1195	15c	green & multi	28	15
1809	A1197	15c	multicolored	28	15
1810	A1195	15c	red & multi	28	15
a.			Vert. strip of 6 #1805-1810	1.75	1.50

1980-81, Coil stamps, Perf. 10 Vertically

1811	A984	1c	dark blue, *greenish*	15	15
a.			Imperf., pair	175.00	
1813	A1199	3.5c	purple, *yellow*	15	15
a.			Untagged (Bureau precanceled, lines only)		15
b.			Imperf., pair	225.00	
1816	A997	12c	brown red, *beige*	24	15
a.			Untagged (Bureau precanceled)		25
b.			Imperf., pair	175.00	

1981

1818	A1207 (18c)		violet	32	15
1819	A1207 (18c)		violet	40	15
a.			Booklet pane of 8	3.50	*1.50*

Coil stamp, Perf. 10 Vertically

1820	A1207 (18c)		violet	40	15
a.			Imperf., pair	100.00	

1980

1821	A1208	15c	Prussian blue	28	15
1822	A1209	15c	red brown & sepia	28	15
1823	A1210	15c	black & red	28	15
a.			Vert. pair, imperf. horiz.	300.00	
1824	A1211	15c	multicolored	28	15
1825	A1212	15c	carmine & violet bl	28	15
a.			Horiz. pair, imperf. vert.	500.00	

HOW TO USE THIS BOOK

The number in the first column is its Scott number or identifying number. The letter and number that come next (A41) indicate the design and refer to the illustration so designated. Following that is the denomination of the stamp and its color. Finally, the value, unused and used is shown.

Scott No.	Illus. No.		Description	Unused Value	Used Value	//////
1826	A1213	15c	multicolored	28	15	
a.			Red, brown & blue (engr.) omitted	800.00		
b.			Red, brn, bl (engr.), bl & yel (litho.) omitted	1,400.		
1827	A1214	15c	multicolored	26	15	
1828	A1215	15c	multicolored	26	15	
1829	A1216	15c	multicolored	26	15	
1830	A1217	15c	multicolored	26	15	
a.			Block of 4, #1827-1830	1.05	85	
b.			As "a," imperf.	1,250.		
c.			As "a," imperf. btwn., vert.	—		
d.			As "a," imperf. vert.	3,000.		
1831	A1218	15c	multicolored	28	15	
a.			Imperf., pair	400.00		
1832	A1219	15c	purple	28	15	
1833	A1220	15c	multicolored	28	15	
a.			Horiz. pair, imperf. btwn.	250.00		
1834	A1221	15c	multicolored	30	15	
1835	A1222	15c	multicolored	30	15	
1836	A1223	15c	multicolored	30	15	
1837	A1224	15c	multicolored	30	15	
a.			Block of 4, #1834-1837	1.25	85	
1838	A1225	15c	black & brick red	30	15	
1839	A1226	15c	black & brick red	30	15	
1840	A1227	15c	black & brick red	30	15	
1841	A1228	15c	black & brick red	30	15	
a.			Block of 4, #1838-1841	1.25	85	
1842	A1229	15c	multicolored	28	15	
a.			Imperf., pair	80.00		
1843	A1230	15c	multicolored	28	15	
a.			Imperf., pair	80.00		
b.			Buff omitted	—		

1980-85

Scott No.	Illus. No.		Description	Unused Value	Used Value	//////
1844	A1231	1c	black	15	15	
a.			Imperf. pair	350.00		
b.			Vert. pair, imperf. btwn.	—		
1845	A1232	2c	brown black	15	15	
1846	A1233	3c	olive green	15	15	
1847	A1234	4c	violet	15	15	
1848	A1235	5c	henna brown	15	15	
1849	A1236	6c	orange vermilion	15	15	
a.			Vert. pair, imperf. btwn.	2,300.		
1850	A1237	7c	brt carmine	15	15	
1851	A1238	8c	olive black	15	15	
1852	A1239	9c	dark green	16	15	

A1225   A1226

A1227   A1228

A1229   A1230   A1261   A1262

A1263   A1264

A1265   A1266

Scott No.	Illus. No.		Description	Unused Value	Used Value	//////
1853	A1240	10c	Prussian blue	18	15	
a.			Vert. pair, imperf. btwn. and at bottom	1,100.		
b.			Horiz. pair, imperf. btwn.	2,250.		
1854	A1241	11c	dark blue	20	15	
1855	A1242	13c	light maroon	24	15	
1856	A1243	14c	slate green	25	15	
a.			Vert. pair, imperf. horiz.	*150.00*		
b.			Horiz. pair, imperf. btwn.	8.50		
c.			Vert. pair, imperf. btwn.	*1,750.*		
1857	A1244	17c	green	32	15	
1858	A1245	18c	dark blue	32	15	
1859	A1246	19c	brown	35	15	
1860	A1247	20c	claret	40	15	
1861	A1248	20c	green	38	15	
1862	A1249	20c	black	38	15	
1863	A1250	22c	dark chalky blue	40	15	
a.			Vert. pair, imperf. horiz.	2,500.		
b.			Vert. pair, imperf. btwn.	—		
c.			Horiz. pair, imperf. btwn.	—		
1864	A1251	30c	olive gray	55	15	
1865	A1252	35c	gray	65	15	
1866	A1253	37c	blue	70	15	
1867	A1254	39c	rose lilac	70	15	
a.			Vert. pair, imperf. horiz.	600.00		
b.			Vert. pair, imperf. btwn.	1,250.		
1868	A1255	40c	dark green	70	15	
1869	A1256	50c	brown	90	15	

1981

Scott No.	Illus. No.		Description	Unused Value	Used Value	//////
1874	A1261	15c	gray	28	15	
1875	A1262	15c	multicolored	28	15	
1876	A1263	18c	multicolored	35	15	
1877	A1264	18c	multicolored	35	15	
1878	A1265	18c	multicolored	35	15	
1879	A1266	18c	multicolored	35	15	
a.			Block of 4, #1876-1879	1.40	85	
1880	A1267	18c	Bighorn	35	15	
1881	A1268	18c	Puma	35	15	
1882	A1269	18c	Harbor seal	35	15	
1883	A1270	18c	Bison	35	15	
1884	A1271	18c	Brown bear	35	15	
1885	A1272	18c	Polar bear	35	15	
1886	A1273	18c	Elk (wapiti)	35	15	
1887	A1274	18c	Moose	35	15	
1888	A1275	18c	White-tailed deer	35	15	
1889	A1276	18c	Pronghorn	35	15	
a.			Bklt. pane of 10, #1880-1889	9.00	—	

A1231 **A1232** **A1233** **A1234** **A1235**

A1236 **A1237** **A1238** **A1239** **A1240**

A1241 **A1242** **A1243** **A1244** **A1245**

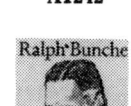 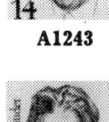    

A1246 **A1247** **A1248** **A1249** **A1250**

A1251 **A1252** **A1253** **A1254** **A1255**

A1256

Scott No.	Illus. No.		Description	Unused Value	Used Value	//////
1890	A1277	18c	multicolored	32	15	
a.			Imperf., pair	100.00		
b.			Vert. pair, imperf. horiz.	—		

Coil stamp, Perf. 10 Vertically

1891	A1278	18c	multicolored	36	15	
a.			Imperf., pair	20.00		
b.			Pair, imperf. btwn.	—		
1892	A1279	6c	multicolored	55	15	
1893	A1280	18c	multicolored	32	15	
a.			Booklet pane of 8 (2 #1892, 6 #1893)	3.25	—	
b.			As "a," vert. imperf. btwn.	80.00		
c.			Pair, #1892, 1893	90	—	
1894	A1281	20c	black, dark blue & red	35	15	
a.			Vert. pair, imperf.	40.00		
b.			Vert. pair, imperf. horiz.	650.00		
c.			Dark blue omitted	90.00		
d.			Black omitted	300.00		

Coil stamp, Perf. 10 Vertically

1895	A1281	20c	black, dark blue & red	35	15	
a.			Imperf., pair	10.00		
b.			Black omitted	40.00		
c.			Dark blue omitted	—		
d.			Pair, imperf. btwn.	900.00		
e.			Untagged (Bureau precanceled)	50	50	
1896	A1281	20c	black, dark blue & red	35	15	
a.			Booklet pane of 6	2.50	—	
b.			Booklet pane of 10	4.25	—	

1981-84, Coil stamps, Perf. 10 Vertically

1897	A1282	1c	violet	15	15	
b.			Imperf., pair	700.00		
1897A	A1283	2c	black	15	15	
e.			Imperf., pair	50.00		
1898	A1284	3c	dark green	15	15	
1898A	A1285	4c	reddish brown	15	15	
b.			Untagged (Bureau precanceled)	15	15	
c.			As "b," imperf., pair	700.00		
d.			No. 1898A, imperf., pair.	900.00	—	
1899	A1286	5c	gray green	15	15	
a.			Imperf., pair	—		
1900	A1287	5.2c	carmine	15	15	
a.			Untagged (Bureau precanceled)	15	15	
1901	A1288	5.9c	blue	18	15	
a.			Untagged (Bureau precanceled, lines only)	18	18	
b.			As "a," imperf., pair	200.00		

 **A1282**
 **A1283**
 **A1284**
 **A1285**

 **A1286**
 **A1287**
 **A1288**
 **A1289**

 **A1290**
 **A1291**
 **A1292**
 **A1293**

 **A1294**
 **A1295**

 **A1296**

Scott No.	Illus. No.		Description	Unused Value	Used Value	/ / / / / /
1902	A1289	7.4c	brown..................................	18	15	
a.			Untagged (Bureau precanceled)	20	20	
1903	A1290	9.3c	carmine rose	25	15	
a.			Untagged (Bureau precanceled, lines only)	22	22	
b.			As "a," imperf., pair........	*140.00*		
1904	A1291	10.9c	purple.............................	24	15	
a.			Untagged (Bureau precanceled, lines only)	24	24	
b.			As "a," imperf., pair........	*175.00*		
1905	A1292	11c	red..................................	24	15	
a.			Untagged	24	15	
1906	A1293	17c	ultra................................	32	15	
a.			Untagged (Bureau precanceled, Presorted First Class)...	35	35	
b.			Imperf., pair.....................	*165.00*		
c.			As "a," imperf., pair........	*650.00*		
1907	A1294	18c	dark brown	34	15	
a.			Imperf., pair....................	*120.00*		
1908	A1295	20c	vermilion	32	15	
a.			Imperf., pair....................	*110.00*		

1983, Booklet stamp, Perf. 10 Vertically

1909	A1296		$9.35 multicolored	22.50	14.00	
a.			Booklet pane of 3	62.50	—	

1981

1910	A1297	18c	multicolored	32	15	
1911	A1298	18c	multicolored	32	15	
1912	A1299	18c	multicolored	32	15	
1913	A1300	18c	multicolored	32	15	
1914	A1301	18c	multicolored	32	15	
1915	A1302	18c	multicolored	32	15	
1916	A1303	18c	multicolored	32	15	
1917	A1304	18c	multicolored	32	15	
1918	A1305	18c	multicolored	32	15	
1919	A1306	18c	multicolored	32	15	
a.			Block of 8, #1912-1919..	3.00	2.75	
b.			As "a," imperf.	*8,000.*		
1920	A1307	18c	blue & black....................	32	15	
1921	A1308	18c	multicolored	35	15	
1922	A1309	18c	multicolored	35	15	
1923	A1310	18c	multicolored	35	15	
1924	A1311	18c	multicolored	35	15	
a.			Block of 4, #1921-1924..	1.40	1.00	
1925	A1312	18c	multicolored	32	15	
a.			Vert. pair, imperf. horiz. .	*2,750.*		

A1207

A1281

A1267  A1268

A1269 A1270

A1271 A1272

A1273 A1274

A1275 A1276

A1277

A1278

A1279

A1280

A1332

A1333

A1334

A1390

Scott No.	Illus. No.		Description	Unused Value	Used Value	/ / / / / /
1926	A1313	18c	multicolored	32	15	
a.			Black (engr., inscriptions) omitted	400.00	—	
1927	A1314	18c	blue & black	42	15	
a.			Imperf., pair	350.00		
b.			Vert. pair, imperf. horiz.	1,250.		
1928	A1315	18c	black & red	42	15	
1929	A1316	18c	black & red	42	15	
1930	A1317	18c	black & red	42	15	
1931	A1318	18c	black & red	42	15	
a.			Block of 4, #1928-1931	1.75	1.00	
1932	A1319	18c	purple	32	15	
1933	A1320	18c	green	32	15	
1934	A1321	18c	gray, green & brown	32	15	
a.			Vert. pair, imperf. btwn.	250.00		
b.			Brown omitted	600.00		
1935	A1322	18c	multicolored	32	16	
1936	A1322	20c	multicolored	35	15	
1937	A1323	18c	multicolored	35	15	
1938	A1324	18c	multicolored	35	15	
a.			Pair, #1937-1938	90	15	
b.			As "a," black (engr., inscriptions) omitted	450.00		
1939	A1325	(20c)	multicolored	38	15	
a.			Imperf., pair	110.00		
b.			Vert. pair, imperf. horiz.	1,650.		
1940	A1326	(20c)	multicolored	38	15	
a.			Imperf., pair	250.00		
b.			Vert. pair, imperf. horiz.	—		
1941	A1327	20c	multicolored	38	15	
1942	A1328	20c	multicolored	35	15	
1943	A1329	20c	multicolored	35	15	
1944	A1330	20c	multicolored	35	15	
1945	A1331	20c	multicolored	35	15	
a.			Block of 4, #1942-1945	1.50	15	
b.			As "a," deep brown omitted	7,500.		
c.			No. 1945 imperf., vert. pair	5,250.		
1946	A1332	(20c)	brown	38	15	

Coil stamp, Perf. 10 Vertically

1947	A1332	(20c)	brown	60	15	
a.			Imperf., pair	1,750.		
1948	A1333	(20c)	brown	38	15	
a.			Booklet pane of 10	4.50	—	

| A1299 | A1300 | A1301 | A1302 |

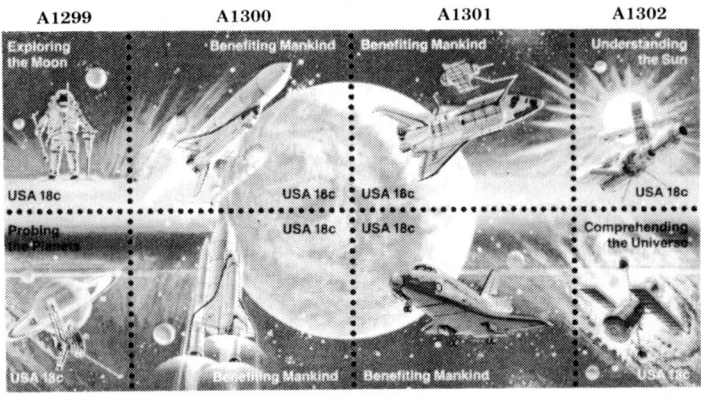

| A1303 | A1304 | A1305 | A1306 |

A1297

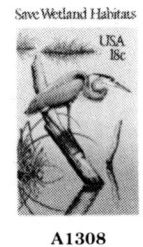

A1308

A1309

A1310 A1311

A1298

Scott No.	Illus. No.		Description	Unused Value	Used Value	/ / / / / /
1982						
1949	A1334	20c	dark blue (from bklt. pane)	50	15	
a.			Booklet pane of 10	5.00	—	
b.			As "a," vert. imperf. btwn.	*100.00*		
c.			Type II	50	15	
d.			As "c," booklet pane of 10	10.00	—	
1950	A1335	20c	blue	38	15	
1951	A1336	20c	multicolored	38	15	
a.			Perf. 11	48	15	
b.			Imperf., pair	*275.00*		
c.			Blue omitted	*200.00*		
1952	A1337	20c	multicolored	38	15	
1953	A1338	20c	Alabama	45	25	
1954	A1339	20c	Alaska	45	25	
1955	A1340	20c	Arizona	45	25	
1956	A1341	20c	Arkansas	45	25	
1957	A1342	20c	California	45	25	
1958	A1343	20c	Colorado	45	25	
1959	A1344	20c	Connecticut	45	25	
1960	A1345	20c	Delaware	45	25	
1961	A1346	20c	Florida	45	25	
1962	A1347	20c	Georgia	45	25	
1963	A1348	20c	Hawaii	45	25	
1964	A1349	20c	Idaho	45	25	
1965	A1350	20c	Illinois	45	25	
1966	A1351	20c	Indiana	45	25	
1967	A1352	20c	Iowa	45	25	
1968	A1353	20c	Kansas	45	25	
1969	A1354	20c	Kentucky	45	25	
1970	A1355	20c	Louisiana	45	25	
1971	A1356	20c	Maine	45	25	
1972	A1357	20c	Maryland	45	25	
1973	A1358	20c	Massachusetts	45	25	
1974	A1359	20c	Michigan	45	25	
1975	A1360	20c	Minnesota	45	25	
1976	A1361	20c	Mississippi	45	25	
1977	A1362	20c	Missouri	45	25	
1978	A1363	20c	Montana	45	25	
1979	A1364	20c	Nebraska	45	25	
1980	A1365	20c	Nevada	45	25	
1981	A1366	20c	New Hampshire	45	25	
1982	A1367	20c	New Jersey	45	25	
1983	A1368	20c	New Mexico	45	25	
1984	A1369	20c	New York	45	25	
1985	A1370	20c	North Carolina	45	25	
1986	A1371	20c	North Dakota	45	25	
1987	A1372	20c	Ohio	45	25	
1988	A1373	20c	Oklahoma	45	25	

A1307   A1312

A1313   A1314   A1327

A1315   A1316

A1317   A1318

A1319   A1320

A1322

A1323

A1324

A1325

A1326

A1329

A1328

A1330

A1331

A1335

A1336

A1337

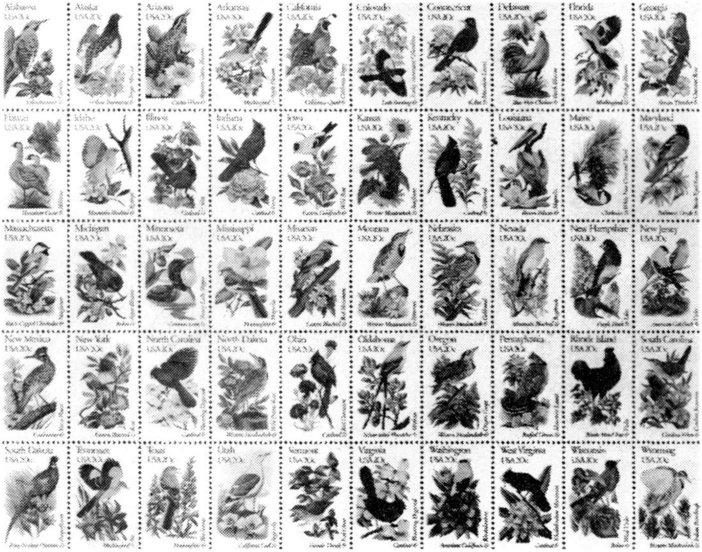

A1338-A1387—State Birds and Flowers

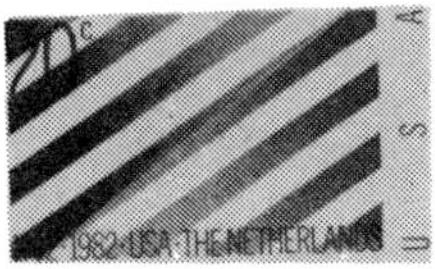

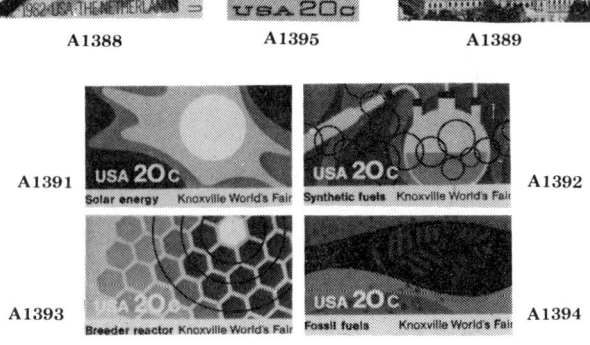

20c
1982·USA THE NETHERLANDS
USA

A1388

Horatio Alger
USA 20c

A1395

Library of Congress
USA 20c

A1389

A1391

USA 20c
Solar energy
Knoxville World's Fair

USA 20c
Synthetic fuels
Knoxville World's Fai

A1392

A1393

USA 20c
Breeder reactor
Knoxville World's Fair

USA 20c
Fossil fuels
Knoxville World's Fai

A1394

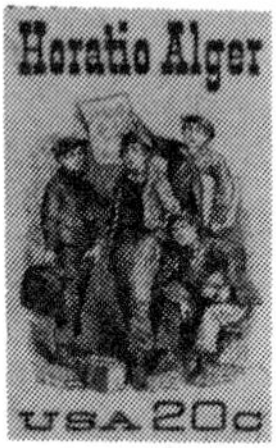

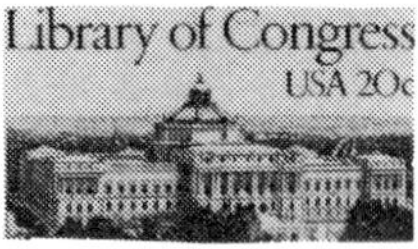

Scott No.	Illus. No.		Description	Unused Value	Used Value	/ / / / / /
1989	A1374	20c	Oregon	45	25	
1990	A1375	20c	Pennsylvania	45	25	
1991	A1376	20c	Rhode Island	45	25	
1992	A1377	20c	South Carolina	45	25	
1993	A1378	20c	South Dakota	45	25	
1994	A1379	20c	Tennessee	45	25	
1995	A1380	20c	Texas	45	25	
1996	A1381	20c	Utah	45	25	
1997	A1382	20c	Vermont	45	25	
1998	A1383	20c	Virginia	45	25	
1999	A1384	20c	Washington	45	25	
2000	A1385	20c	West Virginia	45	25	
2001	A1386	20c	Wisconsin	45	25	
2002	A1387	20c	Wyoming	45	25	
			#1953a-2002a, any single, perf. 11	50	30	
b.			Pane of 50, perf. 10½x11	22.50	—	
c.			Pane of 50, perf. 11	25.00	—	
d.			Pane of 50, imperf.	—		
2003	A1388	20c	ver, brt blue & gray black	38	15	
a.			Imperf., pair	*400.00*		
2004	A1389	20c	red & black	38	15	

Coil stamp, Perf. 10 Vertically

2005	A1390	20c	sky blue	75	15	
a.			Imperf., pair	*100.00*		
2006	A1391	20c	multicolored	40	15	
2007	A1392	20c	multicolored	40	15	
2008	A1393	20c	multicolored	40	15	
2009	A1394	20c	multicolored	40	15	
a.			Block of 4, #2006-2009	1.75	1.00	
2010	A1395	20c	red & black, *tan*	38	15	
2011	A1396	20c	brown	38	15	
2012	A1397	20c	multicolored	38	15	
2013	A1398	20c	multicolored	38	15	
2014	A1399	20c	multicolored	38	15	
a.			Black & green (engr.) omitted	*250.00*		
2015	A1400	20c	red & black	38	15	
a.			Vert. pair, imperf. horiz.	*300.00*		
2016	A1401	20c	multicolored	1.00	15	
2017	A1402	20c	multicolored	38	15	
a.			Imperf., pair	*1,250.*		
2018	A1403	20c	multicolored	38	15	
2019	A1404	20c	black & brown	38	15	
2020	A1405	20c	black & brown	38	15	
2021	A1406	20c	black & brown	38	15	
2022	A1407	20c	black & brown	38	15	
a.			Block of 4, #2019-2022	1.60	1.00	

A1396

A1399

A1397

A1398

A1400

A1401

A1402

A1403

A1404

A1405

A1406

A1407

Scott No.	Illus. No.		Description	Unused Value	Used Value	/ / / / / /
2023	A1408	20c	multicolored	38	15	
2024	A1409	20c	multicolored	38	15	
a.			Imperf., pair	600.00		
a.			Vert. pair, imperf. between and at top	—		
2025	A1410	13c	multicolored	26	15	
2026	A1411	20c	multicolored	38	15	
a.			Imperf., pair	150.00		
b.			Horiz. pair, imperf. vert.	—		
c.			Vert. pair, imperf. horiz.	—		
2027	A1412	20c	multicolored	50	15	
2028	A1413	20c	multicolored	50	15	
2029	A1414	20c	multicolored	50	15	
2030	A1415	20c	multicolored	50	15	
a.			Block of 4, #2027-2030	2.00	1.00	
b.			As "a," imperf.	3,000.		
c.			As "a," imperf. horiz.	—		

1983

Scott No.	Illus. No.		Description	Unused Value	Used Value	/ / / / / /
2031	A1416	20c	multicolored	38	15	
a.			Black (engr.) omitted	1,400.		
2032	A1417	20c	multicolored	38	15	
2033	A1418	20c	multicolored	38	15	
2034	A1419	20c	multicolored	38	15	
2035	A1420	20c	multicolored	38	15	
a.			Block of 4, #2032-2035	1.65	1.00	
b.			As "a," imperf.	—		
2036	A1421	20c	multicolored	38	15	
2037	A1422	20c	multicolored	38	15	
a.			Imperf., pair	2,500.		
2038	A1423	20c	multicolored	38	15	
2039	A1424	20c	red & black	38	15	
a.			Imperf., pair	850.00		
2040	A1425	20c	brown	38	15	
2041	A1426	20c	blue	38	15	
2042	A1427	20c	multicolored	40	15	
2043	A1428	20c	multicolored	38	15	
2044	A1429	20c	multicolored	40	15	
a.			Imperf., pair	500.00		
2045	A1430	20c	multicolored	40	15	
a.			Red omitted	300.00		
2046	A1431	20c	blue	1.00	15	
2047	A1432	20c	multicolored	40	15	
2048	A1433	13c	multicolored	35	15	
2049	A1434	13c	multicolored	35	15	
2050	A1435	13c	multicolored	35	15	
2051	A1436	13c	multicolored	35	15	
a.			Block of 4, #2048-2051	1.50	1.00	

A1408

A1409

A1411

A1410

A1416

A1412

A1413

A1414

A1415

A1421

A1422

Scott No.	Illus. No.	Description	Unused Value	Used Value	/ / / / / /
2052	A1437	20c multicolored	38	15	
2053	A1438	20c buff, blue & red	40	15	
2054	A1439	20c yellow & maroon	38	15	
2055	A1440	20c multicolored	45	15	
2056	A1441	20c multicolored	45	15	
2057	A1442	20c multicolored	45	15	
2058	A1443	20c multicolored	45	15	
a.		Block of 4, #2055-2058	1.90	1.00	
b.		As "a," black omitted	450.00		
2059	A1444	20c multicolored	40	15	
2060	A1445	20c multicolored	40	15	
2061	A1446	20c multicolored	40	15	
2062	A1447	20c multicolored	40	15	
a.		Block of 4, #2059-2062	1.70	1.00	
b.		As "a," black omitted	475.00		
c.		As "a," black omitted on #2059, 2061	—		
2063	A1448	20c multicolored	38	15	
2064	A1449	20c multicolored	38	15	
a.		Imperf., pair	165.00		
2065	A1450	20c multicolored	38	15	

1984

Scott No.	Illus. No.	Description	Unused Value	Used Value	/ / / / / /
2066	A1451	20c multicolored	38	15	
2067	A1452	20c multicolored	42	15	
2068	A1453	20c multicolored	42	15	
2069	A1454	20c multicolored	42	15	
2070	A1455	20c multicolored	42	15	
a.		Block of 4, #2067-2070	1.70	1.00	
2071	A1456	20c multicolored	38	15	
2072	A1457	20c multicolored	40	15	
a.		Horiz. pair, imperf. vert.	200.00		
2073	A1458	20c multicolored	40	15	
a.		Horiz. pair, imperf. vert.	—		
2074	A1459	20c multicolored	38	15	
2075	A1460	20c multicolored	38	15	
2076	A1461	20c Wild pink	42	15	
2077	A1462	20c Yellow lady's-slipper	42	15	
2078	A1463	20c Spreading pogonia	42	15	
2079	A1464	20c Pacific calypso	42	15	
a.		Block of 4, #2076-2079	1.80	1.00	
2080	A1465	20c multicolored	40	15	
2081	A1466	20c multicolored	40	15	
2082	A1467	20c multicolored	60	15	
2083	A1468	20c multicolored	60	15	
2084	A1469	20c multicolored	60	15	
2085	A1470	20c multicolored	60	15	
a.		Block of 4, #2082-2085	2.40	1.00	

 **A1417**

A1418

 **A1419**

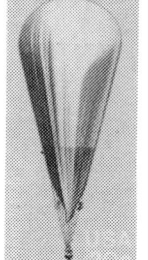 **A1420**

 **A1423**

 **A1429**

A1431

A1432

 **A1424**

 **A1425**

 **A1426**

 **A1427**

 **A1428**

A1430

A1438

A1437

A1433 **A1434**

A1435 **A1436**

A1440 **A1441**

A1442 **A1443**

A1439

A1448

A1449

A1444 A1445

A1446 A1447

A1450

A1452 A1453

A1451

A1454 A1455

A1457

A1456

176

A1458

A1461

A1462

A1459

A1460

A1463

A1464

A1466

A1467　**A1468**

A1473

A1474

A1469　A1470

A1465

A1471

A1472

177

 A1475

 A1478

 A1479

 A1476   A1477

 A1480

 A1481

 A1482

A1483   A1484

A1485   A1486

Scott No.	Illus. No.		Description	Unused Value	Used Value	//////
2086	A1471	20c	multicolored	38	15	
2087	A1472	20c	multicolored	40	15	
2088	A1473	20c	multicolored	38	15	
2089	A1474	20c	dark brown	40	15	
2090	A1475	20c	multicolored	40	15	
2091	A1476	20c	multicolored	40	15	
2092	A1477	20c	blue	50	15	
a.			Horiz. pair, imperf. vert.	400.00		
2093	A1478	20c	multicolored	38	15	
2094	A1479	20c	sage green	38	15	
2095	A1480	20c	orange & dark brown	45	15	
2096	A1481	20c	multicolored	38	15	
a.			Horiz. pair, imperf. btwn.	300.00		
b.			Vert. pair, imperf. btwn.	250.00		
c.			Block of 4, imperf. btwn, vert. and horiz.	4,500.		
2097	A1482	20c	multicolored	1.00	15	
a.			Horiz. pair, imperf. vert.	1,600.		
2098	A1483	20c	multicolored	40	15	
2099	A1484	20c	multicolored	40	15	
2100	A1485	20c	multicolored	40	15	
2101	A1486	20c	multicolored	40	15	
a.			Block of 4, #2098-2101	1.75	1.00	
2102	A1487	20c	multicolored	38	15	
2103	A1488	20c	multicolored	38	15	
a.			Vert. pair, imperf. horiz.	1,500.		
2104	A1489	20c	multicolored	40	15	
a.			Horiz. pair, imperf. vert.	600.00		
2105	A1490	20c	deep blue	38	15	
2106	A1491	20c	brown & maroon	38	15	
2107	A1492	20c	multicolored	40	15	
2108	A1493	20c	multicolored	40	15	
a.			Horiz. pair, imperf. vert.	950.00		
2109	A1494	20c	multicolored	40	15	

1985

Scott No.	Illus. No.		Description	Unused Value	Used Value	
2110	A1495	22c	multicolored	40	15	
2111	A1496	(22c)	green	60	15	
a.			Vert. pair, imperf.	55.00		
b.			Vert. pair, imperf. horiz.	1,350.		

Coil stamp, Perf. 10 Vertically

Scott No.	Illus. No.		Description	Unused Value	Used Value	
2112	A1496	(22c)	green	60	15	
a.			Imperf., pair	50.00		
2113	A1497	(22c)	green	80	15	
a.			Booklet pane of 10	8.00		
b.			As "a," imperf. btwn. horiz.	—		
2114	A1498	22c	blue, red & black	40	15	

A1487  **A1488**  **A1489**

A1490  **A1494**

A1491  **A1492**  **A1493**  **A1495**

A1496  **A1497** **A1498** **A1499**

HOW TO USE THIS BOOK

The number in the first column is its Scott number or identifying number. The letter and number that come next (A41) indicate the design and refer to the illustration so designated. Following that is the denomination of the stamp and its color. Finally, the value, unused and used is shown.

Scott No.	Illus. No.		Description	Unused Value	Used Value	/ / / / / /
Coil stamp, Perf. 10 Vertically						
2115	A1498	22c	blue, red & black............	40	15	
a.			Imperf., pair...................	10.00		
b.			Inscribed "T" at bottom ..	48	15	
c.			Black field of stars	—	—	
2116	A1499	22c	blue, red & black............	48	15	
a.			Booklet pane of 5	2.50	—	
2117	A1500	22c	black & brown................	40	15	
2118	A1501	22c	multicolored	40	15	
2119	A1502	22c	black & brown................	40	15	
2120	A1503	22c	black & violet.................	40	15	
2121	A1504	22c	multicolored	40	15	
a.			Booklet pane of 10	4.00	—	
b.			As "a," violet omitted	*850.00*		
c.			As "a," vert. imperf. btwn.	*600.00*		
d.			As "a," imperf.	—		
e.			Strip of 5, #2117-2121	2.00		
Booklet stamp, Perf. 10 Vertically						
2122	A1505	$1075	multicolored.....................	17.00	6.75	
a.			Booklet pane of 3	52.50	—	
b.			Type II.............................	17.00	—	
c.			As "b," booklet pane of 3	52.50	—	
1985-87, Coil stamps, Perf. 10 Vertically						
2123	A1506	3.4c	dark bluish green............	15	15	
a.			Untagged (Bureau Precancel)	15	15	
2124	A1507	4.9c	brown black....................	15	15	
a.			Untagged (Bureau Precancel)	16	16	
2125	A1508	5.5c	deep magenta..................	15	15	
a.			Untagged (Bureau precancel)	15	15	
2126	A1509	6c	red brown	15	15	
a.			Untagged (Bureau Precancel)	15	15	
b.			As "a," imperf., pair........	190.00		
2127	A1510	7.1c	lake	15	15	
a.			Untagged (Bureau Precancel)	15	15	
2128	A1511	8.3c	green...............................	18	15	
a.			Untagged (Bureau Precancel)	18	18	
2129	A1512	8.5c	dark Prussian green	16	15	
a.			Untagged (Bureau Precancel)	16	16	
2130	A1513	10.1c	slate blue.........................	22	15	
a.			Untagged (Bureau Precancel)	22	22	
b.			As "a," imperf., pair........	15.00		
2131	A1514	11c	dark green.......................	22	15	
2132	A1515	12c	dark blue.........................	24	15	
a.			Untagged (Bureau Precancel)	24	24	
b.			Type II, untagged (Bureau Precancel)......................	24	24	

A1500

A1501

A1502

A1503

A1505

A1504

A1506

A1507

A1508

A1509

A1510

A1511

A1512

A1513

A1514

A1515

A1516

A1517

A1518

A1519

Scott No.	Illus. No.	Description	Unused Value	Used Value	/ / / / / /
2133	A1516	12.5c olive green....................	25	15	
a.		Untagged (Bureau Precancel)	25	25	
b.		As "a," imperf., pair........	50.00		
2134	A1517	14c sky blue	28	15	
a.		Imperf., pair.....................	90.00		
b.		Type II...............................	28	15	
2135	A1518	17c sky blue	30	15	
a.		Imperf., pair.....................	500.00		
2136	A1519	25c orange brown	45	15	
a.		Imperf., pair.....................	10.00		
b.		Pair, imperf. between......	—		

1985

Scott No.	Illus. No.	Description	Unused Value	Used Value	/ / / / / /
2137	A1520	22c multicolored	40	15	
2138	A1521	22c multicolored	60	15	
2139	A1522	22c multicolored	60	15	
2140	A1523	22c multicolored	60	15	
2141	A1524	22c multicolored	60	15	
a.		Block of 4, #2138-2141..	3.00	1.00	
2142	A1525	22c multicolored	40	15	
a.		Vert. pair, imperf. horiz..	650.00		
2143	A1526	22c multicolored	40	15	
a.		Imperf., pair.....................	1,750.		
2144	A1527	22c multicolored	45	15	
2145	A1528	22c multicolored	40	15	
a.		Red, black & blue omitted	225.00		
b.		Red & black omitted.......	1,250.		
c.		Red omitted......................	—		
2146	A1529	22c multicolored	40	15	
a.		Imperf., pair.....................	350.00		
2147	A1530	22c multicolored	40	15	

Coil stamps, Perf. 10 Vertically

Scott No.	Illus. No.	Description	Unused Value	Used Value	/ / / / / /
2149	A1532	18c multicolored	32	15	
a.		Untagged (Bureau Precancel)	35	35	
b.		Imperf., pair.....................	950.00		
c.		As "a," imperf., pair........	700.00		
2150	A1533	21.1c multicolored	40	15	
a.		Untagged (Bureau Precancel)	38	38	

1985

Scott No.	Illus. No.	Description	Unused Value	Used Value	/ / / / / /
2152	A1535	22c gray green & rose red......	40	15	
2153	A1536	22c deep blue & light blue.....	40	15	
2154	A1537	22c gray green & rose red......	40	15	
2155	A1538	22c multicolored	75	15	
2156	A1539	22c multicolored	75	15	
2157	A1540	22c multicolored	75	15	
2158	A1541	22c multicolored	75	15	
a.		Block of 4, #2155-2158..	4.00	1.00	

A1520

A1526

A1527

A1521 A1522

A1523 A1524

A1525

A1528

A1530

A1529

A1535

A1532

A1536

A1533

A1537

A1538

A1539

A1540

A1541

A1543

A1544

A1545

A1546

Scott No.	Illus. No.	Description	Unused Value	Used Value
2159	A1542	22c multicolored	42	15
2160	A1543	22c multicolored	48	15
2161	A1544	22c multicolored	48	15
2162	A1545	22c multicolored	48	15
2163	A1546	22c multicolored	48	15
a.		Block of 4, #2160-2163	2.00	1.00
2164	A1547	22c multicolored	42	15
2165	A1548	22c multicolored	40	15
a.		Imperf., pair	*100.00*	
2166	A1549	22c multicolored	40	15
a.		Imperf., pair	*130.00*	

1986-93

Scott No.	Illus. No.	Description	Unused Value	Used Value
2167	A1550	22c multicolored	40	15
a.		Vert. pair, imperf. horiz.	—	
2168	A1551	1c brownish vermilion	15	15
2169	A1552	2c bright blue	15	15
2170	A1553	3c bright blue	15	15
2171	A1554	4c blue violet	15	15
a.		Untagged	15	15
2172	A1555	5c dark olive green	15	15
2173	A1556	5c carmine	15	15
a.		Untagged	15	15
2176	A1559	10c lake	18	15
b.		Untagged	20	15
2177	A1560	14c crimson	25	15
2178	A1561	15c claret	28	15
2179	A1562	17c dull blue green	30	15
2180	A1563	21c blue violet	38	15
2182	A1565	23c purple	42	15
2183	A1566	25c blue	45	15
a.		Booklet pane of 10	4.50	—
2184	A1567	28c myrtle green	50	15
2184A	A1567a	29c blue	50	15
2184B	A1567b	29c indigo	50	15
2185	A1568	35c black	65	15
2186	A1569	40c dark blue	70	15
2188	A1571	45c bright blue	80	15
2190	A1573	52c purple	90	15
2191	A1574	56c scarlet	90	15
2192	A1575	65c dark blue	1.20	18
2193	A1576	75c deep magenta	1.30	20
2194	A1577	$1 dark Prussian green	2.50	50
2194A	A1577a	$1 deep blue	1.75	50
2195	A1578	$2 bright violet	3.00	50
2196	A1579	$5 copper red	7.00	1.00
2197	A1566	25c blue	45	15
a.		Booklet pane of 6	2.65	—

A1542

A1547

A1548

A1549

A1550

A1585

A1586

A1587

A1594

A1588-1592

A1593

Scott No.	Illus. No.		Description	Unused Value	Used Value	/ / / / / /
1986						
2198	A1581	22c	multicolored	45	15	
2199	A1582	22c	multicolored	45	15	
2200	A1583	22c	multicolored	45	15	
2201	A1584	22c	multicolored	45	15	
a.			Bklt. pane of 4, #2198-2201	2.00	—	
b.			As "a," black omitted on #2198, 2201	45.00		
c.			As "a," blue (litho.) omitted on #2198-2200	2,250.		
d.			As "a," buff (litho.) omitted	—		
2202	A1585	22c	multicolored	40	15	
2203	A1586	22c	multicolored	40	15	
2204	A1587	22c	dk bl, dk red & grysh blk	42	15	
a.			Horiz. pair, imperf. vert.	*1,000.*		
b.			Dark red omitted	*2,750.*		
2205	A1588	22c	multicolored	50	15	
2206	A1589	22c	multicolored	50	15	
2207	A1590	22c	multicolored	50	15	
2208	A1591	22c	multicolored	50	15	
2209	A1592	22c	multicolored	50	15	
a.			Bklt. pane of 5, #2205-2209	3.25	—	
2210	A1593	22c	multicolored	40	15	
a.			Vert. pair, imperf. horiz.	*400.00*		
b.			Horiz. pair, imperf. vert.	*1,350.*		
2211	A1594	22c	multicolored	40	15	
a.			Vert. pair, imperf. horiz.	*1,000.*	—	
2216			Sheet of 9	3.50		
a.-i.	A1599	22c	any single	38	20	
j.			Blue omitted	*3,500.*		
k.			Black inscription omitted	*1,500.*		
l.			Imperf.	*10,500.*		
2217			Sheet of 9	3.50		
a.-i.	A1599	22c	any single	38	20	
j.			Black inscription omitted	*3,750.*		
2218			Sheet of 9	3.50		
a.-i.	A1599	22c	any single	38	20	
j.			Brown omitted	—		
k.			Black inscription omitted	*2,600.*		
2219			Sheet of 9	3.50		
a.-i.	A1599	22c	any single	38	20	
2220	A1600	22c	multicolored	45	15	
2221	A1601	22c	multicolored	45	15	
2222	A1602	22c	multicolored	45	15	
2223	A1603	22c	multicolored	45	15	
a.			Block of 4, #2220-2223	2.00	1.00	
b.			As "a," black (engr.) omitted	*9,000.*		
2224	A1604	22c	scarlet & dark blue	40	15	

A1599a

A1599b

A1599c

A1599d

A1581-1584

A1600-1603

A1605-1608

A1604a   **A1604**   **A1604b**

A1610-1613

A1609   **A1616**

Scott No.	Illus. No.		Description	Unused Value	Used Value	/ / / / / /

1986-87, Coil stamps, Perf. 10 Vertically

Scott No.	Illus. No.		Description	Unused Value	Used Value
2225	A1604a	1c	violet	15	15
a.			Untagged	15	15
b.			Imperf., pair	—	
2226	A1604b	2c	black	15	15
2228	A1285	4c	reddish brown	15	15
b.			Imperf., pair	350.00	
2231	A1511	8.3c	green (Bureau precancel)	16	16

1986

Scott No.	Illus. No.		Description	Unused Value	Used Value
2235	A1605	22c	multicolored	40	15
2236	A1606	22c	multicolored	40	15
2237	A1607	22c	multicolored	40	15
2238	A1608	22c	multicolored	40	15
a.			Block of 4, #2235-2238	1.65	1.00
b.			As "a," black (engr.) omitted	350.00	
2239	A1609	22c	copper red	40	15
2240	A1610	22c	multicolored	42	15
2241	A1611	22c	multicolored	42	15
2242	A1612	22c	multicolored	42	15
2243	A1613	22c	multicolored	42	15
a.			Block of 4, #2240-2243	1.75	1.00
b.			As "a," imperf. vert.	1,500.	
2244	A1614	22c	multicolored	40	15
2245	A1615	22c	multicolored	40	15

1987

Scott No.	Illus. No.		Description	Unused Value	Used Value
2246	A1616	22c	multicolored	40	15
2247	A1617	22c	multicolored	40	15
a.			Silver omitted	1,500.	
2248	A1618	22c	multicolored	40	15
2249	A1619	22c	multicolored	40	15
2250	A1620	22c	multicolored	40	15
a.			Black (engr.) omitted	4,000.	
2251	A1621	22c	multicolored	40	15

1987-88, Coil stamps, Perf. 10 Vertically

Scott No.	Illus. No.		Description	Unused Value	Used Value
2252	A1622	3c	claret	15	15
a.			Untagged	15	15
2253	A1623	5c	black	15	15
2254	A1624	5.3c	black (Bureau precancel in scarlet)	15	15
2255	A1625	7.6c	brown (Bureau precancel in scarlet)	15	15
2256	A1626	8.4c	dp claret (Bureau precancel in red)	15	15
a.			Imperf., pair	750.00	
2257	A1627	10c	sky blue	18	15

A1614

A1615

A1618

A1617

A1637

A1619

A1620

A1638

A1639

A1640

A1641

A1642

A1621

A1643

A1645

A1644

Scott No.	Illus. No.	Description	Unused Value	Used Value	/ / / / / /
2258	A1628 13c	black (Bureau precancel in red)............	22	22	
2259	A1629 13.2c	slate green (Bureau precancel in red)............	22	22	
a.		Imperf., pair.....................	120.00		
2260	A1630 15c	violet..................................	24	15	
c.		Imperf., pair.....................	—		
2261	A1631 16.7c	rose (Bureau precancel in black)	28	28	
a.		Imperf., pair.....................	180.00		
2262	A1632 17.5c	dark violet........................	30	15	
a.		Untagged (Bureau precancel)	30	30	
b.		Imperf., pair.....................	1,750.		
2263	A1633 20c	blue violet........................	35	15	
a.		Imperf., pair.....................	75.00		
2264	A1634 20.5c	rose (Bureau precancel in black)	38	38	
2265	A1635 21c	olive green (Bureau precancel in red)............	38	38	
a.		Imperf., pair.....................	65.00		
2266	A1636 24.1c	deep ultra (Bureau precancel)	42	42	

1987, Perf. 10 on 1, 2 or 3 sides

Scott No.	Illus. No.	Description	Unused Value	Used Value	/ / / / / /
2267	A1637 22c	multicolored.....................	55	15	
2268	A1638 22c	multicolored.....................	55	15	
2269	A1639 22c	multicolored.....................	55	15	
2270	A1640 22c	multicolored.....................	55	15	
2271	A1641 22c	multicolored.....................	55	15	
2272	A1642 22c	multicolored.....................	55	15	
2273	A1643 22c	multicolored.....................	55	15	
2274	A1644 22c	multicolored.....................	55	15	
a.		Bklt. pane of 10, #2268-2271, 2273-2274, 2 each #2267, 2272..................	6.75	—	
2275	A1645 22c	multicolored.....................	40	15	
2276	A1646 22c	multicolored.....................	40	15	
a.		Booklet pane of 20..........	8.50	—	
2277	A1647 (25c)	multicolored.....................	45	15	
2278	A1648 25c	multicolored.....................	40	15	
2279	A1647 (25c)	multicolored.....................	45	15	
a.		Imperf., pair.....................	100.00		
2280	A1649 25c	Green trees	45	15	
a.		Imperf., pair.....................	15.00		
b.		Black trees........................	100.00	—	
d.		Pair, imperf. between	750.00		
2281	A1649d 25c	multicolored.....................	45	15	
a.		Imperf., pair.....................	45.00		
b.		Black (engr.) omitted	60.00		
c.		Black (litho.) omitted.......	350.00		
d.		Pair, imperf. between	900.00		

A1622    **A1623**    **A1624**    **A1625**

A1626    **A1627**    **A1628**    **A1629**

A1630    **A1631**    **A1632**    **A1633**

A1634    **A1635**    **A1636**

HOW TO USE THIS BOOK

The number in the first column is its Scott number or identifying number. The letter and number that come next (A41) indicate the design and refer to the illustration so designated. Following that is the denomination of the stamp and its color. Finally, the value, unused and used is shown.

Scott No.	Illus. No.		Description	Unused Value	Used Value
2282	A1647	(25c)	multicolored	50	15
a.			Booklet pane of 10	6.50	—
2283	A1649a	25c	multicolored	50	15
a.			Booklet pane of 10	6.00	—
b.		25c	multi, red removed from sky	1.00	15
c.			As "b," booklet pane of 10	65.00	—
d.			As "a," horiz. imperf. between	—	
2284	A1649b	25c	multicolored	45	15
2285	A1649c	25c	multicolored	45	15
b.			Bklt. pane of 10, 5 each #2284-2285	4.50	—
d.			Pair, #2284-2285	1.00	—
2285A	A1648	25c	multicolored	45	15
c.			Booklet pane of 6	2.75	—
2286	A1650	22c	Barn swallow	85	15
2287	A1651	22c	Monarch butterfly	85	15
2288	A1652	22c	Bighorn sheep	85	15
2289	A1653	22c	Broad-tailed hummingbird	85	15
2290	A1654	22c	Cottontail	85	15
2291	A1655	22c	Osprey	85	15
2292	A1656	22c	Mountain lion	85	15
2293	A1657	22c	Luna moth	85	15
2294	A1658	22c	Mule deer	85	15
2295	A1659	22c	Gray squirrel	85	15
2296	A1660	22c	Armadillo	85	15
2297	A1661	22c	Eastern chipmunk	85	15
2298	A1662	22c	Moose	85	15
2299	A1663	22c	Black bear	85	15
2300	A1664	22c	Tiger swallowtail	85	15
2301	A1665	22c	Bobwhite	85	15
2302	A1666	22c	Ringtail	85	15
2303	A1667	22c	Red-winged blackbird	85	15
2304	A1668	22c	American lobster	85	15
2305	A1669	22c	Black-tailed jack rabbit	85	15
2306	A1670	22c	Scarlet tanager	85	15
2307	A1671	22c	Woodchuck	85	15
2308	A1672	22c	Roseate spoonbill	85	15
2309	A1673	22c	Bald eagle	85	15
2310	A1674	22c	Alaskan brown bear	85	15
2311	A1675	22c	Iiwi	85	15
2312	A1676	22c	Badger	85	15
2313	A1677	22c	Pronghorn	85	15
2314	A1678	22c	River otter	85	15
2315	A1679	22c	Ladybug	85	15
2316	A1680	22c	Beaver	85	15
2317	A1681	22c	White-tailed deer	85	15
2318	A1682	22c	Blue jay	85	15
2319	A1683	22c	Pika	85	15

HOW TO USE THIS BOOK

The number in the first column is its Scott number or identifying number. The letter and number that come next (A41) indicate the design and refer to the illustration so designated. Following that is the denomination of the stamp and its color. Finally, the value, unused and used is shown.

Scott No.	Illus. No.		Description	Unused Value	Used Value	//////
2320	A1684	22c	Bison	85	15	
2321	A1685	22c	Snowy egret	85	15	
2322	A1686	22c	Gray wolf	85	15	
2323	A1687	22c	Mountain goat	85	15	
2324	A1688	22c	Deer mouse	85	15	
2325	A1689	22c	Black-tailed prairie dog	85	15	
2326	A1690	22c	Box turtle	85	15	
2327	A1691	22c	Wolverine	85	15	
2328	A1692	22c	American elk	85	15	
2329	A1693	22c	California sea lion	85	15	
2330	A1694	22c	Mockingbird	85	15	
2331	A1695	22c	Raccoon	85	15	
2332	A1696	22c	Bobcat	85	15	
2333	A1697	22c	Black-footed ferret	85	15	
2334	A1698	22c	Canada goose	85	15	
2335	A1699	22c	Red fox	85	15	
a.			Pane of 50, #2286-2335	47.50		
			2286b-2335b, any single, red omitted	—		

1987-88

Scott No.	Illus. No.		Description	Unused Value	Used Value	//////
2336	A1700	22c	multicolored	40	15	
2337	A1701	22c	multicolored	42	15	
2338	A1702	22c	multicolored	42	15	
a.			Black (engr.) omitted	5,250.		
2339	A1703	22c	multicolored	40	15	
2340	A1704	22c	multicolored	40	15	
2341	A1705	22c	dark blue & dark red	40	15	
2342	A1706	22c	multicolored	40	15	
2343	A1707	25c	multicolored	45	15	
a.			Strip of 3, vert. imperf. between	—		
2344	A1708	25c	multicolored	45	15	
2345	A1709	25c	multicolored	45	15	
2346	A1710	25c	multicolored	45	15	
2347	A1711	25c	multicolored	45	15	
2348	A1712	25c	multicolored	45	15	
2349	A1713	22c	scarlet & black	40	15	
a.			Black (engr.) omitted	300.00		
2350	A1714	22c	bright green	40	15	
2351	A1715	22c	ultra & white	42	15	
2352	A1716	22c	ultra & white	42	15	
2353	A1717	22c	ultra & white	42	15	
2354	A1718	22c	ultra & white	42	15	
a.			Block of 4, #2351-2354	1.75	1.00	
b.			As "a," white omitted	1,000.		
2355	A1719	22c	multicolored	50	15	
a.			Grayish green (background) omitted	—		

Dec 7, 1787 USA
Delaware 22
A1700

Dec 12, 1787
Pennsylvania
A1701

Dec 18, 1787 USA
New Jersey 22
A1702

22 USA
January 2, 1788
Georgia
A1703

22 USA
January 9, 1788
Connecticut
A1704

22 USA
Feb 6, 1788
Massachusetts
A1705

April 28, 1788 USA
Maryland 22
A1706

25 USA
May 23, 1788
South Carolina
A1707

25 USA
June 21, 1788
New Hampshire
A1708

June 25, 1788 USA
Virginia 25
A1709

July 26, 1788 USA
New York 25
A1710

25 USA
November 21, 1789
North Carolina
A1711

25 USA
May 29, 1790
Rhode Island
A1712

Scott No.	Illus. No.		Description	Unused Value	Used Value
2356	A1720	22c	multicolored....................	50	15
a.			Grayish green (background) omitted.........................	—	
2357	A1721	22c	multicolored....................	50	15
a.			Grayish green (background) omitted.........................	—	
2358	A1722	22c	multicolored....................	50	15
a.			Grayish green (background) omitted.........................	—	
2359	A1723	22c	multicolored....................	50	15
a.			Bklt. pane of 5, #2355-2359	2.75	—
b.			Grayish green (background) omitted.........................	—	
2360	A1724	22c	multicolored....................	40	15
2361	A1725	22c	multicolored....................	1.90	15
a.			Black (engr.) omitted	*850.00*	
2362	A1726	22c	multicolored....................	60	15
2363	A1727	22c	multicolored....................	60	15
2364	A1728	22c	multicolored....................	60	15
2365	A1729	22c	multicolored....................	60	15
a.			Red omitted....................		—
2366	A1730	22c	multicolored....................	60	15
a.			Booklet pane of 5, #2362-2366	3.25	—
b.			As "a," blk omitted on #2366	—	
2367	A1731	22c	multicolored....................	40	15
2368	A1732	22c	multicolored....................	40	15
1988					
2369	A1733	22c	multicolored....................	40	15
2370	A1734	22c	multicolored....................	40	15
2371	A1735	22c	multicolored....................	40	15
2372	A1736	22c	multicolored....................	42	15
2373	A1737	22c	multicolored....................	42	15
2374	A1738	22c	multicolored....................	42	15
2375	A1739	22c	multicolored....................	42	15
a.			Block of 4, #2372-2375 ..	1.90	1.00
2376	A1740	22c	multicolored....................	40	15
2377	A1741	25c	multicolored....................	45	15
2378	A1742	25c	multicolored....................	45	15
2379	A1743	45c	multicolored....................	65	20
2380	A1744	25c	multicolored....................	45	15
2381	A1745	25c	multicolored....................	50	15
2382	A1746	25c	multicolored....................	50	15
2383	A1747	25c	multicolored....................	50	15
2384	A1748	25c	multicolored....................	50	15
2385	A1749	25c	multicolored....................	50	15
a.			Booklet pane of 5, #2381-2385	2.75	—

A1713 **A1714** **A1724** **A1725**

A1715-1718

A1731 **A1733** **A1732**

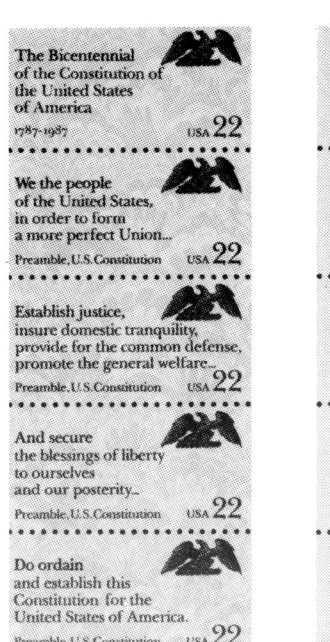

A1719-1723

A1726-1730

A1736-1739

A1735

A1734

A1740

A1741

A1742

A1743

A1744

A1745-1749

A1754-1757

Scott No.	Illus. No.	Description	Unused Value	Used Value	//////
2386	A1750	25c multicolored	55	15	
2387	A1751	25c multicolored	55	15	
2388	A1752	25c multicolored	55	15	
2389	A1753	25c multicolored	55	15	
a.		Block of 4, #2386-2389	2.40	1.00	
b.		Black (engr.) omitted	1,500.		
c.		As "a," imperf. horiz.	3,000.		
2390	A1754	25c multicolored	60	15	
2391	A1755	25c multicolored	60	15	
2392	A1756	25c multicolored	60	15	
2393	A1757	25c multicolored	60	15	
a.		Block of 4, #2390-2393	2.50	1.00	
2394	A1758	$8.75 multicolored	13.50	7.75	
2395	A1759	25c multicolored	45	15	
2396	A1760	25c multicolored	45	15	
a.		Bklt. pane, 3 #2395 + 3 #2396 with gutter btwn.	3.00	—	
2397	A1761	25c multicolored	45	15	
2398	A1762	25c multicolored	45	15	
a.		Bklt. pane, 3 #2397 + 3 #2398 with gutter btwn.	3.00	—	
b.		As "a," imperf. horiz.	—		
2399	A1763	25c multicolored	45	15	
a.		Gold omitted	40.00		
2400	A1764	25c multicolored	45	15	

1989

Scott No.	Illus. No.	Description	Unused Value	Used Value	//////
2401	A1765	25c multicolored	45	15	
2402	A1766	25c multicolored	45	15	
2403	A1767	25c multicolored	45	15	
2404	A1768	25c multicolored	45	15	
2405	A1769	25c multicolored	45	15	
2406	A1770	25c multicolored	45	15	
2407	A1771	25c multicolored	45	15	
2408	A1772	25c multicolored	45	15	
2409	A1773	25c multicolored	45	15	
a.		Bklt. pane of 5, #2405-2409	2.50	—	
2410	A1774	25c grysh brn, blk & car rose	45	15	
2411	A1775	25c multicolored	45	15	

1989-90

Scott No.	Illus. No.	Description	Unused Value	Used Value	//////
2412	A1776	25c multicolored	45	15	
2413	A1777	25c multicolored	45	15	
2414	A1778	25c multicolored	45	15	
2415	A1779	25c multicolored	45	15	

1989

Scott No.	Illus. No.	Description	Unused Value	Used Value	//////
2416	A1780	25c multicolored	45	15	

A1750-1753

A1758

A1759   **A1760**

A1761   **A1762**

A1764   **A1763**   **A1765**

A1766

A1767

A1768

A1769-1773

A1774

A1775

A1776

A1777

A1778

A1779

A1781 **A1782** **A1785** **A1790**

A1780

A1784 **A1783**

A1786-1789

Scott No.	Illus. No.		Description	Unused Value	Used Value	//////
2417	A1781	25c	multicolored	48	15	
2418	A1782	25c	multicolored	45	15	
2419	A1783	$2.40	multicolored	4.00	2.00	
a.			Black (engr.) omitted	*3,000.*		
b.			Imperf., pair	*1,150.*		
c.			Black (litho.) omitted	—		
2420	A1784	25c	multicolored	45	15	
2421	A1785	25c	multicolored	45	15	
a.			Black (engr.) omitted	300.00		
2422	A1786	25c	multicolored	45	15	
2423	A1787	25c	multicolored	45	15	
2424	A1788	25c	multicolored	45	15	
2425	A1789	25c	multicolored	45	15	
a.			Block of 4, #2422-2425	2.00	1.00	
b.			As "a," black (engr.) omitted	*1,100.*		
2426	A1790	25c	multicolored	45	15	
2427	A1791	25c	multicolored	45	15	
a.			Booklet pane of 10	4.50	—	
b.			Red (litho.) omitted	—		
2428	A1792	25c	multicolored	45	15	
a.			Vert. pair, imperf. horiz.	*2,000.*		

Booklet stamp, Perf. 11 ½ on 2 or 3 sides

2429	A1792	25c	multicolored	45	15	
a.			Booklet pane of 10	4.50	—	
b.			As "a," horiz. imperf. between	—		
c.			As "a," red omitted			

Die cut, Self-adhesive

2431	A1793	25c	multicolored	50	20	
a.			Booklet pane of 18	9.00		
b.			Vert. pair, no die cutting between	850.00		
2433	A1794		Sheet of 4	11.00	9.00	
a.		90c	like No. 122	1.90	1.75	
b.		90c	like No. 132TC (blue frame, brown center)	1.90	1.75	
c.		90c	like No. 132TC (green frame, blue center)	1.90	1.75	
d.		90c	like No. 132TC (scarlet frame, blue center)	1.90	1.75	
2434	A1795	25c	multicolored	45	15	
2435	A1796	25c	multicolored	45	15	
2436	A1797	25c	multicolored	45	15	
2437	A1798	25c	multicolored	45	15	
a.			Block of 4, #2434-2437	2.00	2.00	
b.			As "a," dark blue (engr.) omitted	*1,000.*		

A1792

A1791

A1793

A1794

A1795-1798

A1800

A1799 **A1801**

A1802

Scott No.	Illus. No.		Description	Unused Value	Used Value	/ / / / / /
2438			Sheet of 4..........................	4.00	1.75	
a.	A1795	25c	multicolored	60	25	
b.	A1796	25c	multicolored	60	25	
c.	A1797	25c	multicolored	60	25	
d.	A1798	25c	multicolored	60	25	
e.			Dark blue & gray (engr.) omitted.............................	—		

1990

Scott No.	Illus. No.		Description	Unused Value	Used Value	
2439	A1799	25c	multicolored	45	15	
2440	A1800	25c	brt bl, dk pink & emer grn	45	15	
a.			Imperf., pair.....................	850.00		

Booklet stamp, Perf. 11 ½ on 2 or 3 sides

Scott No.	Illus. No.		Description	Unused Value	Used Value	
2441	A1800	25c	ultra, bright pink & dk grn	45	15	
a.			Booklet pane of 10	4.50	—	
b.			As "a," bright pink omitted	2,250.		
2442	A1801	25c	multicolored	45	15	
2443	A1802	15c	multicolored	28	15	
a.			Booklet pane of 10	2.80	—	
b.			As "a," blue omitted........	1,800.		
2444	A1803	25c	multicolored	45	15	
a.			Black (engr.) omitted	2,000.	—	
2445	A1804	25c	multicolored	70	15	
2446	A1805	25c	multicolored	70	15	
2447	A1806	25c	multicolored	70	15	
2448	A1807	25c	multicolored	70	15	
a.			Block of 4, #2445-2448 ..	3.25	1.00	
2449	A1808	25c	multicolored	45	15	

1990-94, Coil stamps, Perf. 10 Vertically

Scott No.	Illus. No.		Description	Unused Value	Used Value	
2451	A1810	4c	claret...............................	15	15	
a.			Imperf., pair.....................	675.00		
b.			Untagged	15	15	
2452	A1811	5c	red...................................	15	15	
a.			Untagged	15	15	
c.			Imperf., pair.....................	—		
2452B	A1811	5c	carmine............................	15	15	
2453	A1812	5c	brown (Bureau precancel in gray)	15	15	
a.			Imperf., pair.....................	600.00		
2454	A1812	5c	red (Bureau precancel in gray)	15	15	
2457	A1816	10c	green, engr. (Bureau precancel in gray).........	18	18	
a.			Imperf., pair.....................	500.00		
2458	A1816	10c	green, photo. (Bureau precancel in black)	20	20	

A1803

A1808

A1804-07

A1810

A1811

A1812

A1816

A1823

A1827

A1829-33

Scott No.	Illus. No.		Description	Unused Value	Used Value	/////
2464	A1823	23c	dark blue..................	42	15	
a.			Imperf., pair................	175.00		
2468	A1827	$1	blue & scarlet.............	1.75	50	

1990
2470	A1829	25c	multicolored.............	45	15	
2471	A1830	25c	multicolored.............	45	15	
2472	A1831	25c	multicolored.............	45	15	
2473	A1832	25c	multicolored.............	45	15	
2474	A1833	25c	multicolored.............	45	15	
a.			Bklt. pane of 5, #2470-2474	2.50	—	
b.			As "a," white (USA 25) omitted....................	75.00		

Die cut, Self-adhesive
2475	A1834	25c	dark red & dark blue.......	50	25	
a.			Pane of 12...................	6.00		

1990-93
2476	A1835	$2	multicolored.............	3.50	1.25	
a.			Black (engr.) omitted......	—		

Die cut, Self-adhesive
2478	A1837	29c	multicolored.............	50	15	
a.			Pane of 18.................	9.00		
2479	A1838	29c	red, green & black........	50	15	
a.			Pane of 18.................	9.00		
2480	A1839	29c	multicolored.............	50	15	
a.			Pane of 18.................	9.00		

1991-92, Perf. 11, 11 ½ (19c)
2481	A1840	1c	multicolored.............	15	15	
2482	A1841	3c	multicolored.............	15	15	
2487	A1846	19c	multicolored.............	35	15	
2489	A1848	30c	multicolored.............	50	15	
2491	A1850	45c	multicolored.............	78	15	
a.			Black (engr.) omitted......	—	—	

1991, Booklet stamp, Perf. 10 on 2 or 3 sides
2493	A1852	29c	black & multi.............	50	15	
a.			Booklet pane of 10.........	5.00		
b.			As "a," horiz. imperf. btwn.	—		

Booklet stamp, Perf. 11 on 2 or 3 sides
2494	A1852	29c	red & multi...............	50	15	
a.			Booklet pane of 10.........	5.00		

A1834

A1835

A1837

A1838

A1839

A1840

A1841

A1855-59

A1860-64

Scott No.	Illus. No.		Description	Unused Value	Used Value	/ / / / / /
Booklet stamp, Perf. 10x11 on 2 or 3 sides						
2495	A1853	29c	multicolored	50	15	
a.			Booklet pane of 10	5.00		
1990						
2496	A1855	25c	multicolored	45	15	
2497	A1856	25c	multicolored	45	15	
2498	A1857	25c	multicolored	45	15	
2499	A1858	25c	multicolored	45	15	
2500	A1859	25c	multicolored	45	15	
a.			Strip of 5, #2496-2500	2.50	—	
2501	A1860	25c	multicolored	45	15	
2502	A1861	25c	multicolored	45	15	
2503	A1862	25c	multicolored	45	15	
2504	A1863	25c	multicolored	45	15	
2505	A1864	25c	multicolored	45	15	
a.			Bklt. pane, 2 each #2501-2505	4.75	—	
b.			As "a," black (engr.) omitted			
c.			Strip of 5, #2501-2505	2.25	—	
d.			As "a," horiz. imperf. btwn.	—		
2506	A1865	25c	multicolored	45	15	
2507	A1866	25c	multicolored	45	15	
a.			Pair, #2506-2507	1.00	16	
b.			As "a," black (engr.) omitted	—		
2508	A1867	25c	multicolored	45	15	
2509	A1868	25c	multicolored	45	15	
2510	A1869	25c	multicolored	45	15	
2511	A1870	25c	multicolored	45	15	
a.			Block of 4, #2508-2511 ..	2.00	—	
b.			As "a," black (engr.) omitted	*1,000.*		
2512	A1871	25c	multicolored	45	15	
2513	A1872	25c	multicolored	45	15	
a.			Imperf., pair	*2,000.*		
2514	A1873	25c	multicolored	45	15	
a.			Booklet pane of 10	4.50		
2515	A1874	25c	multicolored	45	15	
a.			Vert. pair, imperf. horiz. .	*1,100.*		
Booklet stamp, Perf. 11 ½x11 on 2 or 3 sides						
2516	A1874	25c	multicolored	45	15	
a.			Booklet pane of 10	4.50		
1991						
2517	A1875	(29c)	yel, blk, red & yel grn	50	15	
a.			Imperf., pair	*750.00*		
b.			Horiz. pair, imperf. vert. .	—		

A1846 **A1848** **A1850** **A1852**

A1853 **A1865-66**

A1871

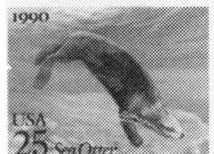 

A1867-70 **A1872**

   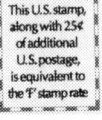

A1873 **A1874** **A1875** **A1876**

A1877

Scott No.	Illus. No.	Description	Unused Value	Used Value	//////

Coil stamp, Perf. 10 Vertically

| 2518 | A1875 (29c) | yel, blk, dull red & dk yel grn | 50 | 15 | |
| a. | | Imperf., pair.................... | *40.00* | | |

Booklet stamps, Perf. 11 on 2 or 3 sides

2519	A1875 (29c)	yel, blk, dull red & dk grn	50	15	
a.		Booklet pane of 10..........	5.00		
2520	A1875 (29c)	pale yel, blk, red & brt grn	50	15	
a.		Booklet pane of 10..........	5.50		
b.		As "a," imperf. horiz.......	—		
2521	A1876 (4c)	bister & carmine..............	15	15	
a.		Vert. pair, imperf. horiz. .	*200.00*		
b.		Double impression of bister	—	—	

Die cut, Self-adhesive

| 2522 | A1877 (29c) | black, dark blue & red..... | 50 | 25 | |
| a. | | Pane of 12....................... | 6.00 | | |

Coil stamps, Perf. 10 Vertically

2523	A1878	29c	blue, red & claret............	50	15	
b.			Imperf., pair....................	*20.00*		
c.			Blue, red & brown	5.00	—	
2523A	A1878	29c	blue, red & brown	50	15	

1991-92

| 2524 | A1879 | 29c | dull yel, blk, red & pale yel grn | 50 | 15 | |
| a. | | | Perf. 13 .... | 50 | 15 | |

Coil stamps, Rouletted 10 Vertically

| 2525 | A1879 | 29c | pale yel, blk, red & yel grn | 50 | 15 | |

Perf. 10 Vertically

2526	A1879	29c	pale yel, blk, red & yel grn	50	15	
2527	A1879	29c	pale yel, blk, red & brt grn	50	15	
a.			Booklet pane of 10..........	5.00	—	
b.			As "a," vert. imperf. between	—		
c.			As "a," imperf. horiz.......	—		

1991

2528	A1880	29c	multicolored	50	15	
a.			Booklet pane of 10..........	5.00	—	
b.			As "a," horiz. imperf. between	—		

Coil stamp, Perf. 10 Vertically

2529	A1881	19c	multicolored, two loops ..	35	15	
a.			Type II (finer dot pattern)	35	15	
b.			As "a," untagged	35	15	
2529C	A1881	19c	multicolored, one loop	35	15	

A1878　　　A1879　　　A1880　　　A1881

A1882　　　A1883　　　A1884

A1887　　　A1888　　　A1889

A1890　　　A1891　　　A1892

Scott No.	Illus. No.		Description	Unused Value	Used Value	/ / / / / /
Booklet stamp, Perf. 10 on 2 or 3 sides						
2530	A1882	19c	multicolored	35	15	
a.			Booklet pane of 10	3.50	—	
2531	A1883	29c	multicolored	50	15	
Die cut, Self-adhesive						
2531A	A1884	29c	black, gold & green	58	25	
b.			Pane of 18	10.50		
2532	A1887	50c	multicolored	1.00	25	
a.			Vert. pair, imperf. horiz.	—		
2533	A1888	29c	multicolored	50	15	
2534	A1889	29c	multicolored	50	15	
Perf. 12½x13						
2535	A1890	29c	multicolored	50	15	
a.			Perf. 11	58	15	
b.			Imperf., pair	—		
Booklet stamp, Perf. 11 on 1 or 2 sides						
2536	A1890	29c	multicolored	50	15	
a.			Booklet pane of 10	5.00		
2537	A1891	52c	multicolored	90	20	
2538	A1892	29c	multicolored	50	15	
2539	A1893	$1	gold & multi	1.75	50	
1991-93						
2540	A1894	$2.90	Priority	5.00	2.50	
2541	A1895	$9.95	Domestic express	17.50	7.50	
2542	A1896	$14	International express	22.50	10.00	
2543	A1897	$2.90	multicolored	5.80	—	
1991						
2545	A1899	29c	multicolored	50	15	
2546	A1900	29c	multicolored	50	15	
2547	A1901	29c	multicolored	50	15	
2548	A1902	29c	multicolored	50	15	
2549	A1903	29c	multicolored	50	15	
a.			Bklt. pane of 5, #2545-2549	2.50	—	
2550	A1904	29c	multicolored	50	15	
a.			Vert. pair, imperf. horiz.	*650.00*		
2551	A1905	29c	multicolored	50	15	
a.			Vert. pair, imperf. horiz.	—		
2552	A1905	29c	multicolored	50	15	
a.			Booklet pane of 5	2.50	—	
2553	A1907	29c	multicolored	50	15	
2554	A1908	29c	multicolored	50	15	
2555	A1909	29c	multicolored	50	15	
2556	A1910	29c	multicolored	50	15	

A1893

A1897

A1894

A1895

A1896

A1899-A1903

A1904

  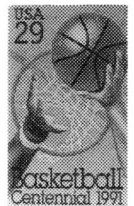

A1905   A1912   A1914

A1915   A1921

A1913

A1907-A1911 **A1916-A1920**

Scott No.	Illus. No.		Description	Unused Value	Used Value	//////
2557	A1911	29c	multicolored	50	15	
a.			Strip of #2553-2557	2.50	—	
2558	A1912	29c	multicolored	50	15	
2559	A1913		Block of 10	5.80	—	
a.-j.		29c	any single	58	29	
k.			Black (engr.) omitted	—		
2560	A1914	29c	multicolored	50	15	
2561	A1915	29c	multicolored	50	15	
a.			Black (engr.) omitted	200.00		
2562	A1916	29c	multicolored	50	15	
2563	A1917	29c	multicolored	50	15	
2564	A1918	29c	multicolored	50	15	
2565	A1919	29c	multicolored	50	15	
2566	A1920	29c	multicolored	50	15	
a.			Bklt. pane, 2 each #2562-2566	5.50	—	
b.			As "a," scarlet & bright violet (engr.) omitted	650.00		
c.			Strip of 5, #2562-2566	2.90	—	
2567	A1921	29c	multicolored	50	15	
a.			Horiz. pair, imperf. vert.	*1,500.*		
b.			Vert. pair, imperf. horiz.	*1,750.*		
2568	A1922	29c	multicolored	50	15	
2569	A1923	29c	multicolored	50	15	
2570	A1924	29c	multicolored	50	15	
2571	A1925	29c	multicolored	50	15	
2572	A1926	29c	multicolored	50	15	
2573	A1927	29c	multicolored	50	15	
2574	A1928	29c	multicolored	50	15	
2575	A1929	29c	multicolored	50	15	
2576	A1930	29c	multicolored	50	15	
2577	A1931	29c	multicolored	50	15	
a.			Bklt. pane of 10, #2568-2577	6.00	—	
2578	A1933	(29c)	multicolored	50	15	
a.			Booklet pane of 10	5.80	—	
b.			As "a," single, red & black (engr.) omitted	*2,500.*		
2579	A1934	(29c)	multicolored	50	15	
a.			Horiz. pair, imperf. vert.	*550.00*		
b.			Vert. pair, imperf. horiz.	—		
2580	A1934	(29c)	Type I	50	15	
2581	A1934	(29c)	Type II	50	15	
a.			Pair, #2580, 2581	1.00	25	
b.			Bklt. pane, 2 each #2580, 2581	2.00	—	
2582	A1935	(29c)	multicolored	50	15	
a.			Booklet pane of 4	2.00	—	

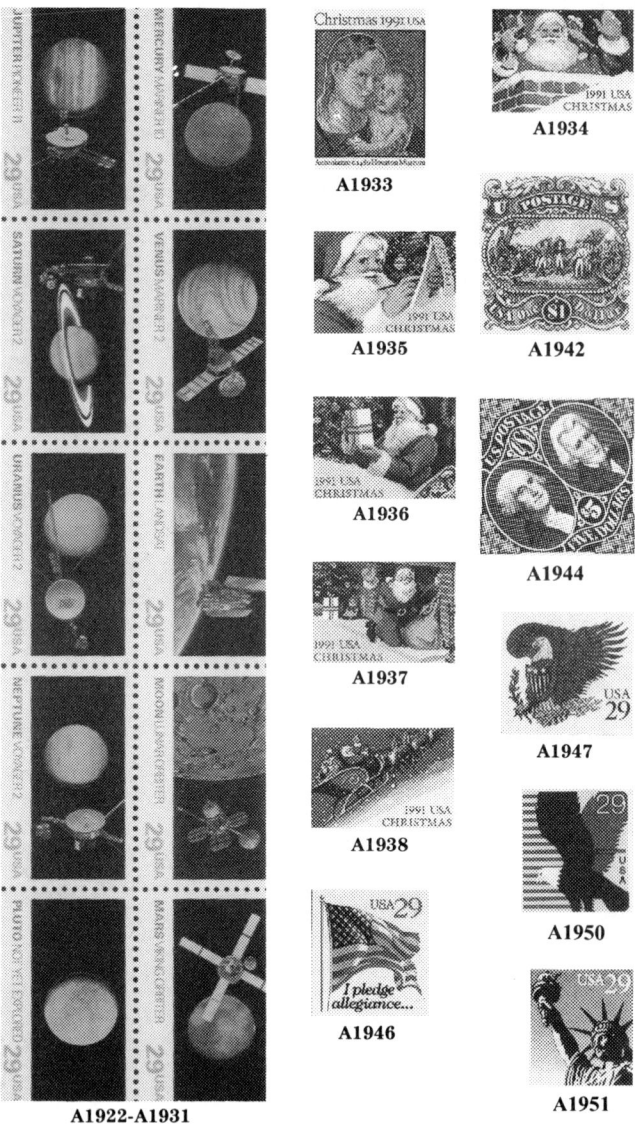

Scott No.	Illus. No.		Description	Unused Value	Used Value	//////
2583	A1936	(29c)	multicolored	50	15	
a.			Booklet pane of 4	2.00	—	
2584	A1937	(29c)	multicolored	50	15	
a.			Booklet pane of 4	2.00	—	
2585	A1938	(29c)	multicolored	50	15	
a.			Booklet pane of 4	2.00	—	

1994, Perf. 11.5

2590	A1942	$1	blue	2.00	50	
2592	A1944	$5	green	10.00	—	

1992-93, Booklet stamps
Perf. 10 on 2 or 3 sides

2594	A1946	29c	black denomination	50	15	
a.			Booklet pane of 10	5.00	—	

Perf. 11x10 on 2 or 3 sides

2594B	A1946	29c	red denomination	50	15	
c.			Booklet pane of 10	5.00	—	

1992-94, Die cut, Self-adhesive

2595	A1947	29c	brown & multi	50	25	
a.			Pane of 17 + label	8.50		
b.			Pair, no die cutting	—		
2596	A1947	29c	green & multi	50	25	
a.			Pane of 17 + label	8.50		
2597	A1947	29c	red & multi	50	25	
a.			Pane of 17 + label	8.50		
2598	A1950	29c	red, cream & blue	50	15	
a.			Pane of 18	9.00		
2599	A1951	29c	multicolored	50	15	
a.			Pane of 18	9.00		

1991-93, Coil stamps, Perf. 10 Vertically

2604	A1956	(10c)	multicolored	20	15	
a.			Imperf. pair	30.00		
2605	A1957	(10c)	orange yellow & multi	20	20	
2606	A1957	(10c)	gold & multi	20	20	
2607	A1959	23c	multi (Bureau precancel in blue)	46	46	
2608	A1960	23c	multi (Bureau precanceled)	40	40	
2608A	A1960	23c	multi (Bureau precanceled)	40	40	
2608B	A1960	23c	First Class 8 ½ mm long	40	40	
2609	A1961	29c	blue & red	50	15	
a.			Imperf. pair	20.00		
b.			Pair, imperf. between	100.00		

A1956

A1957

A1959

A1960

A1961

A1968

A1969

A1970

A1971

A1963-A1967

Scott No.	Illus. No.		Description	Unused Value	Used Value	/ / / / / /
1992						
2611	A1963	29c	multicolored	50	15	
2612	A1964	29c	multicolored	50	15	
2613	A1965	29c	multicolored	50	15	
2614	A1966	29c	multicolored	50	15	
2615	A1967	29c	multicolored	50	15	
a.			Strip of 5, #2611-2615	2.50	—	
2616	A1968	29c	multicolored	50	15	
2617	A1969	29c	multicolored	50	15	
2618	A1970	29c	multicolored	50	15	
a.			Horiz. pair, imperf. vert. .	—		
2619	A1971	29c	multicolored	50	15	
2620	A1972	29c	multicolored	50	15	
2621	A1973	29c	multicolored	50	15	
2622	A1974	29c	multicolored	50	15	
2623	A1975	29c	multicolored	50	15	
a.			Block of 4, #2620-2623 ..	2.00	1.00	
Perf. 10 ½						
2624	A1976		Sheet of 3	1.60	—	
a.	A71	1c	deep blue	15	15	
b.	A74	4c	ultramarine	15	15	
c.	A82	$1	salmon	1.50	1.00	
2625	A1977		Sheet of 3	6.25	—	
a.	A72	2c	brown violet	15	15	
b.	A73	3c	green	15	15	
c.	A85	$4	crimson lake	6.00	4.00	
2626	A1978		Sheet of 3	1.25	—	
a.	A75	5c	chocolate	15	15	
b.	A80	30c	orange brown	45	30	
c.	A81	50c	slate blue	75	50	
2627	A1979		Sheet of 3	4.75	—	
a.	A76	6c	purple	15	15	
b.	A77	8c	magenta	15	15	
c.	A84	$3	yellow green	4.50	3.00	
2628	A1980		Sheet of 3	3.50	—	
a.	A78	10c	black brown	15	15	
b.	A79	15c	dark green	22	15	
c.	A83	$2	brown red	3.00	2.00	
2629	A1981	$5	Sheet of 1, type A86	7.75	—	
2630	A1982	29c	green, red & black	50	15	
2631	A1983	29c	multicolored	50	15	
2632	A1984	29c	multicolored	50	15	
2633	A1985	29c	multicolored	50	15	
2634	A1986	29c	multicolored	50	15	
a.			Block of 4, #2631-2634 ..	2.00	1.00	
2635	A1987	29c	multicolored	50	15	
a.			Black (engr.) omitted	—		

A1972-A1975

A1976-A1981

A1982

A1983-A1986

A1987

A1988

A1989-A1993

A1994-A1998

A2050   **A2051**

A2052-A2055

Scott No.	Illus. No.		Description	Unused Value	Used Value	/ / / / / /
2636	A1988	29c	multicolored	50	15	
2637	A1989	29c	multicolored	50	15	
2638	A1990	29c	multicolored	50	15	
2639	A1991	29c	multicolored	50	15	
2640	A1992	29c	multicolored	50	15	
2641	A1993	29c	multicolored	50	15	
a.			Strip of 5, #2637-2641	2.50	—	
2642	A1994	29c	multicolored	50	15	
2643	A1995	29c	multicolored	50	15	
2644	A1996	29c	multicolored	50	15	
2645	A1997	29c	multicolored	50	15	
2646	A1998	29c	multicolored	50	15	
a.			Bklt. pane of 5, #2642-2646	2.50	—	
2647	A1999	29c	Indian paintbrush	50	15	
2648	A2000	29c	Fragrant water lily	50	15	
2649	A2001	29c	Meadow beauty	50	15	
2650	A2002	29c	Jack-in-the-pulpit	50	15	
2651	A2003	29c	California poppy	50	15	
2652	A2004	29c	Large-flowered trillium	50	15	
2653	A2005	29c	Tickseed	50	15	
2654	A2006	29c	Shooting star	50	15	
2655	A2007	29c	Stream violet	50	15	
2656	A2008	29c	Bluets	50	15	
2657	A2009	29c	Herb Robert	50	15	
2658	A2010	29c	Marsh marigold	50	15	
2659	A2011	29c	Sweet white violet	50	15	
2660	A2012	29c	Claret cup cactus	50	15	
2661	A2013	29c	White mountain avens	50	15	
2662	A2014	29c	Sessile bellwort	50	15	
2663	A2015	29c	Blue flag	50	15	
2664	A2016	29c	Harlequin lupine	50	15	
2665	A2017	29c	Twinflower	50	15	
2666	A2018	29c	Common sunflower	50	15	
2667	A2019	29c	Sego lily	50	15	
2668	A2020	29c	Virginia bluebells	50	15	
2669	A2021	29c	Ohia lehua	50	15	
2670	A2022	29c	Rosebud orchid	50	15	
2671	A2023	29c	Showy evening primrose	50	15	
2672	A2024	29c	Fringed gentian	50	15	
2673	A2025	29c	Yellow ladys slipper	50	15	
2674	A2026	29c	Passionflower	50	15	
2675	A2027	29c	Bunchberry	50	15	
2676	A2028	29c	Pasqueflower	50	15	
2677	A2029	29c	Round-lobed hepatica	50	15	
2678	A2030	29c	Wild columbine	50	15	
2679	A2031	29c	Fireweed	50	15	
2680	A2032	29c	Indian pond lily	50	15	

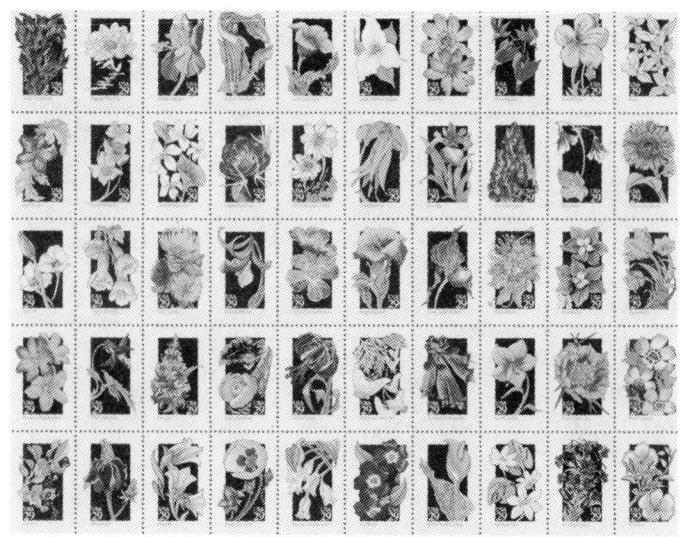

A1999-A2048

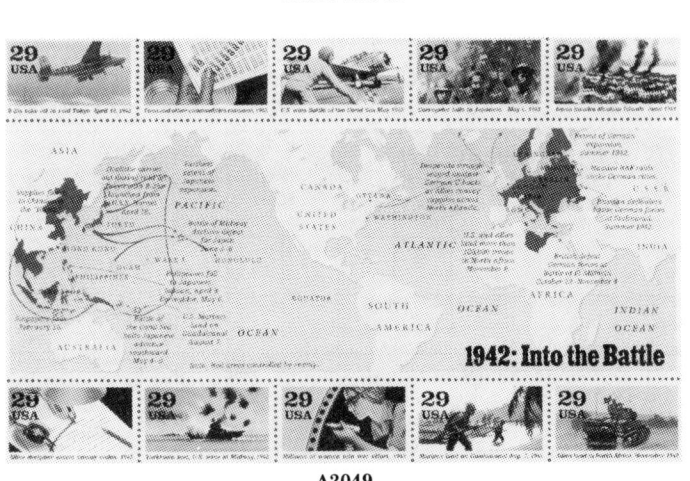

A2049

Scott No.	Illus. No.		Description	Unused Value	Used Value	/ / / / / /
2681	A2033	29c	Turks cap lily	50	15	
2682	A2034	29c	Dutchmans breeches	50	15	
2683	A2035	29c	Trumpet honeysuckle	50	15	
2684	A2036	29c	Jacobs ladder	50	15	
2685	A2037	29c	Plains prickly pear	50	15	
2686	A2038	29c	Moss campion	50	15	
2687	A2039	29c	Bearberry	50	15	
2688	A2040	29c	Mexican hat	50	15	
2689	A2041	29c	Harebell	50	15	
2690	A2042	29c	Desert five spot	50	15	
2691	A2043	29c	Smooth Solomons seal	50	15	
2692	A2044	29c	Red maids	50	15	
2693	A2045	29c	Yellow skunk cabbage	50	15	
2694	A2046	29c	Rue anemone	50	15	
2695	A2047	29c	Standing cypress	50	15	
2696	A2048	29c	Wild flax	50	15	
a.			Pane of 50, #2647-2696	25.00	—	
2697	A2049		Block of 10	5.25	2.90	
a.-j.		29c	any single	52	29	
k.			Red (litho.) omitted	—		
2698	A2050	29c	multicolored	50	15	
2699	A2051	29c	multicolored	50	15	
2700	A2052	29c	multicolored	50	15	
2701	A2053	29c	multicolored	50	15	
2702	A2054	29c	multicolored	50	15	
2703	A2055	29c	multicolored	50	15	
a.			Block or strip of 4, #2700-2703	2.00	1.10	
b.			As "a," silver (litho.) omitted	—		
2704	A2056	29c	multicolored	50	15	
2705	A2057	29c	multicolored	50	15	
2706	A2058	29c	multicolored	50	15	
2707	A2059	29c	multicolored	50	15	
2708	A2060	29c	multicolored	50	15	
2709	A2061	29c	multicolored	50	15	
a.			Booklet pane of 5, #2705-2709	2.50	—	
b.			As "a," imperforate	—		
2710	A2062	29c	multicolored	50	15	
a.			Booklet pane of 10	5.00	—	
2711	A2063	29c	multicolored	50	15	
2712	A2064	29c	multicolored	50	15	
2713	A2065	29c	multicolored	50	15	
2714	A2066	29c	multicolored	50	15	
a.			Block of 4, #2711-2714	2.00	1.10	
2715	A2063	29c	multicolored	50	15	
2716	A2064	29c	multicolored	50	15	
2717	A2065	29c	multicolored	50	15	

A2056

A2062

A2067

A2068

A2057-A2061

A2063-A2066

Scott No.	Illus. No.		Description	Unused Value	Used Value	//////
2718	A2066	29c	multicolored....................	50	15	☐☐☐☐☐
a.			Booklet pane of 4, #2715-2718................	2.00	—	☐☐☐☐☐
b.			As "a," imperf. horiz.......	—		

Die cut, Self-adhesive

2719	A2064	29c	multicolored....................	58	15	☐☐☐☐☐
a.			Booklet pane of 18.........	10.50	—	☐☐☐☐☐
2720	A2067	29c	multicolored....................	50	15	☐☐☐☐☐

1993

2721	A2068	29c	multicolored ("Elvis" only)	50	15	☐☐☐☐☐
2722	A2068	29c	Oklahoma.......................	50	15	☐☐☐☐☐

Perf. 10

2723	A2068	29c	Hank Williams (27 ½mm inscription)...	50	15	☐☐☐☐☐
2724	A2068	29c	Elvis Presley....................	50	15	☐☐☐☐☐
2725	A2068	29c	Bill Haley........................	50	15	☐☐☐☐☐
2726	A2068	29c	Clyde McPhatter.............	50	15	☐☐☐☐☐
2727	A2068	29c	Ritchie Valens................	50	15	☐☐☐☐☐
2728	A2068	29c	Otis Redding..................	50	15	☐☐☐☐☐
2729	A2068	29c	Buddy Holly...................	50	15	☐☐☐☐☐
2730	A2068	29c	Dinah Washington	50	15	☐☐☐☐☐
a.			Vert. strip of 7, #2724-2730	3.50	—	☐☐☐☐☐

Booklet stamps, Perf. 11 Horiz.

2731	A2068	29c	Presley............................	50	15	☐☐☐☐☐
2732	A2068	29c	Haley...............................	50	15	☐☐☐☐☐
2733	A2068	29c	McPhatter.......................	50	15	☐☐☐☐☐
2734	A2068	29c	Valens.............................	50	15	☐☐☐☐☐
2735	A2068	29c	Redding..........................	50	15	☐☐☐☐☐
2736	A2068	29c	Holly...............................	50	15	☐☐☐☐☐
2737	A2068	29c	Washington	50	15	☐☐☐☐☐
a.			Booklet pane, 2 #2731, 1 each #2732-2737.......	4.00	—	☐☐☐☐☐
b.			Booklet pane, #2731, 2735-2737 + tab...........	2.00	—	☐☐☐☐☐
2741	A2086	29c	multicolored....................	50	15	☐☐☐☐☐
2742	A2087	29c	multicolored....................	50	15	☐☐☐☐☐
2743	A2088	29c	multicolored....................	50	15	☐☐☐☐☐
2744	A2089	29c	multicolored....................	50	15	☐☐☐☐☐
2745	A2090	29c	multicolored....................	50	15	☐☐☐☐☐
a.			Booklet pane of 5, #2741-2745	2.50	—	☐☐☐☐☐
2746	A2091	29c	multicolored....................	50	15	☐☐☐☐☐
2747	A2092	29c	multicolored....................	50	15	☐☐☐☐☐
2748	A2093	29c	multicolored....................	50	15	☐☐☐☐☐

A2086-A2090

A2091

A2092

A2093

A2094

A2095-A2098

A2099

A2100

A2101-A2104 **A2111**

A2105-A2109

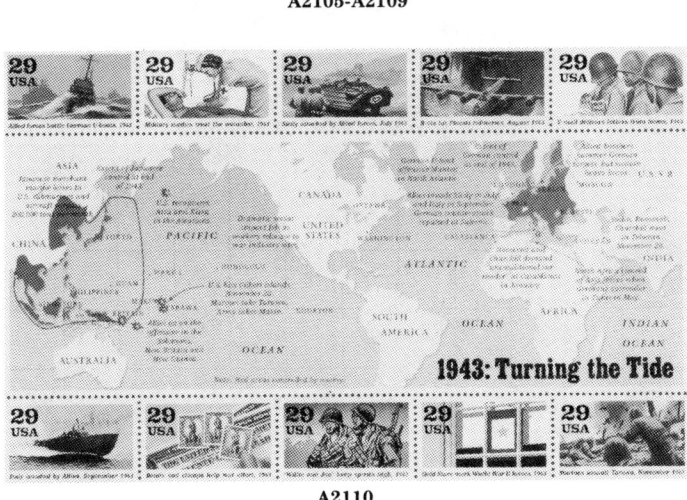

A2110

A2118-A2121

A2122-A2123

A2124-A2127

Scott No.	Illus. No.		Description	Unused Value	Used Value
2749	A2094	29c	blue	50	15
2750	A2095	29c	multicolored	50	15
2751	A2096	29c	multicolored	50	15
2752	A2097	29c	multicolored	50	15
2753	A2098	29c	multicolored	50	15
a.			Block of 4, #2750-2753	2.00	1.10
2754	A2099	29c	multicolored	50	15
2755	A2100	29c	greenish gray	50	15
2756	A2101	29c	multicolored	50	15
2757	A2102	29c	multicolored	50	15
2758	A2103	29c	multicolored	50	15
2759	A2104	29c	multicolored	50	15
a.			Block of 4, #2756-2759	2.00	1.10
b.			As "a," black (engr.) omitted	—	
2760	A2105	29c	multicolored	50	15
2761	A2106	29c	multicolored	50	15
2762	A2107	29c	multicolored	50	15
2763	A2108	29c	multicolored	50	15
2764	A2109	29c	multicolored	50	15
a.			Booklet pane of 5, #2760-2764	2.50	—
b.			As "a," black (engr.) omitted	—	
c.			As "a," imperf.	—	
2765	A2110		Block of 10	5.80	3.00
a.-j.		29c	any single	58	30
2766	A2111	29c	multicolored	50	15
2767	A2068	29c	Show Boat	50	15
2768	A2068	29c	Porgy & Bess	50	15
2769	A2068	29c	Oklahoma	50	15
2770	A2068	29c	My Fair Lady	50	15
a.			Booklet pane of 4, #2767-2770	2.00	—
2771	A2068	29c	Hank Williams (27mm inscription)	50	15
2772	A2068	29c	Patsy Cline	50	15
2773	A2068	29c	Carter Family	50	15
2774	A2068	29c	Bob Wills	50	15
a.			Block or horiz. strip of 4, #2771-2774	2.00	—

Booklet stamps, Perf. 11 Horiz.

Scott No.	Illus. No.		Description	Unused Value	Used Value
2775	A2068	29c	Hank Williams (22mm inscription)	50	15
2776	A2068	29c	Patsy Cline	50	15
2777	A2068	29c	Carter Family	50	15
2778	A2068	29c	Bob Wills	50	15
a.			Booklet pane of 4, #2775-2778	2.00	—

A2128 **A2129-2132** **A2133**

A2134 **A2135**

A2136-A2140

A2141 **A2142** **A2143**

Scott No.	Illus. No.		Description	Unused Value	Used Value	/ / / / / /
2779	A2118	29c	multicolored	50	15	
2780	A2119	29c	multicolored	50	15	
2781	A2120	29c	multicolored	50	15	
2782	A2121	29c	multicolored	50	15	
a.			Block of 4, #2779-2782..	2.00	1.10	
2783	A2122	29c	multicolored	50	15	
2784	A2123	29c	multicolored	50	15	
a.			Pair, #2783-2784............	1.00	20	
2785	A2124	29c	multicolored	50	15	
2786	A2125	29c	multicolored	50	15	
2787	A2126	29c	multicolored	50	15	
2788	A2127	29c	multicolored	50	15	
a.			Block or horiz. strip of 4, #2785-2788	2.00	1.10	
2789	A2128	29c	multicolored	50	15	

Booklet stamp, Perf. 11 1/2x11 on 2 or 3 sides

2790	A2128	29c	multicolored	50	15	

Perf. 11 1/2

2791	A2129	29c	multicolored	50	15	
2792	A2130	29c	multicolored	50	15	
2793	A2131	29c	multicolored	50	15	
2794	A2132	29c	multicolored	50	15	
a.			Block or strip of 4, #2791-2794	2.00	1.10	

Booklet stamps, Perf. 11x10 on 2 or 3 sides

2795	A2132	29c	multicolored	50	15	
2796	A2131	29c	multicolored	50	15	
2797	A2130	29c	multicolored	50	15	
2798	A2129	29c	multicolored	50	15	
a.			Booklet pane, 3 each #2795-2796, 2 each #2797-2798	5.00	—	
b.			Booklet pane, 3 each #2797-2798, 2 each #2795-2796	5.00	—	

Die cut, Self-adhesive, 19 1/2x26 1/2mm

2799	A2131	29c	multicolored	50	15	
2800	A2132	29c	multicolored	50	15	
2801	A2129	29c	multicolored	50	15	
2802	A2130	29c	multicolored	50	15	
a.			Pane, 3 each #2799-2802	6.00		

Die cut, Self-adhesive, 17x20mm

2803	A2131	29c	multicolored	50	15	
a.			Pane of 18......................	9.00		

A2144 **A2145** **A2146** **A2147**

A2148-A2157

A2158-A2162

Scott No.	Illus. No.		Description	Unused Value	Used Value	/ / / / / /

Perf. 11

| 2804 | A2133 | 29c | multicolored | 50 | 15 | |

Perf. 11.2

2805	A2134	29c	multicolored	50	15	
2806	A2135	29c	black & red	50	15	
a.			Perf. 11 vert on 1 or 2 sides	50	15	
a.			As "a," booklet pane of 5	2.50	—	

1994

2807	A2136	29c	multicolored	50	15	
2808	A2137	29c	multicolored	50	15	
2809	A2138	29c	multicolored	50	15	
2810	A2139	29c	multicolored	50	15	
2811	A2140	29c	multicolored	50	15	
a.			Strip of 5, #2807-2811	2.50	—	
2812	A2141	29c	brown	50	15	

Die cut, Self-adhesive

| 2813 | A2142 | 29c | multicolored | 50 | 15 | |
| a. | | | Pane of 18 | 9.00 | | |

Booklet stamp, Perf. 10.9x11.1

2814	A2143	29c	multicolored	50	15	
a.			Booklet pane of 10	5.00	—	
b.			As "a," imperf.	—	—	

Perf. 11.1

| 2814C | A2143 | 29c | multicolored | 50 | 15 | |

Perf. 11.2

2815	A2144	52c	multicolored	1.00	20	
2816	A2145	29c	red brown & brown	50	15	
2817	A2146	29c	multicolored	50	15	

Perf. 11.5x11.2

| 2818 | A2147 | 29c | multicolored | 50 | 15 | |

Perf. 11.2

2819	A2148	29c	red, black & bright violet	50	15	
2820	A2149	29c	red, black & bright violet	50	15	
2821	A2150	29c	red, black & bright violet	50	15	
2822	A2151	29c	red, black & bright violet	50	15	
2823	A2152	29c	red, black & bright violet	50	15	
2824	A2153	29c	red, black & bright violet	50	15	
2825	A2154	29c	red, black & bright violet	50	15	
2826	A2155	29c	red, black & bright violet	50	15	
2827	A2156	29c	red, black & bright violet	50	15	

A2163

A2164

A2165

A2167

A2168

A2169

A2170

A2171-A2175

A2176

Scott No.	Illus. No.	Description	Unused Value	Used Value	//////
2828	A2157	29c red, black & bright violet	50	15	
a.		Block of 10, #2819-2828	2.50	—	
b.		As "a," black (engr.) omitted	—		
c.		As "a," red, black & bright violet (engr.) omitted ...	—		

Booklet stamps, Perf. 10.9 Vert.

2829	A2158	29c multicolored	50	15	
2830	A2159	29c multicolored	50	15	
2831	A2160	29c multicolored	50	15	
2832	A2161	29c multicolored	50	15	
2833	A2162	29c multicolored	50	15	
a.		Booklet pane of 5, #2829-2833	2.50	—	
b.		As "a," imperf.	—		
c.		As "a," black (engr.) omitted	—		

Perf. 11.1

2834	A2163	29c multicolored	50	15	
2835	A2163	40c multicolored	80	18	
2836	A2164	50c multicolored	1.00	20	
2837	A2165	Sheet of 3, #a.-c. (like Nos. 2834-2836)..	2.50	—	

Perf. 10.9

2838	A2166	Block of 10	5.80	3.00	
a.-j.		29c any single	58	30	

Perf. 10.9x11.1

2839	A2167	29c multicolored	50	15	
2840	A2168	Sheet of 4	4.00	—	
a.		50c Freedom from Want	1.00	65	
b.		50c Freedom from Fear	1.00	65	
c.		50c Freedom of Speech	1.00	65	
d.		50c Freedom of Worship	1.00	65	

Perf. 11.2x11.1

2841		Sheet of 12	7.00	—	
a.	A2169	29c Single stamp	60	50	

Perf. 10.7x11.1

2842	A2170	$9.95 multicolored	17.50	7.50	

Booklet stamps, Perf. 11 Horiz.

2843	A2171	29c multicolored	50	15	
2844	A2172	29c multicolored	50	15	
2845	A2173	29c multicolored	50	15	
2846	A2174	29c multicolored	50	15	
2847	A2175	29c multicolored	50	15	
a.		Booklet pane of 5, #2843-2847	2.50	—	

Perf. 11.1x11

2848	A2176	29c blue	50	15	

SCOTT
UNITED STATES
NATIONAL ALBUM

Pages printed on one side.

Includes Scott numbers.

All major variety stamps are either illustrated or described.

Chemically neutral paper protects stamps.

"The" album demanded by serious collectors of United States material. The Scott National postage stamp album provides spaces for commemoratives, definitives, air post, special delivery, registration, certified mail, postage due, parcel post, special handling, officials, newspapers, offices abroad, hunting permits, confederates and much more.

100NTL1	Part 1, 1845-1934	$29.95
100NTL2	Part 2, 1935-1976	$29.95
100NTL3	Part 3, 1977-1993	$29.95

All albums are sold as pages-only sections.

Available from your local dealer or direct from:
Scott Publishing Co.
P.O. Box 828, Sidney, OH 45365

UNITED STATES
PLATE BLOCK
CATALOG

From America's Largest and Most Respected Company Offering Fine – Very Fine, Never Hinged Plate Blocks. Prices on Plate Blocks from the 1920'S to the Present Time.

PLUS...

Our Quarterly Newsletter That Explains Why Plate Blocks Are The Smartest Buy For U.S. Stamp Collectors AND Identifies The Specific Plate Blocks Most Likely To Increase In Value

STARTER ORDER only $9.95

This sampler contains Mint Fine – Very Fine Never Hinged Plate Blocks – some over Fifty Years Old. You'll find Commemoratives, Regular Issues, Air Mails, and Others. IT'S A GREAT VALUE AND A GREAT WAY TO GET STARTED.

ACT TODAY! Get Your FREE Catalog and Newsletter or the STARTER ORDER!
IT'S SO EASY, JUST CALL TOLL FREE
1-800-829-6777 or write to:

 **PLATE BLOCK STAMP COMPANY**

P.O. Box 6417-C • Leawood, KS 66206

AP1 AP2 AP3 AP4

AP5 AP6

AP7

AP8

AP9 AP10

AP11 AP12

AP13

AP14 AP15

Scott No.	Illus. No.	Description		Unused Value	Used Value	/ / / / / /

AIR POST STAMPS

1918
Scott No.	Illus. No.		Description	Unused Value	Used Value	
C1	AP1	6c	orange	55.00	25.00	
C2	AP1	16c	green	80.00	27.50	
C3	AP1	24c	carmine rose & blue	75.00	32.50	
a.			Center inverted	*135,000.*		

1923
C4	AP2	8c	dark green	20.00	12.00	
C5	AP3	16c	dark blue	75.00	27.50	
C6	AP4	24c	carmine	75.00	22.50	

1926-28, Perf. 11
C7	AP5	10c	dark blue	2.25	25	
C8	AP5	15c	olive brown	2.75	1.90	
C9	AP5	20c	yellow green (27)	7.00	1.65	
C10	AP6	10c	dark blue	6.00	1.65	
a.			Booklet pane of 3	75.00	*50.00*	
C11	AP7	5c	carmine & blue	4.50	40	
a.			Vertical pair, imperf. btwn.	*5,500.*		
C12	AP8	5c	violet	8.00	25	
a.			Horiz. pair, imperf. btwn.	*4,500.*		

1930
C13	AP9	65c	green	250.00	150.00	
C14	AP10	$1.30	brown	500.00	350.00	
C15	AP11	$2.60	blue	850.00	500.00	

1931-32, Perf. 10 1/2 x11
C16	AP8	5c	violet	4.75	35	
C17	AP8	8c	olive bister	1.90	20	

1933
C18	AP12	50c	green	75.00	65.00	

1934
C19	AP8	6c	dull orange	2.25	15	

1935
C20	AP13	25c	blue	1.10	75	

1937
C21	AP14	20c	green	8.00	1.25	
C22	AP14	50c	carmine	7.50	4.00	

1938
C23	AP15	6c	dark blue & carmine	40	15	
a.			Vert. pair, imperf. horiz.	300.00		
b.			Horiz. pair, imperf. vert.	*10,000.*		

AP16

AP17

AP19

AP18

AP20

AP21

AP22

AP24

AP23

AP25

AP26 **AP27**
AP28

AP29

AP30

Scott No.	Illus. No.		Description	Unused Value	Used Value	/ / / / / /
1939						
C24	AP16	30c	dull blue	8.50	1.00	☐☐☐☐☐
1941-44						
C25	AP17	6c	carmine	15	15	☐☐☐☐☐
a.			Booklet pane of 3	3.50	1.00	☐☐☐☐☐
b.			Horiz. pair, imperf. between	*1,500.*		☐☐☐☐☐
C26	AP17	8c	olive green (44)	16	15	☐☐☐☐☐
C27	AP17	10c	violet	1.10	20	☐☐☐☐☐
C28	AP17	15c	brown carmine	2.25	35	☐☐☐☐☐
C29	AP17	20c	bright green	1.75	30	☐☐☐☐☐
C30	AP17	30c	blue	2.00	30	☐☐☐☐☐
C31	AP17	50c	orange	9.00	3.75	☐☐☐☐☐
1946						
C32	AP18	5c	carmine	15	15	☐☐☐☐☐
1947, Perf. 10 1/2x11						
C33	AP19	5c	carmine	15	15	☐☐☐☐☐
C34	AP20	10c	black	25	15	☐☐☐☐☐
C35	AP21	15c	bright blue green	35	15	☐☐☐☐☐
a.			Horiz. pair, imperf. between	*1,750.*		☐☐☐☐☐
C36	AP22	25c	blue	85	15	☐☐☐☐☐
1948, Coil stamp, Perf. 10 horizontally						
C37	AP19	5c	carmine	80	75	☐☐☐☐☐
1948						
C38	AP23	5c	bright carmine	15	15	☐☐☐☐☐
1949, Perf. 10 1/2x11						
C39	AP19	6c	carmine	15	15	☐☐☐☐☐
a.			Booklet pane of 6	9.50	*4.00*	☐☐☐☐☐
1949						
C40	AP24	6c	carmine	15	15	☐☐☐☐☐
Coil stamp, Perf. 10 horizontally						
C41	AP19	6c	carmine	2.75	15	☐☐☐☐☐
1949						
C42	AP25	10c	violet	20	18	☐☐☐☐☐
C43	AP26	15c	ultramarine	30	25	☐☐☐☐☐
C44	AP27	25c	rose carmine	50	40	☐☐☐☐☐
C45	AP28	6c	magenta	15	15	☐☐☐☐☐
1952-58						
C46	AP29	80c	bright red violet	5.50	1.00	☐☐☐☐☐
C47	AP30	6c	carmine	15	15	☐☐☐☐☐

AP31

AP32

AP33

AP34

AP35

AP36

AP38

AP37

AP39

AP40

AP42

AP41-Redrawn

AP43

AP44

AP45

AP47

AP46

Scott No.	Illus. No.	Description	Unused Value	Used Value	//////
C48	AP31	4c bright blue	15	15	
C49	AP32	6c blue	15	15	
C50	AP31	5c rose red	15	15	

Perf. 10 1/2x11

C51	AP33	7c blue	15	15	
a.		Booklet pane of 6	11.00	6.00	

Coil stamp, Perf. 10 horizontally

C52	AP33	7c blue	2.25	15	

1959

C53	AP34	7c dark blue	15	15	
C54	AP35	7c dark blue & red	15	15	
C55	AP36	7c rose red	15	15	
C56	AP37	10c violet blue & bright red	24	24	

1959-66

C57	AP38	10c black & green	1.25	70	
C58	AP39	15c black & orange	35	15	
C59	AP40	25c black & maroon	45	15	
a.		Tagged	50	30	

Perf. 10 1/2x11

C60	AP33	7c carmine	15	15	
a.		Booklet pane of 6	15.00	7.00	

Coil stamp, Perf. 10 horizontally

C61	AP33	7c carmine	4.00	25	

1961-67

C62	AP38	13c black & red	40	15	
a.		Tagged	75	50	
C63	AP41	15c black & orange	30	15	
a.		Tagged	32	20	
b.		As "a," horiz.pair, imperf. vert.	15,000.		

Perf. 10 1/2x11

C64	AP42	8c carmine	15	15	
a.		Tagged	20	15	
b.		Booklet pane 5 + label	6.75	2.50	
c.		As "b," tagged	1.65	50	

Coil stamp, Perf. 10 horizontally

C65	AP42	8c carmine	40	15	
a.		Tagged	35	15	

1963-67

C66	AP43	15c carmine, deep claret & blue	60	55	

AP50

AP48

AP51

AP49

AP52

AP53

AP54

AP55

AP56

AP57

AP58

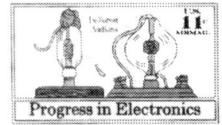
AP59

AP60

AP61

AP62

AP63

AP70

Scott No.	Illus. No.		Description	Unused Value	Used Value	//////
C67	AP44	6c	red...............................	15	15	
a.			Tagged.........................	2.75	1.00	
C68	AP45	8c	carmine & maroon	20	15	
C69	AP46	8c	blue, red & bister............	40	15	
C70	AP47	8c	brown.............................	24	15	
C71	AP48	20c	multicolored	80	15	

1968, Perf. 11x10 1/2

C72	AP49	10c	carmine...........................	18	15	
b.			Booklet pane of 8	2.00	75	
c.			Booklet pane of 5 + label	3.75	75	

Coil stamp, Perf. 10 vertically

C73	AP49	10c	carmine...........................	30	15	
a.			Imperf., pair....................	600.00		

1968

C74	AP50	10c	blue, black & red.............	25	15	
a.			Red (tail stripe) omitted..		—	
C75	AP51	20c	red, blue & black.............	35	15	

1969

C76	AP52	10c	multicolored	20	15	
a.			Rose red (litho.) omitted.	450.00	—	

1971-73

C77	AP53	9c	red...............................	18	15	
C78	AP54	11c	carmine...........................	20	15	
a.			Booklet pane of 4 + 2 labels	1.10	75	
b.			Untagged (Bureau precanceled)		30	
C79	AF55	13c	carmine...........................	22	15	
a.			Booklet pane of 5 + label	1.25	75	
b.			Untagged (Bureau precanceled)		28	
C80	AP56	17c	bluish black, red & dark green	35	15	
C81	AP51	21c	red, blue & black.............	35	15	

Coil stamps, Perf. 10 vertically

C82	AP54	11c	carmine...........................	25	15	
a.			Imperf., pair....................	250.00		
C83	AP55	13c	carmine...........................	26	15	
a.			Imperf., pair....................	80.00		

1972-74

C84	AP57	11c	orange & multi	20	15	
a.			Blue & green (litho.) omitted	1,250.		
C85	AP58	11c	multicolored	22	15	
C86	AP59	11c	rose lilac & multi	22	15	
a.			Vermilion & olive (litho.) omitted............................	1,500.		

AP64

AP66

AP68

AP65

AP67

AP69

AP72

AP71

AP73

AP81

AP86

AP87

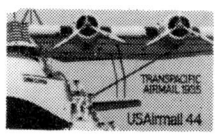
AP88

AP89

AP90

Scott No.	Illus. No.		Description	Unused Value	Used Value	/ / / / / /
C87	AP60	18c	carmine, black & ultra	38	25	
C88	AP61	26c	ultra, black & carmine	48	15	
1976						
C89	AP62	25c	ultra, red & black	45	15	
C90	AP63	31c	ultra, red & black	55	15	
1978						
C91	AP64	31c	ultra & multi....................	60	30	
C92	AP65	31c	ultra & multi....................	60	30	
a.			Vert. pair, #C91-C92	1.20	85	
b.			As "a," ultramarine & black (engr.) omitted...............	900.00		
c.			As "a," black (engr.) omitted	—		
d.			As "a," black, yellow, magenta, blue & brown (litho.) omitted	2,250.		
1979						
C93	AP66	21c	ultra & multi....................	70	32	
C94	AP67	21c	ultra & multi....................	70	32	
a.			Vert. pair, #C93-C94	1.40	95	
b.			As "a," ultramarine & black (engr.) omitted................	4,000.		
C95	AP68	25c	ultra & multi....................	1.10	35	
C96	AP69	25c	ultra & multi....................	1.10	35	
a.			Vert. pair, #C95-C96	2.25	95	
C97	AP70	31c	multicolored	65	30	
1980						
C98	AP71	40c	multicolored	70	15	
a.			Perf. 10 1/2x11...............	3.00	—	
b.			Imperf., pair....................	3,000.		
c.			Horiz. pair, imperf. vert. .	—		
C99	AP72	28c	multicolored	55	15	
C100	AP73	35c	multicolored	60	15	
1983						
C101	AP81	28c	Gymnast	60	28	
C102	AP81	28c	Hurdler	60	28	
C103	AP81	28c	Basketball.......................	60	28	
C104	AP81	28c	Soccer.............................	60	28	
a.			Block of 4, #C101-C104.	2.50	1.75	
b.			As "a," imperf. vert.........	—		
C105	AP81	40c	Shot put	90	40	
a.			Perf. 11x10 1/2...............	1.00	45	
C106	AP81	40c	Gymnast	90	40	
a.			Perf. 11x10 1/2...............	1.00	45	

AP91

AP92

AP93

AP94

AP95-98

AP99

AP100

AP101

AP102

AP102

AP103

Scott No.	Illus. No.		Description	Unused Value	Used Value	/ / / / / /
C107	AP81	40c	Swimmer	90	40	
a.			Perf. 11x10 1/2	1.00	45	
C108	AP81	40c	Weightlifting	90	40	
a.			Block of 4, #C105-C108.	3.60	2.00	
b.			As "a," imperf.	*1,350.*		
c.			Perf. 11x10 1/2	1.00	45	
d.			As "a," perf. 11x10 1/2	4.25	—	
C109	AP81	35c	Women's fencing	90	35	
C110	AP81	35c	Cycling	90	35	
C111	AP81	35c	Women's volleyball	90	35	
C112	AP81	35c	Pole vaulting	90	35	
a.			Block of 4, #C109-C112.	3.60	1.85	

1985

Scott No.	Illus. No.		Description	Unused Value	Used Value	/ / / / / /
C113	AP86	33c	multicolored	60	20	
a.			Imperf., pair	*850.00*		
C114	AP87	39c	multicolored	70	20	
a.			Imperf., pair	*1,250.*		
C115	AP88	44c	multicolored	80	20	
a.			Imperf., pair	*800.00*		
C116	AP89	44c	multicolored	80	20	
a.			Imperf., pair	—		

1988

Scott No.	Illus. No.		Description	Unused Value	Used Value	/ / / / / /
C117	AP90	44c	multicolored	1.00	20	
C118	AP91	45c	multicolored	80	20	
C119	AP92	36c	multicolored	65	20	

1989

Scott No.	Illus. No.		Description	Unused Value	Used Value	/ / / / / /
C120	AP93	45c	multicolored	80	22	
C121	AP94	45c	multicolored	80	22	
C122	AP95	45c	multicolored	90	30	
C123	AP96	45c	multicolored	90	30	
C124	AP97	45c	multicolored	90	30	
C125	AP98	45c	multicolored	90	30	
a.			Block of 4, #C122-C125.	3.60	2.25	
b.			As "a," light blue (engr.) omitted	*1,000.*		
C126			Sheet of 4	4.25	3.25	
a.	AP95	45c	multicolored	90	50	
b.	AP96	45c	multicolored	90	50	
c.	AP97	45c	multicolored	90	50	
d.	AP98	45c	multicolored	90	50	

1990

Scott No.	Illus. No.		Description	Unused Value	Used Value	/ / / / / /
C127	AP99	45c	multicolored	80	20	

Scott No.	Illus. No.	Description	Unused Value	Used Value	/ / / / / /
1991, Perf. 11					
C128	AP100	50c multicolored	90	24	
a.		Vert. pair, imperf. horiz.	—		
b.		Perf. 11.2	90	24	
C129	AP101	40c multicolored	80	22	
C130	AP102	50c multicolored	90	24	
C131	AP103	50c multicolored	90	24	
1993, Perf. 11.2					
C132	AP101	40c multicolored, hair touches top edge	80	22	

SCOTT

UNITED STATES
NATIONAL ALBUM

Pages printed on one side.

Includes Scott numbers.

All major variety stamps are either illustrated or described.

Chemically neutral paper protects stamps.

"The" album demanded by serious collectors of United States material. The Scott National postage stamp album provides spaces for commemoratives, definitives, air post, special delivery, registration, certified mail, postage due, parcel post, special handling, officials, newspapers, offices abroad, hunting permits, confederates and much more.

>   100NTL1   Part 1, 1845-1934.......$29.95
>   100NTL2   Part 2, 1935-1976.......$29.95
>   100NTL3   Part 3, 1977-1993.......$29.95
>   *All albums are sold as pages-only sections.*

Available from your local dealer or direct from:
Scott Publishing Co.
P.O. Box 828, Sidney, OH 45365

ASPD1

SD1

SD2

SD3

SD4

SD5

SD6

SD7

SD8

SD9

HOW TO USE THIS BOOK

The number in the first column is its Scott number or identifying number. The letter and number that come next (A41) indicate the design and refer to the illustration so designated. Following that is the denomination of the stamp and its color. Finally, the value, unused and used is shown.

Scott No.	Illus. No.	Description	Unused Value	Used Value	/ / / / / /
AIR POST SPECIAL DELIVERY STAMPS					
1934					
CE1	APSD1	16c dark blue..........................	55	65	☐☐☐☐☐
1936					
CE2	APSD1	16c red & blue......................	30	20	☐☐☐☐☐
a.		Horiz. pair, imperf. vert..	*4,000.*		☐☐☐☐☐
SPECIAL DELIVERY STAMPS					
1885-93					
E1	SD1	10c blue....................................	185.00	29.00	☐☐☐☐☐
E3	SD2	10c orange.............................	110.00	15.00	☐☐☐☐☐
1894, Line under "TEN CENTS"					
E4		10c blue.....................................	450.00	14.00	☐☐☐☐☐
1895, Watermark 191					
E5	SD3	10c blue.....................................	90.00	1.90	☐☐☐☐☐
b.		Printed on both sides.......	—		☐☐☐☐☐
1902					
E6	SD4	10c ultramarine	55.00	1.90	☐☐☐☐☐
1908					
E7	SD5	10c green.................................	40.00	24.00	☐☐☐☐☐
1911, Watermark 190, Perf. 12					
E8	SD4	10c ultramarine	55.00	2.50	☐☐☐☐☐
b.		10c violet blue........................	55.00	2.50	☐☐☐☐☐
1914, Perf. 10					
E9	SD4	10c ultramarine	110.00	3.00	☐☐☐☐☐
1916, Perf. 10, Unwatermarked					
E10	SD4	10c pale ultramarine...............	200.00	15.00	☐☐☐☐☐
1917-25, Perf. 11					
E11	SD4	10c ultramarine	10.00	25	☐☐☐☐☐
b.		10c gray violet........................	10.00	25	☐☐☐☐☐
c.		10c blue	30.00	60	☐☐☐☐☐
E12	SD6	10c gray violet........................	18.00	15	☐☐☐☐☐
a.		10c deep ultramarine..............	25.00	20	☐☐☐☐☐
E14	SD7	20c black	1.65	85	☐☐☐☐☐
1927-51, Perf. 11x10 1/2					
E15	SD6	10c gray violet........................	60	15	☐☐☐☐☐
a.		10c red lilac............................	60	15	☐☐☐☐☐
b.		10c gray lilac..........................	60	15	☐☐☐☐☐
c.		Horiz. pair, imperf. between	275.00		☐☐☐☐☐

Scott No.	Illus. No.	Description	Unused Value	Used Value	/ / / / / /
E17	SD6	13c blue	60	15	
E19	SD7	20c black	1.25	15	

1954-57

E20	SD8	20c deep blue	40	15	

1969-71

E22	SD9	45c carmine & violet blue	1.25	15	

RS1   CM1

Scott No.	Illus. No.	Description	Unused Value	Used Value	/ / / / / /

REGISTRATION STAMP
1911
F1   RS1   10c ultramarine 55.00   3.00

CERTIFIED MAIL STAMP
1955
FA1 CM1   15c red.................................   35   20

D1 D2

D3 D4 D5

HOW TO USE THIS BOOK
The number in the first column is its Scott number or identifying number. The letter and number that come next (A41) indicate the design and refer to the illustration so designated. Following that is the denomination of the stamp and its color. Finally, the value, unused and used is shown.

Scott No.	Illus. No.		Description	Unused Value	Used Value	/ / / / / /

POSTAGE DUE STAMPS

1879, Perf. 12

J1	D1	1c	brown	30.00	5.00	
J2	D1	2c	brown	200.00	4.00	
J3	D1	3c	brown	25.00	2.50	
J4	D1	5c	brown	300.00	30.00	
J5	D1	10c	brown	350.00	15.00	
a.			Imperf., pair	*1,600.*		
J6	D1	30c	brown	175.00	35.00	
J7	D1	50c	brown	225.00	40.00	

1879, Special Printing

J8	D1	1c	deep brown	*6,250.*		
J9	D1	2c	deep brown	*4,250.*		
J10	D1	3c	deep brown	*3,900.*		
J11	D1	5c	deep brown	*3,250.*		
J12	D1	10c	deep brown	*2,250.*		
J13	D1	30c	deep brown	*2,250.*		
J14	D1	50c	deep brown	*2,400.*		

1884-89

J15	D1	1c	red brown	30.00	2.50	
J16	D1	2c	red brown	40.00	2.50	
J17	D1	3c	red brown	500.00	100.00	
J18	D1	5c	red brown	250.00	15.00	
J19	D1	10c	red brown	225.00	10.00	
J20	D1	30c	red brown	110.00	30.00	
J21	D1	50c	red brown	1,000.	125.00	

1891-93

J22	D1	1c	bright claret	14.00	50	
J23	D1	2c	bright claret	15.00	45	
J24	D1	3c	bright claret	32.50	5.00	
J25	D1	5c	bright claret	35.00	5.00	
J26	D1	10c	bright claret	70.00	11.00	
J27	D1	30c	bright claret	250.00	90.00	
J28	D1	50c	bright claret	275.00	90.00	

1894

J29	D2	1c	vermilion	650.00	200.00	
J30	D2	2c	vermilion	300.00	60.00	
J31	D2	1c	deep claret	22.50	3.00	
b.			Vert. pair, imperf. horiz.	—		
J32	D2	2c	deep claret	17.50	1.75	
J33	D2	3c	deep claret	75.00	20.00	
J34	D2	5c	deep claret	100.00	22.50	
J35	D2	10c	deep claret	100.00	17.50	

Scott No.	Illus. No.	Description	Unused Value	Used Value	/ / / / / /
J36	D2	30c deep claret	225.00	60.00	
a.		30c carmine	225.00	60.00	
b.		30c pale rose	210.00	55.00	
J37	D2	50c deep claret	500.00	150.00	
a.		50c pale rose	450.00	135.00	

1895, Watermark 191

J38	D2	1c deep claret	5.00	30	
J39	D2	2c deep claret	5.00	20	
J40	D2	3c deep claret	35.00	1.00	
J41	D2	5c deep claret	37.50	1.00	
J42	D2	10c deep claret	40.00	2.00	
J43	D2	30c deep claret	300.00	25.00	
J44	D2	50c deep claret	190.00	20.00	

1910-12, Watermark 190

J45	D2	1c deep claret	20.00	2.00	
a.		1c rose carmine	17.50	1.75	
J46	D2	2c deep claret	20.00	30	
a.		2c rose carmine	17.50	30	
J47	D2	3c deep claret	350.00	17.50	
J48	D2	5c deep claret	60.00	3.50	
a.		5c rose carmine	—	—	
J49	D2	10c deep claret	75.00	7.50	
a.		10c rose carmine	—	—	
J50	D2	50c deep claret	600.00	75.00	

1914-15, Perf. 10

J52	D2	1c carmine lake	40.00	7.50	
a.		1c dull rose	40.00	7.50	
J53	D2	2c carmine lake	32.50	20	
a.		2c dull rose	32.50	20	
b.		2c vermilion	32.50	20	
J54	D2	3c carmine lake	425.00	20.00	
a.		3c dull rose	425.00	20.00	
J55	D2	5c carmine lake	25.00	1.50	
a.		5c dull rose	25.00	1.50	
J56	D2	10c carmine lake	40.00	1.00	
a.		10c dull rose	40.00	1.00	
J57	D2	30c carmine lake	145.00	12.00	
J58	D2	50c carmine lake	*6,500.*	375.00	

1916, Perf. 10, Unwatermarked

J59	D2	1c rose	1,100.	175.00	
J60	D2	2c rose	85.00	10.00	

Scott No.	Illus. No.	Description	Unused Value	Used Value	//////
1917, Perf. 11					
J61	D2	1c carmine rose	1.75	15	
a.		1c rose red	1.75	15	
b.		1c deep claret	1.75	15	
J62	D2	2c carmine rose	1.50	15	
a.		2c rose red	1.50	15	
b.		2c deep claret	1.50	15	
J63	D2	3c carmine rose	8.50	15	
a.		3c rose red	8.50	15	
b.		3c deep claret	8.50	25	
J64	D2	5c carmine	8.50	15	
a.		5c rose red	8.50	15	
b.		5c deep claret	8.50	15	
J65	D2	10c carmine rose	12.50	20	
a.		10c rose red	12.50	15	
b.		10c deep claret	12.50	15	
J66	D2	30c carmine rose	60.00	40	
a.		30c deep claret	60.00	40	
J67	D2	50c carmine rose	75.00	15	
a.		50c rose red	75.00	15	
b.		50c deep claret	75.00	15	
1925					
J68	D2	1/2c dull red	70	15	
1930-31, Perf. 11					
J69	D3	1/2c carmine	3.50	1.00	
J70	D3	1c carmine	2.50	15	
J71	D3	2c carmine	3.00	15	
J72	D3	3c carmine	15.00	1.00	
J73	D3	5c carmine	14.00	1.50	
J74	D3	10c carmine	30.00	50	
J75	D3	30c carmine	85.00	1.00	
J76	D3	50c carmine	100.00	30	
J77	D4	$1 carmine	25.00	15	
a.		$1 scarlet	20.00	15	
J78	D4	$5 carmine	30.00	15	
a.		$5 scarlet	25.00	15	
1931-56, Perf. 11x10 1/2, 10 1/2x11					
J79	D3	1/2c dull carmine	75	15	
J80	D3	1c dull carmine	15	15	
J81	D3	2c dull carmine	15	15	
J82	D3	3c dull carmine	25	15	
J83	D3	5c dull carmine	35	15	
J84	D3	10c dull carmine	1.10	15	
J85	D3	30c dull carmine	8.00	15	
J86	D3	50c dull carmine	9.50	15	

Scott No.	Illus. No.	Description	Unused Value	Used Value	/ / / / / /
J79a	D3	1/2c scarlet	75	15	
J80a	D3	1c scarlet	15	15	
J81a	D3	2c scarlet	15	15	
J82a	D3	3c scarlet	25	15	
J83a	D3	5c scarlet	35	15	
J84a	D3	10c scarlet	1.10	15	
J85a	D3	30c scarlet	8.00	15	
J86a	D3	50c scarlet	9.50	15	
J87	D4	$1 scarlet	35.00	20	

1959

J88	D5	1/2c carmine rose	1.25	85	
J89	D5	1c carmine rose	15	15	
a.		"1 CENT" omitted	375.00		
b.		Pair, one without "1 CENT"	—		
J90	D5	2c carmine rose	15	15	
J91	D5	3c carmine rose	15	15	
a.		Pair, one without "3 CENTS"	800.00		
J92	D5	4c carmine rose	15	15	
J93	D5	5c carmine rose	15	15	
a.		Pair, one without "5 CENTS"	—		
J94	D5	6c carmine rose	15	15	
a.		Pair, one without "6 CENTS"	800.00		
J95	D5	7c carmine rose	15	15	
J96	D5	8c carmine rose	16	15	
a.		Pair, one without "8 CENTS"	800.00		
J97	D5	10c carmine rose	20	15	
J98	D5	30c carmine rose	55	15	
J99	D5	50c carmine rose	90	15	
J100	D5	$1 carmine rose	1.50	15	
J101	D5	$5 carmine rose	8.00	15	

1978

J102	D5	11c carmine rose	25	15	
J103	D5	13c carmine rose	25	15	

1985

J104	D5	17c carmine rose	40	15	

United States Stamps of 1917-19 Surcharged

SHANGHAI 2¢ CHINA

Scott No.	Illus. No.	Description	Unused Value	Used Value	/ / / / / /
U.S. OFFICES IN CHINA					
1919					
K1	A140	2c on 1c green	17.50	20.00	
K2	A140	4c on 2c rose, type I	17.50	20.00	
K3	A140	6c on 3c violet, type II	32.50	45.00	
K4	A140	8c on 4c brown	40.00	45.00	
K5	A140	10c on 5c blue	45.00	52.50	
K6	A140	12c on 6c red orange	55.00	67.50	
K7	A140	14c on 7c black	60.00	72.50	
K8	A148	16c on 8c olive bister	45.00	50.00	
a.		16c on 8c olive green	40.00	42.50	
K9	A148	18c on 9c salmon red	45.00	55.00	
K10	A148	20c on 10c orange yellow	40.00	47.50	
K11	A148	24c on 12c brown carmine	47.50	60.00	
a.		24c on 12c claret brown	67.50	90.00	
K12	A148	30c on 15c gray	57.50	80.00	
K13	A148	40c on 20c deep ultra	85.00	125.00	
K14	A148	60c on 30c orange red	80.00	100.00	
K15	A148	$1 on 50c light violet	300.00	400.00	
K16	A148	$2 on $1 violet brown	275.00	325.00	
a.		Double surcharge	*3,000.*	*3,250.*	

Nos. 498 and 528B Surcharged

SHANGHAI 2 Cts. CHINA

1922, Surcharged locally

K17	A140	2c on 1c green	80.00	80.00	
K18	A140	4c on 2c carmine, type VII	70.00	70.00	

O1   O8   O6

O11   O12   O13   O14

Scott No.	Illus. No.	Description	Unused Value	Used Value	/ / / / / /

OFFICIAL STAMPS
1873, AGRICULTURE DEPT.

Scott No.	Illus. No.	Description	Unused Value	Used Value
O1	O1	1c yellow	90.00	70.00
O2	O1	2c yellow	70.00	25.00
O3	O1	3c yellow	65.00	3.50
O4	O1	6c yellow	75.00	15.00
O5	O1	10c yellow	150.00	70.00
O6	O1	12c yellow	200.00	95.00
O7	O1	15c yellow	150.00	80.00
O8	O1	24c yellow	175.00	80.00
O9	O1	30c yellow	225.00	120.00

EXECUTIVE DEPT.

Scott No.	Illus. No.	Description	Unused Value	Used Value
O10	O1	1c carmine	350.00	175.00
O11	O1	2c carmine	225.00	100.00
O12	O1	3c carmine	275.00	85.00
a.		3c violet rose	275.00	85.00
O13	O1	6c carmine	400.00	250.00
O14	O1	10c carmine	375.00	200.00

INTERIOR DEPT.

Scott No.	Illus. No.	Description	Unused Value	Used Value
O15	O1	1c vermilion	20.00	3.50
O16	O1	2c vermilion	17.50	2.00
O17	O1	3c vermilion	27.50	2.00
O18	O1	6c vermilion	20.00	2.00
O19	O1	10c vermilion	19.00	4.00
O20	O1	12c vermilion	30.00	3.00
O21	O1	15c vermilion	50.00	6.00

Scott No.	Illus. No.	Description	Unused Value	Used Value	//////
O22	O1	24c vermilion	37.50	5.00	
O23	O1	30c vermilion	50.00	6.00	
O24	O1	90c vermilion	110.00	15.00	

JUSTICE DEPT.

Scott No.	Illus. No.	Description	Unused Value	Used Value	//////
O25	O1	1c purple	60.00	40.00	
O26	O1	2c purple	95.00	40.00	
O27	O1	3c purple	95.00	6.00	
O28	O1	6c purple	90.00	10.00	
O29	O1	10c purple	100.00	27.50	
O30	O1	12c purple	75.00	15.00	
O31	O1	15c purple	165.00	50.00	
O32	O1	24c purple	450.00	135.00	
O33	O1	30c purple	400.00	75.00	
O34	O1	90c purple	600.00	200.00	

NAVY DEPT.

Scott No.	Illus. No.	Description	Unused Value	Used Value	//////
O35	O1	1c ultramarine	45.00	10.00	
a.		1c dull blue	52.50	12.50	
O36	O1	2c ultramarine	32.50	9.00	
a.		2c dull blue	42.50	9.00	
O37	O1	3c ultramarine	37.50	4.00	
a.		3c dull blue	42.50	5.50	
O38	O1	6c ultramarine	32.50	5.00	
a.		6c dull blue	42.50	5.00	
O39	O1	7c ultramarine	225.00	70.00	
a.		7c dull blue	250.00	70.00	
O40	O1	10c ultramarine	45.00	15.00	
a.		10c dull blue	50.00	15.00	
O41	O1	12c ultramarine	57.50	10.00	
O42	O1	15c ultramarine	95.00	20.00	
O43	O1	24c ultramarine	95.00	25.00	
a.		24c dull blue	110.00	—	
O44	O1	30c ultramarine	85.00	10.00	
O45	O1	90c ultramarine	400.00	70.00	
a.		Double impression		3,250.	

POST OFFICE DEPT.

Scott No.	Illus. No.	Description	Unused Value	Used Value	//////
O47	O6	1c black	7.25	3.00	
O48	O6	2c black	7.00	2.50	
a.		Double impression	300.00		
O49	O6	3c black	2.50	55	
a.		Printed on both sides		2,750.	
O50	O6	6c black	8.00	1.40	
a.		Diagonal half used as 3c on cover		2,750.	
O51	O6	10c black	40.00	15.00	
O52	O6	12c black	22.50	3.50	

Scott No.	Illus. No.	Description	Unused Value	Used Value	/ / / / / /
STATE DEPT.					
O53	O6	15c black	25.00	5.00	
a.		Imperf., pair	*600.00*		
O54	O6	24c black	32.50	6.00	
O55	O6	30c black	32.50	5.50	
O56	O6	90c black	47.50	7.50	
O57	O1	1c dark green	60.00	20.00	
O58	O1	2c dark green	125.00	25.00	
O59	O1	3c bright green	50.00	10.00	
O60	O1	6c bright green	47.50	10.00	
O61	O1	7c dark green	90.00	20.00	
O62	O1	10c dark green	75.00	13.50	
O63	O1	12c dark green	110.00	35.00	
O64	O1	15c dark green	125.00	25.00	
O65	O1	24c dark green	250.00	75.00	
O66	O1	30c dark green	250.00	45.00	
O67	O1	90c dark green	500.00	125.00	
O68	O8	$2 green & black	550.00	400.00	
O69	O8	$5 green & black	4,250.	2,000.	
O70	O8	$10 green & black	3,000.	1,500.	
O71	O8	$20 green & black	2,250.	800.00	
TREASURY DEPT.					
O72	O1	1c brown	22.50	1.75	
O73	O1	2c brown	25.00	1.75	
O74	O1	3c brown	16.00	75	
O75	O1	6c brown	22.50	1.50	
O76	O1	7c brown	57.50	10.00	
O77	O1	10c brown	57.50	3.00	
O78	O1	12c brown	57.50	1.75	
O79	O1	15c brown	50.00	2.50	
O80	O1	24c brown	250.00	30.00	
O81	O1	30c brown	82.50	3.00	
O82	O1	90c brown	87.50	3.00	
WAR DEPT.					
O83	O1	1c rose	82.50	3.25	
O84	O1	2c rose	75.00	4.50	
O85	O1	3c rose	72.50	1.00	
O86	O1	6c rose	250.00	2.00	
O87	O1	7c rose	75.00	40.00	
O88	O1	10c rose	22.50	4.00	
O89	O1	12c rose	75.00	2.00	
O90	O1	15c rose	20.00	2.50	
O91	O1	24c rose	20.00	3.00	
O92	O1	30c rose	22.50	2.50	
O93	O1	90c rose	50.00	10.00	

Scott No.	Illus. No.	Description	Unused Value	Used Value	//////

1879, AGRICULTURE DEPT.
O94	O1	1c yellow, no gum	1,500.		
O95	O1	3c yellow	175.00	35.00	

INTERIOR DEPT.
O96	O1	1c vermilion	110.00	90.00	
O97	O1	2c vermilion	2.50	1.00	
O98	O1	3c vermilion	2.00	60	
O99	O1	6c vermilion	3.00	2.50	
O100	O1	10c vermilion	32.50	27.50	
O101	O1	12c vermilion	65.00	40.00	
O102	O1	15c vermilion	150.00	65.00	
O103	O1	24c vermilion	2,000.	—	

JUSTICE DEPT.
O106	O1	3c bluish purple	50.00	25.00	
O107	O1	6c bluish purple	110.00	90.00	

POST OFFICE DEPT.
O108	O6	3c black	7.50	1.75	

TREASURY DEPT.
O109	O1	3c brown	27.50	2.50	
O110	O1	6c brown	50.00	16.00	
O111	O1	10c brown	70.00	17.50	
O112	O1	30c brown	800.00	125.00	
O113	O1	90c brown	825.00	125.00	

WAR DEPT.
O114	O1	1c rose red	2.00	1.50	
O115	O1	2c rose red	3.00	1.50	
O116	O1	3c rose red	3.00	75	
a.		Imperf., pair	*800.00*		
b.		Double impression	500.00		
O117	O1	6c rose red	2.50	80	
O118	O1	10c rose red	20.00	17.50	
O119	O1	12c rose red	15.00	3.00	
O120	O1	30c rose red	47.50	35.00	

1875, SPECIAL PRINTINGS, Ovptd. "SPECIMEN" (Type D)
Thin hard white paper

AGRICULTURE DEPT., Carmine Overprint
O1S	O1	1c yellow	8.00		
a.		"Sepcimen" error	475.00		
b.		Small dotted "i" in "Specimen"	165.00		
c.		Ribbed paper	15.00		

Scott No.	Illus. No.	Description	Unused Value	Used Value	/ / / / / /
O2S	O1	2c yellow		15.00	
a.		"Sepcimen" error		525.00	
O3S	O1	3c yellow		45.00	
a.		"Sepcimen" error		2,100.	
O4S	O1	6c yellow		80.00	
a.		"Sepcimen" error		5,500.	
O5S	O1	10c yellow		80.00	
a.		"Sepcimen" error		2,250.	
O6S	O1	12c yellow		75.00	
a.		"Sepcimen" error		2,250.	
O7S	O1	15c yellow		75.00	
a.		"Sepcimen" error		2,250.	
O8S	O1	24c yellow		75.00	
a.		"Sepcimen" error		2,250.	
O9S	O1	30c yellow		75.00	
a.		"Sepcimen" error		2,250.	

EXECUTIVE DEPT., Blue Overprint

Scott No.	Illus. No.	Description	Unused Value	Used Value	
O10S	O1	1c carmine		8.00	
a.		Small dotted "i" in "Specimen"		175.00	
b.		Ribbed paper		15.00	
O11S	O1	2c carmine		15.00	
O12S	O1	3c carmine		15.00	
O13S	O1	6c carmine		15.00	
O14S	O1	10c carmine		15.00	

INTERIOR DEPT., Blue Overprint

Scott No.	Illus. No.	Description	Unused Value	Used Value	
O15S	O1	1c vermilion		14.00	
O16S	O1	2c vermilion		20.00	
a.		"Sepcimen" error		1,150.	
O17S	O1	3c vermilion		325.00	
O18S	O1	6c vermilion		300.00	
O19S	O1	10c vermilion		300.00	
O20S	O1	12c vermilion		325.00	
O21S	O1	15c vermilion		325.00	
O22S	O1	24c vermilion		325.00	
O23S	O1	30c vermilion		325.00	
O24S	O1	90c vermilion		325.00	

JUSTICE DEPT., Blue Overprint

Scott No.	Illus. No.	Description	Unused Value	Used Value	
O25S	O1	1c purple		8.00	
a.		"Sepcimen" error		450.00	
b.		Small dotted "i" in "Specimen"		150.00	
c.		Ribbed paper		15.00	
O26S	O1	2c purple		15.00	
a.		"Sepcimen" error		750.00	
O27S	O1	3c purple		140.00	
a.		"Sepcimen" error		3,000.	

Scott No.	Illus. No.		Description	Unused Value	Used Value	//////
O28S	O1	6c	purple..............................		140.00	
O29S	O1	10c	purple..............................		135.00	
O30S	O1	12c	purple..............................		135.00	
a.			"Sepcimen" error		3,000.	
O31S	O1	15c	purple..............................		160.00	
a.			"Sepcimen" error		3,000.	
O32S	O1	24c	purple..............................		175.00	
a.			"Sepcimen" error		3,000.	
O33S	O1	30c	purple..............................		175.00	
a.			"Sepcimen" error		3,000.	
O34S	O1	90c	purple..............................		175.00	

NAVY DEPT., Carmine Overprint

Scott No.	Illus. No.		Description	Unused Value	Used Value	//////
O35S	O1	1c	ultramarine		10.00	
a.			"Sepcimen" error		375.00	
b.			Broken "i" in "Specimen"		—	
O36S	O1	2c	ultramarine		20.00	
a.			"Sepcimen" error		475.00	
b.			Broken "i" in "Specimen"		—	
O37S	O1	3c	ultramarine		175.00	
O38S	O1	6c	ultramarine		200.00	
O39S	O1	7c	ultramarine		80.00	
a.			"Sepcimen" error		1,200.	
O40S	O1	10c	ultramarine		200.00	
a.			"Sepcimen" error		3,000.	
O41S	O1	12c	ultramarine		185.00	
a.			"Sepcimen" error		3,000.	
O42S	O1	15c	ultramarine		185.00	
a.			"Sepcimen" error		3,000.	
O43S	O1	24c	ultramarine		180.00	
a.			"Sepcimen" error		3,000.	
O44S	O1	30c	ultramarine		180.00	
a.			"Sepcimen" error		3,000.	
O45S	O1	90c	ultramarine		180.00	

POST OFFICE DEPT., Carmine Overprint

Scott No.	Illus. No.		Description	Unused Value	Used Value	//////
O47S	O6	1c	black		14.00	
a.			"Sepcimen" error		450.00	
b.			Inverted overprint............		375.00	
O48S	O6	2c	black		40.00	
a.			"Sepcimen" error		1,200.	
O49S	O6	3c	black		240.00	
a.			"Sepcimen" error		3,000.	
O50S	O6	6c	black		240.00	
O51S	O6	10c	black		165.00	
a.			"Sepcimen" error		3,000.	
O52S	O6	12c	black		240.00	

Scott No.	Illus. No.	Description	Unused Value	Used Value	/ / / / / /
O53S	O6	15c black		260.00	
a.		"Sepcimen" error		3,000.	
O54S	O6	24c black		240.00	
a.		"Sepcimen" error		3,000.	
O55S	O6	30c black		250.00	
O56S	O6	90c black		250.00	
a.		"Sepcimen" error		3,000.	

STATE DEPT., Carmine Overprint

Scott No.	Illus. No.	Description	Unused Value	Used Value	/ / / / / /
O57S	O1	1c dark green		8.00	
a.		"Sepcimen" error		275.00	
b.		Small dotted "i" in "Specimen" error		225.00	
c.		Ribbed paper		15.00	
O58S	O1	2c dark green		15.00	
a.		"Sepcimen" error		375.00	
O59S	O1	3c bright green		27.50	
a.		"Sepcimen" error		1,200.	
O60S	O1	6c bright green		55.00	
a.		"Sepcimen" error		1,300.	
O61S	O1	7c dark green		27.50	
a.		"Sepcimen" error		1,200.	
O62S	O1	10c dark green		100.00	
a.		"Sepcimen" error		7,250.	
O63S	O1	12c dark green		110.00	
a.		"Sepcimen" error		2,750.	
O64S	O1	15c dark green		110.00	
O65S	O1	24c dark green		110.00	
a.		"Sepcimen" error		2,750.	
O66S	O1	30c dark green		110.00	
a.		"Sepcimen" error		2,750.	
O67S	O1	90c dark green		110.00	
a.		"Sepcimen" error		2,750.	
O68S	O8	$2 green & black		4,500.	
O69S	O8	$5 green & black		6,500.	
O70S	O8	$10 green & black		8,500.	
O71S	O8	$20 green & black		10,000.	

TREASURY DEPT., Blue Overprint

Scott No.	Illus. No.	Description	Unused Value	Used Value	/ / / / / /
O72S	O1	1c brown		15.00	
O73S	O1	2c brown		80.00	
O74S	O1	3c brown		240.00	
O75S	O1	6c brown		275.00	
O76S	O1	7c brown		155.00	
O77S	O1	10c brown		240.00	
O78S	O1	12c brown		250.00	
O79S	O1	15c brown		250.00	
O80S	O1	24c brown		240.00	
O81S	O1	30c brown		360.00	

Scott No.	Illus. No.	Description	Unused Value	Used Value	//////
O82S	O1	90c brown		360.00	

WAR DEPT., Blue Overprint

O83S	O1	1c rose		10.00	
a.		"Sepcimen" error		375.00	
O84S	O1	2c rose		20.00	
a.		"Sepcimen" error		675.00	
O85S	O1	3c rose		200.00	
a.		"Sepcimen" error		2,750.	
O86S	O1	6c rose		240.00	
a.		"Sepcimen" error		2,750.	
O87S	O1	7c rose		40.00	
a.		"Sepcimen" error		1,000.	
O88S	O1	10c rose		190.00	
a.		"Sepcimen" error		2,750.	
O89S	O1	12c rose		240.00	
a.		"Sepcimen" error		2,750.	
O90S	O1	15c rose		240.00	
a.		"Sepcimen" error		2,750.	
O91S	O1	24c rose		240.00	
a.		"Sepcimen" error		2,750.	
O92S	O1	30c rose		240.00	
a.		"Sepcimen" error		2,750.	
O93S	O1	90c rose		240.00	
a.		"Sepcimen" error		2,750.	

Soft, porous paper

EXECUTIVE DEPT., Blue Overprint

O10xS	O1	1c violet rose		25.00	

NAVY DEPT., Carmine Overprint

O35xS	O1	1c gray blue		30.00	
a.		Double overprint		550.00	

STATE DEPT., Carmine Overprint

O57xS	O1	1c yellow green		110.00	

OFFICIAL POSTAL SAVINGS MAIL
1911, Watermark 191

O121	O11	2c black	9.00	1.10	
O122	O11	50c dark green	110.00	25.00	
O123	O11	$1 ultramarine	100.00	7.00	

Watermark 190

O124	O11	1c dark violet	5.50	1.00	
O125	O11	2c black	30.00	3.50	
O126	O11	10c carmine	10.00	1.00	

Scott No.	Illus. No.	Description	Unused Value	Used Value	/ / / / / /
1983-85					
O127	O12	1c red, blue & black	15	15	
O128	O12	4c red, blue & black	15	25	
O129	O12	13c red, blue & black	26	75	
O129A	O12	14c red, blue & black	28	50	
O130	O12	17c red, blue & black	34	40	
O132	O12	$1 red, blue & black	1.75	1.00	
O133	O12	$5 red, blue & black	9.00	5.00	
Coil stamps, Perf 10 vertically					
O135	O12	20c red, blue & black	2.00	*2.00*	
a.		Imperf., pair	*2,000.*		
O136	O12	22c red, blue & black	60	*2.00*	
1985					
O138	O12	(14c) red, blue & black	3.50	*5.00*	
1985-88, Coil stamps, Perf. 10 vertically					
O138A	O13	15c red, blue & black	30	50	
O138B	O13	20c red, blue & black	40	30	
O139	O12	(22c) red, blue & black	4.50	*3.00*	
O140	O13	(25c) red, blue & black	50	*2.00*	
O141	O13	25c red, blue & black	50	50	
a.		Imperf., pair	2,000.	—	
1989					
O143	O13	1c red, blue & black	15	15	
1991, Coil stamps, Perf. 10 vertically					
O144	O14	(29c) red, blue & black	58	50	
O145	O13	29c red, blue & black	58	25	
1991-93					
O146	O13	4c red, blue & black	15	15	
O146A	O13	10c red, blue & black	20	—	
O147	O13	19c red, blue & black	38	50	
O148	O13	23c red, blue & black	46	25	
O151	O13	$1 red, blue & black	2.00	—	

SUBSCRIBE TO SCOTT STAMP MONTHLY MAGAZINE

INCLUDING THE SCOTT CATALOGUE UPDATE SECTION

LIVELY, ENGAGING ARTICLES

THAT CAPTURE

THE SPECIAL FASCINATION

STAMPS HOLD,

PLUS THE LATEST

INFORMATION ON NEW ISSUES,

INCLUDING SCOTT NUMBERS.

ONE YEAR, 12 ISSUES – $16.95

TWO YEARS, 24 ISSUES – $28.95

CALL TODAY...
1-800-488-5351

OR WRITE TODAY TO: SCOTT PUBLISHING CO., P.O. BOX 828, SIDNEY, OH 45365

N1

N2

N3

N4

N5

N6

N7

N8

N9

N10

N11

N12

N13

N14

Scott No.	Illus. No.	Description	Unused Value	Used Value	//////

NEWSPAPER STAMPS

1865, Thin hard paper, no gum

Scott No.	Illus. No.	Description	Unused Value	Used Value
PR1	N1	5c dark blue	185.00	—
a.		5c light blue	185.00	—
PR2	N2	10c blue green	85.00	—
a.		10c green	85.00	—
b.		Pelure paper	125.00	—
PR3	N3	25c orange red	125.00	—
a.		25c carmine red	150.00	—
b.		Pelure paper	125.00	—

White border, Yellowish paper

Scott No.	Illus. No.	Description	Unused Value	Used Value
PR4	N1	5c light blue	50.00	30.00
a.		5c dark blue	50.00	30.00
b.		Pelure paper	50.00	—

1875, Reprints, Hard white paper, no gum

Scott No.	Illus. No.	Description	Unused Value	Used Value
PR5	N1	5c dull blue	70.00	
a.		Printed on both sides	—	
PR6	N2	10c dark bluish green	50.00	
a.		Printed on both sides	1,750.	
PR7	N3	25c dark carmine	80.00	

1880, Reprint, Soft porous paper, White Border

Scott No.	Illus. No.	Description	Unused Value	Used Value
PR8	N1	5c dark blue	125.00	

1875, Thin hard paper

Scott No.	Illus. No.	Description	Unused Value	Used Value
PR9	N4	2c black	14.00	11.00
PR10	N4	3c black	17.50	14.50
PR11	N4	4c black	15.00	12.50
PR12	N4	6c black	20.00	17.00
PR13	N4	8c black	27.50	22.50
PR14	N4	9c black	60.00	50.00
PR15	N4	10c black	27.50	20.00
PR16	N5	12c rose	65.00	40.00
PR17	N5	24c rose	82.50	45.00
PR18	N5	36c rose	92.50	50.00
PR19	N5	48c rose	165.00	85.00
PR20	N5	60c rose	82.50	45.00
PR21	N5	72c rose	200.00	110.00
PR22	N5	84c rose	300.00	135.00
PR23	N5	96c rose	165.00	100.00
PR24	N6	$1.92 dark brown	225.00	125.00
PR25	N7	$3 vermilion	300.00	135.00
PR26	N8	$6 ultramarine	500.00	185.00
PR27	N9	$9 yellow	650.00	250.00
PR28	N10	$12 blue green	750.00	350.00
PR29	N11	$24 dark gray violet	750.00	325.00

Scott No.	Illus. No.	Description	Unused Value	Used Value
PR30	N12	$36 brown rose	800.00	450.00
PR31	N13	$48 red brown	1,050.	500.00
PR32	N14	$60 violet	1,050.	500.00

1880, Special Printing, Hard white paper, no gum

Scott No.	Illus. No.	Description	Unused Value	Used Value
PR33	N4	2c gray black	100.00	
PR34	N4	3c gray black	105.00	
PR35	N4	4c gray black	110.00	
PR36	N4	6c gray black	150.00	
PR37	N4	8c gray black	175.00	
PR38	N4	9c gray black	200.00	
PR39	N4	10c gray black	250.00	
PR40	N5	12c pale rose	300.00	
PR41	N5	24c pale rose	425.00	
PR42	N5	36c pale rose	500.00	
PR43	N5	48c pale rose	600.00	
PR44	N5	60c pale rose	675.00	
PR45	N5	72c pale rose	825.00	
PR46	N5	84c pale rose	850.00	
PR47	N5	96c pale rose	1,500.	
PR48	N6	$1.92 dark brown	*3,500.*	
PR49	N7	$3 vermilion	*7,000.*	
PR50	N8	$6 ultramarine	*8,500.*	
PR51	N9	$9 yellow	*20,000.*	
PR52	N10	$12 blue green	*18,500.*	
PR53	N11	$24 dark gray violet	—	
PR54	N12	$36 brown rose	—	
PR55	N13	$48 red brown	—	
PR56	N14	$60 violet	—	

1879, Soft porous paper

Scott No.	Illus. No.	Description	Unused Value	Used Value
PR57	N4	2c black	6.00	4.50
PR58	N4	3c black	7.50	5.00
PR59	N4	4c black	7.50	5.00
PR60	N4	6c black	15.00	11.00
PR61	N4	8c black	15.00	11.00
PR62	N4	10c black	15.00	11.00
PR63	N5	12c red	55.00	25.00
PR64	N5	24c red	55.00	22.50
PR65	N5	36c red	170.00	95.00
PR66	N5	48c red	135.00	60.00
PR67	N5	60c red	100.00	60.00
a.		Imperf., pair	*600.00*	
PR68	N5	72c red	210.00	115.00
PR69	N5	84c red	165.00	85.00
PR70	N5	96c red	110.00	60.00
PR71	N6	$1.92 pale brown	90.00	55.00
PR72	N7	$3 red vermilion	90.00	55.00

Scott No.	Illus. No.	Description	Unused Value	Used Value	//////
PR73	N8	$6 blue	150.00	90.00	
PR74	N9	$9 orange	110.00	60.00	
PR75	N10	$12 yellow green	160.00	85.00	
PR76	N11	$24 dark violet	200.00	110.00	
PR77	N12	$36 indian red	250.00	135.00	
PR78	N13	$48 yellow brown	325.00	165.00	
PR79	N14	$60 purple	325.00	165.00	

1883, Special Printing

Scott No.	Illus. No.	Description	Unused Value	Used Value	
PR80	N4	2c intense black	275.00		

1885

Scott No.	Illus. No.	Description	Unused Value	Used Value	
PR81	N4	1c black	8.50	5.00	
PR82	N5	12c carmine	27.50	12.50	
PR83	N5	24c carmine	30.00	15.00	
PR84	N5	36c carmine	42.50	17.50	
PR85	N5	48c carmine	60.00	30.00	
PR86	N5	60c carmine	85.00	40.00	
PR87	N5	72c carmine	95.00	45.00	
PR88	N5	84c carmine	200.00	110.00	
PR89	N5	96c carmine	140.00	85.00	

1894

Scott No.	Illus. No.	Description	Unused Value	Used Value	
PR90	N4	1c intense black	55.00		
PR91	N4	2c intense black	55.00		
PR92	N4	4c intense black	75.00		
PR93	N4	6c intense black	950.00		
PR94	N4	10c intense black	125.00		
PR95	N5	12c pink	550.00	—	
PR96	N5	24c pink	575.00		
PR97	N5	36c pink	*3,500.*		
PR98	N5	60c pink	*3,500.*	—	
PR99	N5	96c pink	*4,000.*		
PR100	N7	$3 scarlet	*5,500.*		
PR101	N8	$6 pale blue	*7,500.*	—	

1895

Scott No.	Illus. No.	Description	Unused Value	Used Value	
PR102	N15	1c black	25.00	7.50	
PR103	N15	2c black	25.00	7.50	
PR104	N15	5c black	35.00	12.50	
PR105	N15	10c black	75.00	32.50	
PR106	N16	25c carmine	100.00	35.00	
PR107	N16	50c carmine	235.00	95.00	
PR108	N17	$2 scarlet	275.00	65.00	
PR109	N18	$5 ultramarine	375.00	150.00	
PR110	N19	$10 green	350.00	165.00	
PR111	N20	$20 slate	675.00	300.00	
PR112	N21	$50 dull rose	700.00	300.00	
PR113	N22	$100 purple	775.00	350.00	

N15   **N16**

N17   **N18**   **N19**

N20   **N21**   **N22**

Scott No.	Illus. No.		Description	Unused Value	Used Value
1895-97, Watermark 191					
PR114	N15	1c	black	3.50	3.00
PR115	N15	2c	black	4.00	3.50
PR116	N15	5c	black	6.00	5.00
PR117	N15	10c	black	4.00	3.50
PR118	N16	25c	carmine	8.00	8.00
PR119	N16	50c	carmine	10.00	12.50
PR120	N17	$2	scarlet	12.00	15.00
PR121	N18	$5	dark blue	20.00	25.00
a.			$5 light blue	100.00	45.00
PR122	N19	$10	green	18.00	25.00
PR123	N20	$20	slate	20.00	27.50
PR124	N21	$50	dull rose	25.00	30.00
PR125	N22	$100	purple	30.00	37.50

PP1

PP2

PP3

PP4

PP5

PP6

PP7

PP8

PP9

PP10

PP11

PP12

PP13

PPD1

Scott No.	Illus. No.	Description	Unused Value	Used Value	/ / / / / /

PARCEL POST STAMPS
1913

Q1	PP1	1c carmine rose	2.50	85	
Q2	PP2	2c carmine rose	3.00	60	
Q3	PP3	3c carmine	5.75	4.50	
Q4	PP4	4c carmine rose	16.00	1.90	
Q5	PP5	5c carmine rose	15.00	1.25	
Q6	PP6	10c carmine rose	25.00	1.75	
Q7	PP7	15c carmine rose	35.00	7.75	
Q8	PP8	20c carmine rose	77.50	15.00	
Q9	PP9	25c carmine rose	35.00	4.00	
Q10	PP10	50c carmine rose	150.00	27.50	
Q11	PP11	75c carmine rose	45.00	22.50	
Q12	PP12	$1 carmine rose	235.00	17.00	

SPECIAL HANDLING STAMPS
1925-28

QE1	PP13	10c yellow green	1.00	80	
QE2	PP13	15c yellow green	1.10	70	
QE3	PP13	20c yellow green	1.75	1.00	
QE4	PP13	25c yellow green	14.00	5.50	
a.		25c deep green	22.50	4.50	

PARCEL POST POSTAGE DUE STAMPS
1912

JQ1	PPD1	1c dark green	5.00	2.75	
JQ2	PPD1	2c dark green	45.00	13.00	
JQ3	PPD1	5c dark green	6.50	3.50	
JQ4	PPD1	10c dark green	100.00	30.00	
JQ5	PPD1	25c dark green	50.00	3.25	

CVP1　　　　　　　　　　　　CVP2

CVP3　　　　　　　　　　　　CVP4

Scott No.	Illus. No.	Description	Unused Value	Used Value	/ / / / / /
COMPUTER VENDED POSTAGE					
1989, Aug. 23, Washington, D.C., Machine 82					
1	CVP1	25c 1st Class	6.00	—	☐☐☐☐☐
a.		1st day dated, serial #12501-15500	4.50	—	☐☐☐☐☐
b.		1st day dated, serial #00001-12500	4.50	—	☐☐☐☐☐
c.		1st day dated, serial over #27500	—	—	☐☐☐☐☐
2	CVP1	$1 3rd Class	—	—	☐☐☐☐☐
a.		1st day dated, serial #24501-27500	—	—	☐☐☐☐☐
b.		1st day dated, serial over #27500	—	—	☐☐☐☐☐
3	CVP2	$1.69 Parcel Post	—	—	☐☐☐☐☐
a.		1st day dated, serial #21501-24500	—	—	☐☐☐☐☐
b.		1st day dated, serial over #27500	—	—	☐☐☐☐☐
4	CVP1	$2.40 Priority Mail	—	—	☐☐☐☐☐
a.		1st day dated, serial #18501-21500	—	—	☐☐☐☐☐
b.		Priority Mail ($2.74), with bar code (CVP2)	100.00		☐☐☐☐☐
c.		1st day dated, serial over #27500	—	—	☐☐☐☐☐
5	CVP1	$8.75 Express Mail	—	—	☐☐☐☐☐
a.		1st day dated, serial #15501-18500	—	—	☐☐☐☐☐
b.		1st day dated, serial over #27500	—	—	☐☐☐☐☐

Scott No.	Illus. No.	Description	Unused Value	Used Value	/ / / / / /
Washington, D.C., Machine 83					
6	CVP1	25c 1st Class	6.00	—	☐☐☐☐☐
a.		1st day dated, serial #12501-15500	4.50	—	☐☐☐☐☐
b.		1st day dated, serial #00001-12500	4.50	—	☐☐☐☐☐
c.		1st day dated, serial over #27500	—	—	☐☐☐☐☐
7	CVP1	$1 3rd Class	—	—	☐☐☐☐☐
a.		1st day dated, serial #24501-27500	—	—	☐☐☐☐☐
b.		1st day dated, serial over #27500	—	—	☐☐☐☐☐
8	CVP2	$1.69 Parcel Post	—	—	☐☐☐☐☐
a.		1st day dated, serial #21501-24500	—	—	☐☐☐☐☐
b.		1st day dated, serial over #27500	—	—	☐☐☐☐☐
9	CVP1	$2.40 Priority Mail	—	—	☐☐☐☐☐
a.		1st day dated, serial #18501-21500	—	—	☐☐☐☐☐
b.		1st day dated, serial over #27500	—	—	☐☐☐☐☐
c.		Priority Mail ($2.74), with bar code (CVP2)	*100.00*		☐☐☐☐☐
10	CVP1	$8.75 Express Mail	—	—	☐☐☐☐☐
a.		1st day dated, serial #15501-18500	—	—	☐☐☐☐☐
b.		1st day dated, serial over #27500	—	—	☐☐☐☐☐
1989, Sept. 1, Kensington, MD, Machine 82					
11	CVP1	25c 1st Class	6.00	—	☐☐☐☐☐
a.		1st day dated, serial #12501-15500	4.50	—	☐☐☐☐☐
b.		1st day dated, serial #00001-12500	4.50	—	☐☐☐☐☐
c.		1st day dated, serial over #27500	—	—	☐☐☐☐☐
12	CVP1	$1 3rd Class	—	—	☐☐☐☐☐
a.		1st day dated, serial #24501-27500	—	—	☐☐☐☐☐
b.		1st day dated, serial over #27500	—	—	☐☐☐☐☐
13	CVP2	$1.69 Parcel Post	—	—	☐☐☐☐☐
a.		1st day dated, serial #21501-24500	—	—	☐☐☐☐☐
b.		1st day dated, serial over #27500	—	—	☐☐☐☐☐
14	CVP1	$2.40 Priority Mail	—	—	☐☐☐☐☐
a.		1st day dated, serial #18501-21500	—	—	☐☐☐☐☐
b.		1st day dated, serial over #27500	—	—	☐☐☐☐☐
c.		Priority Mail ($2.74), with bar code (CVP2)	*100.00*		☐☐☐☐☐

Scott No.	Illus. No.	Description	Unused Value	Used Value	//////
15	CVP1 $8.75	Express Mail	—	—	☐☐☐☐☐
a.		1st day dated, serial #15501-18500	—	—	☐☐☐☐☐
b.		1st day dated, serial over #27500	—	—	☐☐☐☐☐

Kensington, MD, Machine 83

Scott No.	Illus. No.	Description	Unused Value	Used Value	//////
16	CVP1 25c	1st Class	6.00	—	☐☐☐☐☐
a.		1st day dated, serial #12501-15500	4.50	—	☐☐☐☐☐
b.		1st day dated, serial #00001-12500	4.50	—	☐☐☐☐☐
c.		1st day dated, serial over #27500	—	—	☐☐☐☐☐
17	CVP1 $1	3rd Class	—	—	☐☐☐☐☐
a.		1st day dated, serial #24501-27500	—	—	☐☐☐☐☐
b.		1st day dated, serial over #27500	—	—	☐☐☐☐☐
18	CVP2 $1.69	Parcel Post	—	—	☐☐☐☐☐
a.		1st day dated, serial #21501-24500	—	—	☐☐☐☐☐
b.		1st day dated, serial over #27500	—	—	☐☐☐☐☐
19	CVP1 $2.40	Priority Mail	—	—	☐☐☐☐☐
a.		1st day dated, serial #18501-21500	—	—	☐☐☐☐☐
b.		1st day dated, serial over #27500	—	—	☐☐☐☐☐
c.		Priority Mail ($2.74), with bar code (CVP2)	100.00		☐☐☐☐☐
20	CVP1 $8.75	Express Mail	—	—	☐☐☐☐☐
a.		1st day dated, serial #15501-18500	—	—	☐☐☐☐☐
b.		1st day dated, serial over #27500	—	—	☐☐☐☐☐

1989, Nov., Washington, D.C., Machine 11

Scott No.	Illus. No.	Description	Unused Value	Used Value	//////
21	CVP1 25c	1st Class	*150.00*		☐☐☐☐☐
a.		1st Class, with bar code (CVP2)	—		☐☐☐☐☐
22	CVP1 $1	3rd Class	*500.00*		☐☐☐☐☐
23	CVP2 $1.69	Parcel Post	*500.00*		☐☐☐☐☐
24	CVP1 $2.40	Priority Mail	*500.00*		☐☐☐☐☐
a.		Priority Mail ($2.74), with bar code (CVP2)	—		☐☐☐☐☐
25	CVP1 $8.75	Express Mail	*500.00*		☐☐☐☐☐

Washington, D.C., Machine 12

Scott No.	Illus. No.	Description	Unused Value	Used Value	//////
26	CVP1 25c	1st Class	*150.00*		☐☐☐☐☐
27	CVP1 $1	3rd Class	—		☐☐☐☐☐
28	CVP2 $1.69	Parcel Post	—		☐☐☐☐☐
29	CVP1 $2.40	Priority Mail	—		☐☐☐☐☐
a.		Priority Mail ($2.74), with bar code (CVP2)	—		☐☐☐☐☐

Scott No.	Illus. No.	Description	Unused Value	Used Value	///////
30	CVP1	$8.75 Express Mail	—		☐☐☐☐☐

1992, Coil Stamp
| 31 | CVP3 | 29c red & blue........................ | 60 | — | ☐☐☐☐☐ |

1994, Coil Stamp
| 32 | CVP4 | 29c red & blue........................ | 60 | 25 | ☐☐☐☐☐ |

OC1 　　OC2

C1 　　C2 　　C3

C6 　　C7 　　C8 　　C10

C11 　　C13 　　C14 　　C15

C16 　　C17 　　C18

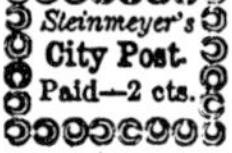

C19 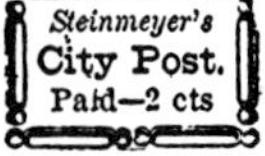　　C20

C20a

C20b

C20c

Scott No.	Illus. No.	Description	Unused Value	Used Value	//////
CARRIER'S STAMPS					
OFFICIAL ISSUES					
1851					
LO1	OC1	(1c) dull blue, *rose*	*2,750.*	*3,500.*	
LO2	OC2	1c blue	15.00	*30.00*	
1875 REPRINT, No gum					
LO3	OC1	(1c) blue, *rose,* imperf.	40.00		
SPECIAL PRINTING					
LO4	OC1	(1c) blue, perf. 12	*2,500.*		
REPRINT					
LO5	OC2	1c blue, imperf.	20.00		
SPECIAL PRINTING					
LO6	OC2	1c blue, perf. 12	175.00		
SEMI-OFFICIAL ISSUES					
1850-55					
1LB1	C1	1c red, *bluish*	100.00	150.00	
1LB2	C1	1c blue, *bluish*	125.00	90.00	
a.		Bluish laid paper	—	—	
1LB3	C1	1c blue	75.00	50.00	
a.		Laid paper	150.00	100.00	
1LB4	C1	1c green	—	600.00	
1LB5	C1	1c red	350.00	275.00	
1856					
1LB6	C2	1c blue	90.00	60.00	
1LB7	C2	1c red	90.00	60.00	
1857					
1LB8	C3	1c black	40.00	30.00	
a.		SENT	45.00	35.00	
b.		Short rays	45.00	35.00	
1LB9	C3	1c red	60.00	45.00	
a.		SENT	75.00	50.00	
b.		Short rays	75.00	50.00	
1849-50					
3LB1	C6	1c blue	150.00	75.00	
1851					
3LB2	C7	1c blue (shades), *slate*	125.00	65.00	
1849					
4LB1	C8	2c black, *brown rose*	*2,500.*	*2,500.*	
4LB2	C8	2c black, *yellow*		*2,500.*	

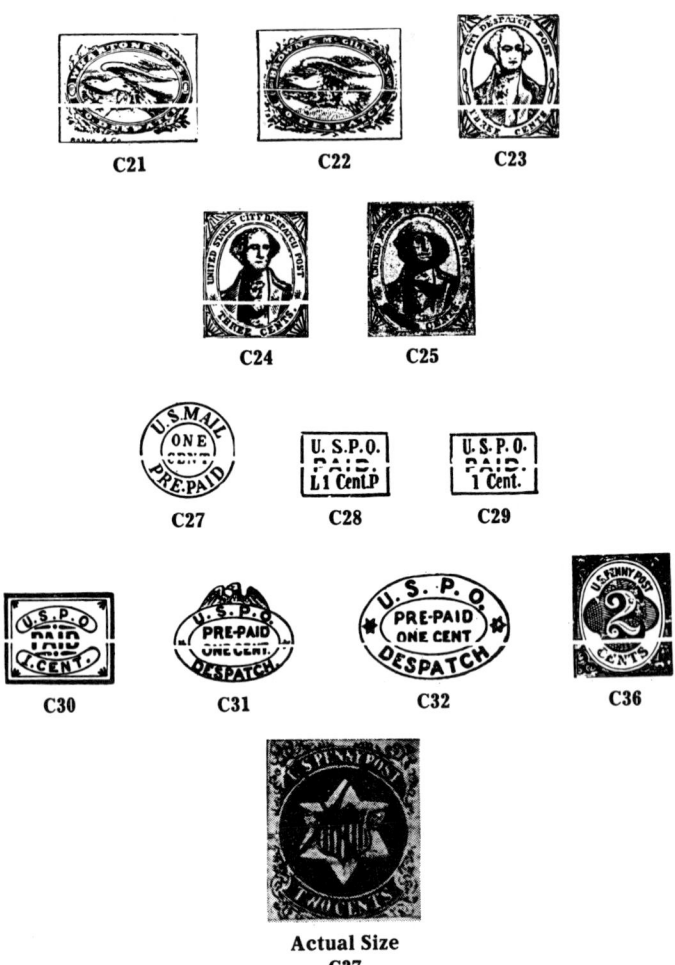

Actual Size
C37

HOW TO USE THIS BOOK
The number in the first column is its Scott number or identifying number. The letter and number that come next (A41) indicate the design and refer to the illustration so designated. Following that is the denomination of the stamp and its color. Finally, the value, unused and used is shown.

Scott No.	Illus. No.	Description	Unused Value	Used Value	/ / / / / /
1854					
4LB3	C10	2c black		1,000.	☐☐☐☐☐
1849-50					
4LB5	C11	2c black, *bluish*, pelure	400.00	300.00	☐☐☐☐☐
4LB7	C11	2c black, *yellow*	400.00	400.00	☐☐☐☐☐
1851-58					
4LB8	C13	2c black, *bluish*	175.00	100.00	☐☐☐☐☐
a.		Period after Paid	350.00	150.00	☐☐☐☐☐
b.		Cens		700.00	☐☐☐☐☐
c.		Conours and Bents		—	☐☐☐☐☐
4LB9	C13	2c black, *bluish*, pelure	375.00	425.00	☐☐☐☐☐
4LB11	C14	(2c) black, *bluish*	—	250.00	☐☐☐☐☐
4LB12	C14	(2c) black, *bluish*, pelure	—	250.00	☐☐☐☐☐
4LB13	C15	(2c) black, *bluish*	250.00	125.00	☐☐☐☐☐
a.		Comma after PAID	600.00		☐☐☐☐☐
b.		No period after Post	800.00		☐☐☐☐☐
1851(?)-58(?)					
4LB14	C16	2c black, *bluish*	400.00	450.00	☐☐☐☐☐
4LB15	C17	2c black, *bluish*	500.00	500.00	☐☐☐☐☐
1858					
4LB16	C18	2c black, *bluish*	2,000.		☐☐☐☐☐
1860					
4LB17	C19	2c black		—	☐☐☐☐☐
1859					
4LB18	C19	2c black, *bluish*	2,500.		☐☐☐☐☐
4LB19	C20	2c black, *bluish*	2,500.	—	☐☐☐☐☐
4LB20	C20	2c black, *pink*	150.00	—	☐☐☐☐☐
4LB21	C20	2c black, *yellow*	125.00		☐☐☐☐☐
1854					
9LB1	C20a	2c brown	1,500.	1,500.	☐☐☐☐☐
1854					
10LB1	C20b	blue	1,000.	1,000.	☐☐☐☐☐
10LB2	C20c	2c black, *bluish*	750.00	750.00	☐☐☐☐☐
1857					
5LB1	C21	(2c) bluish green	75.00		☐☐☐☐☐
1858					
5LB2	C22	(2c) blue (58)	150.00	150.00	☐☐☐☐☐
5LB3	C22	(2c) black	600.00	1,750.	☐☐☐☐☐

Scott No.	Illus. No.	Description	Unused Value	Used Value	/ / / / /
1842					
6LB1	C23	3c black, *grayish*		1,250.	
1842-45					
6LB2	C24	3c black, *rosy buff*	600.00		
6LB3	C24	3c black, *light blue*	400.00	400.00	
6LB4	C24	3c black, *green*	2,000.		
6LB5	C24	3c black, *blue green (shades)*	125.00	100.00	
a.		Double impression		500.00	
b.		3c black, *blue*	400.00	125.00	
c.		As "b," double impression		750.00	
d.		3c black, *green*	650.00	600.00	
e.		As "d," double impression	—		
1846					
6LB7	C25	2c on 3c, on cover		—	
1849					
6LB9	C27	1c black, *rose*	60.00	50.00	
1849-50					
6LB10	C27	1c black, *yellow*	60.00	60.00	
6LB11	C27	1c black, *buff*	60.00	50.00	
a.		Pair, one stamp sideways	1,000.		
1849-50					
7LB1	C28	1c black, *rose* (with letters L.P.)	175.00		
7LB2	C28	1c black, *rose* (with letter S)	500.00		
7LB3	C28	1c black, *rose* (with letter H)	175.00		
7LB4	C28	1c black, *rose* (with letters L.S.)	175.00		
7LB5	C28	1c black, *rose* (with letters J.J.)	2,000.		
7LB6	C29	1c black, *rose*	150.00	125.00	
7LB7	C29	1c black, *blue*, glazed	600.00		
7LB8	C29	1c black, *vermilion*, glazed	500.00		
7LB9	C29	1c black, *yellow*, glazed	2,000.		
1850-52					
7LB11	C30	1c gold, *black*, glazed	100.00	75.00	
7LB12	C30	1c blue	200.00	150.00	
7LB13	C30	1c black	—	500.00	
7LB14	C31	1c blue, *buff*	3,500.		
1855(?)					
7LB16	C31	1c black		1,650.	
1856(?)					
7LB18	C32	1c black	900.00	1,400.	

Scott No.	Illus. No.	Description	Unused Value	Used Value	//////
1849					
8LB1	C36	2c black	4,000.	5,000.	☐☐☐☐☐
1857					
8LB2	C37	2c blue		5,000.	☐☐☐☐☐

HP1

HP2

HP3

HP4

HP5

HP6

HP7

HP8

HP9

HP10

Scott No.	Illus. No.	Description	Unused Value	Used Value	/ / / / / /
HUNTING PERMIT STAMPS					
1934					
RW1	HP1	$1 blue..................................	450.00	85.00	☐☐☐☐☐
a.		Imperf., pair....................	—		☐☐☐☐☐
b.		Vert. pair, imperf. horiz..	—		☐☐☐☐☐
1935					
RW2		$1 *Canvasback Ducks Taking to Flight*..............	400.00	100.00	☐☐☐☐☐
1936					
RW3		$1 *Canada Geese in Flight*..	210.00	50.00	☐☐☐☐☐
1937					
RW4		$1 *Scaup Ducks Taking to Flight*	170.00	35.00	☐☐☐☐☐
1938					
RW5		$1 *Pintail Drake and Duck Alighting*	175.00	35.00	☐☐☐☐☐
1939					
RW6	HP2	$1 chocolate	125.00	15.00	☐☐☐☐☐
1940					
RW7		$1 *Black Mallards*................	125.00	15.00	☐☐☐☐☐
1941					
RW8		$1 *Family of Ruddy Ducks*...	115.00	15.00	☐☐☐☐☐
1942					
RW9		$1 *Baldpates*.........................	115.00	15.00	☐☐☐☐☐
1943					
RW10		$1 *Wood Ducks*	50.00	15.00	☐☐☐☐☐
1944					
RW11		$1 *White-fronted Geese*	40.00	15.00	☐☐☐☐☐
1945					
RW12		$1 *Shoveller Ducks in Flight*	40.00	10.00	☐☐☐☐☐
1946					
RW13		$1 *Redhead Ducks*................	35.00	9.00	☐☐☐☐☐
a.		$1 bright rose pink	—		☐☐☐☐☐
1947					
RW14		$1 *Snow Geese*	35.00	9.00	☐☐☐☐☐

Scott No.	Illus. No.	Description	Unused Value	Used Value	//////
1948					
RW15		$1 *Bufflehead Ducks in Flight*	30.00	9.00	☐☐☐☐☐
1949					
RW16	HP3	$2 bright green	40.00	7.00	☐☐☐☐☐
1950					
RW17		$2 *Trumpeter Swans in Flight*	45.00	7.00	☐☐☐☐☐
1951					
RW18		$2 *Gadwall Ducks*...............	45.00	5.00	☐☐☐☐☐
1952					
RW19		$2 *Harlequin Ducks*.............	45.00	5.00	☐☐☐☐☐
1953					
RW20		$2 *Blue-winged Teal*............	50.00	5.00	☐☐☐☐☐
1954					
RW21		$2 *Ring-necked Ducks*.........	45.00	5.00	☐☐☐☐☐
1955					
RW22		$2 *Blue Geese*......................	45.00	5.00	☐☐☐☐☐
1956					
RW23		$2 *American Merganser*......	45.00	5.00	☐☐☐☐☐
1957					
RW24		$2 *American Eider*...............	45.00	5.00	☐☐☐☐☐
1958					
RW25		$2 *Canada Geese*.................	45.00	5.00	☐☐☐☐☐
1959					
RW26	HP4	$3 blue, ocher & black.........	60.00	5.00	☐☐☐☐☐
1960					
RW27	HP5	$3 red brown, dark blue & bister	60.00	5.00	☐☐☐☐☐
1961					
RW28		$3 *Mallard Hen and Ducklings*	65.00	5.00	☐☐☐☐☐
1962					
RW29	HP6	$3 dk bl, dk red brn & black	70.00	6.00	☐☐☐☐☐
1963					
RW30		$3 *Pair of Brant landing*......	70.00	6.00	☐☐☐☐☐

Scott No.	Illus. No.	Description	Unused Value	Used Value	/ / / / /
1964 RW31		$3 *Hawaiian Nene Geese*.....	70.00	6.00	☐☐☐☐☐
1965 RW32		$3 *3 Canvasback Drakes*	65.00	6.00	☐☐☐☐☐
1966 RW33	HP7	$3 ultra, slate grn & blk	65.00	5.00	☐☐☐☐☐
1967 RW34		$3 *Old Squaw Ducks*............	65.00	5.00	☐☐☐☐☐
1968 RW35		$3 *Hooded Mergansers*........	50.00	5.00	☐☐☐☐☐
1969 RW36	HP8	$3 gray, brn, indigo & brn red	50.00	5.00	☐☐☐☐☐
1970 RW37		$3 *Ross Geese*	47.50	5.00	☐☐☐☐☐
1971 RW38		$3 *3 Cinnamon Teal*............	27.50	5.00	☐☐☐☐☐
1972 RW39		$5 *Emperor Geese*................	20.00	5.00	☐☐☐☐☐
1973 RW40		$5 *Stellers Eiders*	17.00	5.00	☐☐☐☐☐
1974 RW41		$5 *Wood Ducks*	15.00	5.00	☐☐☐☐☐
1975 RW42		$5 *Weathered canvasback duck decoy and flying ducks*	10.00	5.00	☐☐☐☐☐
1976 RW43		$5 *Family of Canada Geese*	10.00	5.00	☐☐☐☐☐
1977 RW44		$5 *Ross Geese, pair*..............	12.00	5.00	☐☐☐☐☐
1978 RW45	HP9	$5 multicolored	10.00	5.00	☐☐☐☐☐
1979 RW46		$7.50 *Green-winged teal*...........	12.00	5.00	☐☐☐☐☐

Scott No.	Illus. No.		Description	Unused Value	Used Value	/ / / / / /
1980						
RW47		$7.50	*Mallards*	12.00	5.00	☐☐☐☐☐
1981						
RW48		$7.50	*Ruddy Ducks*	12.00	5.00	☐☐☐☐☐
1982						
RW49		$7.50	*Canvasbacks*	11.00	5.00	☐☐☐☐☐
1983						
RW50		$7.50	*Pintails*	11.00	5.00	☐☐☐☐☐
1984						
RW51		$7.50	*Widgeon*............................	11.00	5.00	☐☐☐☐☐
1985						
RW52		$7.50	*Cinnamon Teal*.................	11.00	5.00	☐☐☐☐☐
1986						
RW53		$7.50	*Fulvous Whistling Duck*..	11.00	5.00	☐☐☐☐☐
a.			Black omitted	3,250.		☐☐☐☐☐
1987						
RW54		$10	*Redheads*	14.00	5.00	☐☐☐☐☐
1988						
RW55		$10	*Snow Goose*......................	14.00	5.00	☐☐☐☐☐
1989						
RW56		$12.50	*Lesser Scaups*...................	17.50	5.00	☐☐☐☐☐
1990						
RW57		$12.50	*Black Bellied Whistling Duck*	17.50	6.00	☐☐☐☐☐
a.			Back printing omitted	850.00		☐☐☐☐☐
1991						
RW58	HP10	$15	multicolored	20.00	6.00	☐☐☐☐☐
a.			Black (engr.) omitted	—		☐☐☐☐☐
1992						
RW59		$15	*Spectacled Eider*	20.00	6.00	☐☐☐☐☐
1993						
RW60		$15	*Canvasbacks*	20.00	5.00	☐☐☐☐☐
a.			Black (engr.) omitted	—		☐☐☐☐☐
1994						
RW61		$15	*Red-breasted Mergansers*	20.00	4.00	☐☐☐☐☐

Scott No.	Illus. No.	Description	Unused Value	Used Value	/ / / / / /

A5

A6

A7

A8

A9

A10

A11

A12

A13

A14

Scott No.	Illus. No.	Description	Unused Value	Used Value	//////
MARSHALL ISLANDS					
1984					
31	A5	20c Outrigger canoe................	50	50	
32	A5	20c Fishnet...........................	50	50	
33	A5	20c Navigational stick chart ..	50	50	
34	A5	20c Islet.................................	50	50	
a.		Block of 4, #31-34	2.00	2.00	
1984-85					
35	A6	1c shown	15	15	
36	A6	3c Likiep, Azimuth compass	15	15	
37	A6	5c Ebon, 16th cent. compass	15	15	
38	A6	10c Jaluit, anchor buoys	20	20	
39	A6	13c Ailinginae, Nocturnal......	26	26	
a.		Booklet pane of 10...........	7.00	—	
40	A6	14c Wotho Atoll, navigational stick chart	28	28	
a.		Booklet pane of 10...........	7.00	—	
41	A6	20c Kwajalein and Ebeye, stick chart	40	40	
a.		Booklet pane of 10...........	9.00	—	
b.		Booklet pane, 5 each 13c, 20c	8.00	—	
42	A6	22c Eniwetok, 18th cent. lodestone storage case.....	44	44	
a.		Booklet pane of 10...........	9.00	—	
b.		Booklet pane, 5 each 14c, 22c	8.00	—	
43	A6	28c Ailinglaplap, printed compass	56	56	
44	A6	30c Majuro, navigational stick-chart	60	60	
45	A6	33c Namu, stick chart	66	66	
46	A6	37c Rongelap, quadrant	74	74	
47	A6	39c Taka, map compass, 16th cent. sea chart..........	78	78	
48	A6	44c Ujelang, chronograph......	88	88	
49	A6	50c Maloelap and Aur, nocturlabe	1.00	1.00	
49A	A6	$1 Arno, 16th cent. sector compass	2.00	2.00	
1984					
50	A7	40c shown	75	75	
51	A7	40c No. 13.............................	75	75	
52	A7	40c No. 4...............................	75	75	
53	A7	40c No. 25.............................	75	75	
a.		Block of 4, #50-53	3.00	3.00	
54	A8	20c Common.........................	45	45	
55	A8	20c Rissos.............................	45	45	
56	A8	20c Spotter............................	45	45	
57	A8	20c Bottlenose.......................	45	45	
a.		Block of 4, #54-57	1.80	1.80	
58		Strip of 4........................	2.00	2.00	
a.-d.	A9	20c any single	45	45	
e.		Sheet of 16.....................	9.00		

307

start your
U.S. Collection
with Scott Minuteman

Scott's U.S. Minuteman stamp album features:

- The famous Scott Catalogue identification number for every stamp.
- Exciting stories of almost every stamp.
- Attractive vinyl binder.
- Supplemented annually.

" A must for every collector of U.S. postage stamps. "

Available at your local dealer or direct from:

SCOTT Scott Publishing Co.
P.O. Box 828, Sidney, OH 45365

Scott No.	Illus. No.	Description	Unused Value	Used Value	//////
59	A10	20c Traditional chief............	45	45	
60	A10	20c Amata Kabua	45	45	
61	A10	20c Chester Nimitz	45	45	
62	A10	20c Trygve Lie.....................	45	45	
a.		Block of 4, #59-62	1.80	1.80	

1985

Scott No.	Illus. No.	Description	Unused Value	Used Value	//////
63	A11	22c Forked-tailed Petrel........	60	60	
64	A11	22c Pectoral Sandpiper	60	60	
a.		Pair, #63-64	1.20	1.20	
65	A12	22c Cymatium lotorium.........	50	50	
66	A12	22c Chicoreus cornucervi	50	50	
67	A12	22c Strombus aurisdanae	50	50	
68	A12	22c Turbo marmoratus..........	50	50	
69	A12	22c Chicoreus palmarosae	50	50	
a.		Strip of 5, #65-69	2.50	2.50	
70	A13	22c Native drum....................	50	50	
71	A13	22c Palm branches	50	50	
72	A13	22c Pounding stone...............	50	50	
73	A13	22c Ak bird	50	50	
a.		Block of 4, #70-73	2.00	2.00	
74	A14	22c Acanthurus dussumieri ...	50	50	
75	A14	22c Adioryx caudimaculatus .	50	50	
76	A14	22c Ostracion meleacaris.......	50	50	
77	A14	22c Chaetodon ephippium.....	50	50	
a.		Block of 4, #74-77	2.00	2.00	
78	A15	22c multicolored	50	50	
79	A15	22c multicolored	50	50	
80	A15	22c multicolored	50	50	
81	A15	22c multicolored	50	50	
a.		Block of 4, #78-81	2.00	2.00	
82	A16	14c multicolored	25	25	
83	A16	22c multicolored	45	45	
84	A16	33c multicolored	65	65	
85	A16	44c multicolored	90	90	
86	A17	22c multicolored	1.10	1.10	
87	A17	22c multicolored	1.10	1.10	
88	A17	22c multicolored	1.10	1.10	
89	A17	22c multicolored	1.10	1.10	
90	A17	22c multicolored	1.10	1.10	
a.		Strip of 5, #86-90	5.50	5.50	
91	A18	22c Sida fallax.......................	50	50	
92	A18	22c Scaevola frutescens.........	50	50	
93	A18	22c Guettarda speciosa	50	50	
94	A18	22c Cassytha filiformis	50	50	
a.		Block of 4, #91-94	2.00	2.00	

A15

A16

A17

A18

A19

A20

A21

A22

Scott No.	Illus. No.		Description	Unused Value	Used Value	//////
1986-87						
107	A6	$2	Wotje and Erikub, terrestrial globe, 1571	4.00	4.00	
108	A6	$5	Bikini, Stick chart	10.00	10.00	
109	A6	$10	Stick chart of the atolls	16.00	16.00	
1986						
110	A19	14c	Tritons trumpet	35	35	
111	A19	14c	Giant clam	35	35	
112	A19	14c	Small giant clam	35	35	
113	A19	14c	Coconut crab	35	35	
a.			Block of 4, #110-113	1.40	1.40	
114	A20	$1	Douglas C-54 Globester, souvenir sheet	3.25	3.25	
115	A21	22c	multicolored	50	50	
116	A21	22c	multicolored	50	50	
117	A21	22c	multicolored	50	50	
118	A21	22c	multicolored	50	50	
a.			Block of 4, #115-118	2.00	2.00	
119	A12	22c	Ramose murex	50	50	
120	A12	22c	Orange spider	50	50	
121	A12	22c	Red-mouth frog shell	50	50	
122	A12	22c	Laciniate conch	50	50	
123	A12	22c	Giant frog shell	50	50	
a.			Strip of 5, #119-123	2.50	2.50	
124	A22	22c	Blue marlin	50	50	
125	A22	22c	Wahoo	50	50	
126	A22	22c	Dolphin fish	50	50	
127	A22	22c	Yellowfin tuna	50	50	
a.			Block of 4, #124-127	2.00	2.00	
128	A23	22c	United Nations UR	70	70	
129	A23	22c	United Nations UL	70	70	
130	A23	22c	United Nations LR	70	70	
131	A23	22c	United Nations LL	70	70	
a.			Block of 4, #128-131	2.80	2.80	
1987						
132	A24	22c	James Arnold, 1854	50	50	
133	A24	22c	General Scott, 1859	50	50	
134	A24	22c	Charles W. Morgan, 1865	50	50	
135	A24	22c	Lucretia, 1884	50	50	
a.			Block of 4, #132-135	2.00	2.00	
136	A25	33c	multicolored	70	70	
137	A25	33c	multicolored	70	70	
a.			Pair, #136-137	1.40	1.40	
138	A25	39c	multicolored	75	75	
139	A25	39c	multicolored	75	75	
a.			Pair, #138-139	1.50	1.50	

A24

A23

A25

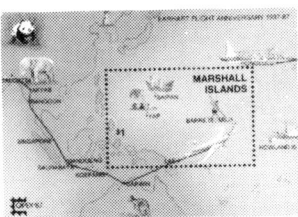
A26

A27

A28

A29

A30

A31

Scott No.	Illus. No.		Description	Unused Value	Used Value	/ / / / / /
140	A25	44c	multicolored....................	80	80	
141	A25	44c	multicolored....................	80	80	
a.			Pair, #140-141...............	1.60	1.60	
142	A26	$1	Map of flight, souvenir sheet	2.75	2.75	
143	A27	14c	We,... Marshall...............	35	35	
144	A27	14c	National seals.................	35	35	
145	A27	14c	We,... United States.........	35	35	
a.			Strip of 3, #143-145........	1.05	1.05	
146	A27	22c	All we have....................	45	45	
147	A27	22c	Flags..............................	45	45	
148	A27	22c	to establish.....................	45	45	
a.			Strip of 3, #146-148........	1.35	1.35	
149	A27	44c	With this Constitution.....	90	90	
150	A27	44c	Stick chart, Liberty Bell..	90	90	
151	A27	44c	to promote...	90	90	
a.			Strip of 3, #149-151........	2.70	2.70	
152	A12	22c	Magnificent cone............	50	50	
153	A12	22c	Partridge tun...................	50	50	
154	A12	22c	Scorpion spider conch.....	50	50	
155	A12	22c	Hairy triton.....................	50	50	
156	A12	22c	Chiragra spider conch.....	50	50	
a.			Strip of 5, #152-156........	2.50	2.50	
157	A28	44c	Planting coconut.............	75	75	
158	A28	44c	Making copra	75	75	
159	A28	44c	Bottling coconut oil........	75	75	
a.			Strip of 3, #157-159........	2.25	2.25	
160	A29	14c	Matthew 2:1....................	30	30	
161	A29	22c	Luke 2:14	45	45	
162	A29	33c	Psalms 33:3	70	70	
163	A29	44c	Pslams 150:5...................	90	90	

1988

164	A30	44c	Pacific reef herons...........	85	85	
165	A30	44c	Bar-tailed godwit	85	85	
166	A30	44c	Masked booby................	85	85	
167	A30	44c	Northern shoveler............	85	85	

1988-89

168	A31	1c	Damselfish......................	15	15	
169	A31	3c	Blackface butterflyfish	15	15	
170	A31	14c	Hawkfish	25	25	
a.			Booklet pane of 10..........	3.00	—	
171	A31	15c	Balloonfish	25	25	
a.			Booklet pane of 10..........	2.50	—	
172	A31	17c	Trunk fish	30	30	
173	A31	22c	Lyretail wrasse	35	35	
a.			Booklet pane of 10..........	4.00	—	
b.			Bklt. pane, 5 each 14c, 22c	4.00	—	

| A32 | A33 |

A34

A35

A36

A37

A38

A39

A42

Scott No.	Illus. No.		Description	Unused Value	Used Value	//////
174	A31	25c	Parrotfish	40	40	
a.			Booklet pane of 10	4.00	—	
b.			Bklt. pane, 5 each 15c, 25c	4.00	—	
175	A31	33c	White-spotted boxfish	60	60	
176	A31	36c	Spotted boxfish	65	65	
177	A31	39c	Surgeonfish	70	70	
178	A31	44c	Long-snouted butterflyfish	75	75	
179	A31	45c	Trumpetfish	70	70	
180	A31	56c	Sharp-nosed puffer	1.00	1.00	
181	A31	$1	Seahorse	1.75	1.75	
182	A31	$2	Ghost pipefish	3.50	3.50	
183	A31	$5	Big-spotted triggerfish	8.75	8.75	
184	A31	$10	Blue jack (89)	15.00	15.00	

1988

Scott No.	Illus. No.		Description	Unused Value	Used Value	//////
188			Strip of 5	1.75	1.75	
a.-e.	A32	15c	any single	30	30	
189			Strip of 5	2.25	2.25	
a.-e.	A33	25c	any single	45	45	
190			Sheet of 9	5.75	5.75	
a.-i.	A34	25c	any single	50	50	
191	A35	25c	multicolored	55	55	
192	A35	25c	multicolored	55	55	
193	A35	25c	multicolored	55	55	
194	A35	25c	multicolored	55	55	
a.			Block of 4, #191-194	2.20	2.20	
195	A36	25c	multicolored	50	50	
196	A36	25c	multicolored	50	50	
197	A36	25c	multicolored	50	50	
198	A36	25c	multicolored	50	50	
199	A36	25c	multicolored	50	50	
a.			Strip of 5, #195-199	2.50	2.50	
200	A37	25c	Nuclear threat diminished	60	60	
201	A37	25c	Signing the Test Ban Treaty	60	60	
202	A37	25c	Portrait	60	60	
203	A37	25c	US-USSR Hotline	60	60	
204	A37	25c	Peace Corps enactment	60	60	
a.			Strip of 5, #200-204	3.00	3.00	
205	A38	25c	multicolored	55	55	
206	A38	25c	multicolored	55	55	
207	A38	25c	multicolored	55	55	
208	A38	25c	multicolored	55	55	
a.			Strip of 4, #205-208	2.20	2.20	

1989

Scott No.	Illus. No.		Description	Unused Value	Used Value	//////
209	A39	45c	multicolored	85	85	
210	A39	45c	multicolored	85	85	
211	A39	45c	multicolored	85	85	

Scott No.	Illus. No.		Description	Unused Value	Used Value	/ / / / / /
212	A39	45c	multicolored	85	85	
a.			Block of 4, #209-212	3.40	3.40	
213	A40	45c	Island Woman	85	85	
214	A40	45c	Kotzebue, Alaska	85	85	
215	A40	45c	Marshallese Madonna	85	85	
a.			Strip of 3, #213-215	2.55	2.55	
216	A12	25c	Pontifical miter.................	55	55	
217	A12	25c	Tapestry turban	55	55	
218	A12	25c	Flame-mouthed helmet ...	55	55	
219	A12	25c	Prickly Pacific drupe........	55	55	
220	A12	25c	Blood-mouthed conch.....	55	55	
a.			Strip of 5, #216-220	2.75	2.75	
221	A41	$1	multicolored, souvenir sheet	2.00	2.00	
222	A42	45c	Wandering tattler	85	85	
223	A42	45c	Ruddy turnstone...............	85	85	
224	A42	45c	Pacific golden plover	85	85	
225	A42	45c	Sanderling	85	85	
a.			Block of 4, #222-225	3.40	3.40	
226	A43	45c	multicolored	85	85	
227	A43	45c	multicolored	85	85	
228	A43	45c	multicolored	85	85	
229	A43	45c	multicolored	85	85	
a.			Block of 4, #226-229	3.40	3.40	
230			Sheet of 6........................	10.00	3.00	
a.-f.	A44	25c	any single	1.25	1.25	
231	A43	$1	multicolored, souvenir sheet	10.00	3.00	
232	A45	25c	multicolored	1.25	1.25	
233	A45	25c	multicolored	1.25	1.25	
234	A45	25c	multicolored	1.25	1.25	
235	A45	25c	multicolored	1.25	1.25	
236	A45	25c	multicolored	1.25	1.25	
237	A45	25c	multicolored	1.25	1.25	
238	A45	$1	multicolored	5.00	5.00	
a.			Booklet pane of 7, #232-238	13.00	—	
239	A46	25c	W1 (1-1)...........................	45	45	
240	A46	45c	W2 (1-1)...........................	75	75	
241	A46	45c	W3 (1-1)...........................	75	75	
242	A46	45c	W4 (4-1)...........................	75	75	
243	A46	45c	W4 (4-2)...........................	75	75	
244	A46	45c	W4 (4-3)...........................	75	75	
245	A46	45c	W4 (4-4)...........................	75	75	
a.			Block of 4, #242-245	3.00	3.00	

1990

246	A46	25c	W5 (2-1)...........................	50	50	
247	A46	25c	W5 (2-2)...........................	50	50	
a.			Pair, #246-247.................	1.00	1.00	
248	A47	25c	W6 (1-1)...........................	50	50	

Scott No.	Illus. No.		Description	Unused Value	Used Value	/ / / / / /
249	A46	25c	W8 (2-1)........................	50	50	
250	A46	25c	W8 (2-2)........................	50	50	
a.			Pair, #249-250...............	1.00	1.00	
251	A46	45c	W7 (1-1)........................	90	90	
252	A46	45c	W9 (2-1)........................	90	90	
253	A46	45c	W9 (2-2)........................	90	90	
254	A47	45c	W10 (1-1)......................	90	90	
255	A46	25c	W11 (1-1)......................	50	50	
256	A47	25c	W12 (1-1)......................	50	50	
257	A46	45c	W13 (4-1)......................	90	90	
258	A46	45c	W13 (4-2)......................	90	90	
259	A46	45c	W13 (4-3)......................	90	90	
260	A46	45c	W13 (4-4)......................	90	90	
a.			Block of 4, #257-260	3.60	3.60	
261	A46	45c	W14 (4-1)......................	90	90	
262	A46	45c	W14 (4-2)......................	90	90	
263	A46	45c	W14 (4-3)......................	90	90	
264	A46	45c	W14 (4-4)......................	90	90	
a.			Block of 4, #261-264	3.60	3.60	
265	A46	45c	W15	90	90	
266	A47	25c	W16	50	50	
267	A46	25c	W17 (4-1)......................	50	50	
268	A46	25c	W17 (4-2)......................	50	50	
269	A46	25c	W17 (4-3)......................	50	50	
270	A46	25c	W17 (4-4)......................	50	50	
a.			Block of 4, #266-270	2.00	2.00	

1991

Scott No.	Illus. No.		Description	Unused Value	Used Value	
271	A46	30c	W18 (4-1)......................	60	60	
272	A46	30c	W18 (4-2)......................	60	60	
273	A46	30c	W18 (4-3)......................	60	60	
274	A46	30c	W18 (4-4)......................	60	60	
a.			Block of 4, #271-274	2.40	2.40	
275	A46	30c	Tanks, W19	60	60	
276	A47	29c	W20 (2-1)......................	58	58	
277	A47	29c	W20 (2-2)......................	58	58	
a.			Pair, #276-277...............	1.16	1.16	
278	A46	50c	W21 (4-1)......................	1.00	1.00	
279	A46	50c	W21 (4-2)......................	1.00	1.00	
280	A46	50c	W21 (4-3)......................	1.00	1.00	
281	A46	50c	W21 (4-4)......................	1.00	1.00	
a.			Block of 4, #278-281	4.00	4.00	
282	A46	30c	Tanks, W22	60	60	
283	A47	29c	W23 (2-1)......................	58	58	
284	A47	29c	W23 (2-2)......................	58	58	
a.			Pair, #283-284...............	1.16	1.16	
285	A46	29c	W24	58	58	
286	A46	30c	W25 (2-1)......................	60	60	

A40

A41

A43

A44

A45

A46

A47

A57

A58

Scott No.	Illus. No.		Description	Unused Value	Used Value	/ / / / / /
287	A46	30c	W25 (2-1)	60	60	
a.			Pair, #286-287	1.20	1.20	
288	A47	50c	W26 (4-1)	1.00	1.00	
289	A47	50c	W26 (4-2)	1.00	1.00	
290	A47	50c	W26 (4-3)	1.00	1.00	
291	A47	50c	W26 (4-4)	1.00	1.00	
a.			Block of 4, #288-291	4.00	4.00	
292	A47	29c	W27	58	58	
293	A46	29c	W28	58	58	
294	A46	50c	W29 (2-1)	1.00	1.00	
295	A46	50c	W29 (2-2)	1.00	1.00	
a.			Pair, #294-295	2.00	2.00	
296	A46	29c	W30	58	58	

1992

Scott No.	Illus. No.		Description	Unused Value	Used Value	
297	A46	29c	W31	58	58	
298	A46	50c	W32	1.00	1.00	
299	A46	29c	W33	58	58	
300	A46	29c	W34	58	58	
301	A47	50c	W35	1.00	1.00	
302	A46	29c	W36	58	58	
303	A46	29c	W37	58	58	
304	A46	29c	W38	58	58	
305	A47	29c	W39	58	58	
306	A47	50c	W40	1.00	1.00	
307	A46	29c	W41	58	58	
308	A46	50c	W42 (4-1)	1.00	1.00	
309	A46	50c	W42 (4-2)	1.00	1.00	
310	A46	50c	W42 (4-3)	1.00	1.00	
311	A46	50c	W42 (4-4)	1.00	1.00	
a.			Block of 4, #308-311	4.00	4.00	
312	A46	50c	W43 (4-1)	1.00	1.00	
313	A46	50c	W43 (4-3)	1.00	1.00	
314	A46	50c	W43 (4-2)	1.00	1.00	
315	A46	50c	W43 (4-4)	1.00	1.00	
a.			Block of 4, #312-315	4.00	4.00	
316	A46	29c	W44	58	58	
317	A47	29c	W45	58	58	
318	A46	29c	W46 (2-1)	58	58	
319	A46	29c	W46 (2-2)	58	58	
a.			Pair, #318-319	1.16	1.16	
320	A46	29c	W47	58	58	
321	A47	29c	W48	58	58	
322	A46	29c	W49	58	58	
323	A47	50c	W50	1.00	1.00	
324	A46	29c	W51	58	58	
325	A46	50c	W52	1.00	1.00	
326	A46	29c	W53	58	58	

A59a

A59

A60

A61 A62

A63

A64

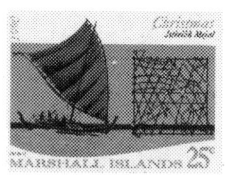
A65

A66

A67

A77

Scott No.	Illus. No.		Description	Unused Value	Used Value	//////
327	A46	29c	W54 (2-1)	58	58	
328	A46	29c	W54 (2-2)	58	58	
a.			Pair, #327-328	1.16	1.16	

1993

329	A46	29c	W55	58	58	
330	A46	29c	W56	58	58	
331	A46	50c	W57 (4-1)	1.00	1.00	
332	A46	50c	W57 (4-2)	1.00	1.00	
333	A46	50c	W57 (4-3)	1.00	1.00	
334	A46	50c	W57 (4-4)	1.00	1.00	
a.			Block of 4, #331-334	4.00	4.00	
335	A46	50c	W58	1.00	1.00	
336	A46	29c	W59 (2-1)	58	58	
337	A46	29c	W59 (2-2)	58	58	
a.			Pair, #336-337	1.16	1.16	

1989

341	A57	25c	Horn	75	75	
342	A57	25c	Singing carol	75	75	
343	A57	25c	Lute	75	75	
344	A57	25c	Lyre	75	75	
a.			Block of 4, #341-344	3.00	3.00	
345			Sheet of 25	30.00	30.00	
a.-y.	A58	45c	any single	1.00	1.00	

1990-92

346	A59	1c	Black noddy	15	15	
347	A59	5c	Red-tailed tropic bird	15	15	
348	A59	10c	Sanderling	20	20	
349	A59	12c	Black-naped tern	24	24	
350	A59	15c	Wandering tattler	30	30	
351	A59	20c	Bristle-thighed curlew	40	40	
352	A59	23c	Northern shoveler	46	46	
353	A59	25c	Brown noddy	50	50	
354	A59	27c	Sooty tern	54	54	
355	A59	29c	Wedge-tailed shearwater	58	58	
356	A59a	29c	Northern pintail	58	58	
357	A59	30c	Pacific golden plover	60	60	
358	A59	35c	Brown booby	70	70	
359	A59	36c	Red footed booby	72	72	
360	A59	40c	White tern	80	80	
361	A59	50c	Great frigate bird	1.00	1.00	
a.			Min. sheet of 4, #347, 350, 353, 361	1.90	1.90	
362	A59	52c	Great crested tern	1.04	1.04	
363	A59	65c	Lesser sand plover	1.30	1.30	
364	A59	75c	Little tern	1.50	1.50	

A68

A69

A70

A71

A72

A73

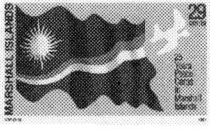
A74

A75

A76

A78

Scott No.	Illus. No.		Description	Unused Value	Used Value	//////
365	A59	$1	Pacific reef heron	2.00	2.00	
365A	A59	$2	Masked booby	4.00	4.00	

1990

Scott No.	Illus. No.		Description	Unused Value	Used Value	//////
366	A60	25c	Lodidean	75	75	
367	A60	25c	Lejonjon	75	75	
368	A60	25c	Etobobo	75	75	
369	A60	25c	Didmakol	75	75	
a.			Block of 4, #366-369	3.00	3.00	
370	A61	25c	multicolored	75	75	
371	A61	25c	multicolored	75	75	
372	A61	25c	multicolored	75	75	
373	A61	25c	multicolored	75	75	
374	A61	25c	multicolored	75	75	
375	A61	25c	multicolored	75	75	
376	A61	$1	multicolored	3.50	3.50	
a.			Booklet pane of 7, #370-376	8.00	—	
377	A62	25c	multicolored	75	75	
378	A62	25c	multicolored	75	75	
379	A62	25c	multicolored	75	75	
380	A62	25c	multicolored	75	75	
a.			Block of 4, #377-380	3.00	3.00	
381	A63	25c	multicolored	60	60	
382	A64	45c	multicolored	1.25	1.25	
383	A65	25c	Canoe, stick chart	75	75	
384	A65	25c	Missionary preaching	75	75	
385	A65	25c	Sailors dancing	75	75	
386	A65	25c	Youths dancing	75	75	
a.			Block of 4, #383-386	3.00	3.00	
387	A66	25c	Harvesting	75	75	
388	A66	25c	Peeling, slicing	75	75	
389	A66	25c	Preserving	75	75	
390	A66	25c	Kneading dough	75	75	
a.			Block of 4, #387-390	3.00	3.00	

1991

Scott No.	Illus. No.		Description	Unused Value	Used Value	//////
391	A67	50c	747 ferry	1.00	1.00	
392	A67	50c	Orbital release of LDEF	1.00	1.00	
393	A67	50c	Lift-off	1.00	1.00	
394	A67	50c	Landing	1.00	1.00	
a.			Block of 4, #391-394	4.00	4.00	
395	A68	52c	Ixora carolinensis	1.00	1.00	
396	A68	52c	Clerodendrum inerme	1.00	1.00	
397	A68	52c	Messerchmidia argentea	1.00	1.00	
398	A68	52c	Vigna marina	1.00	1.00	
a.			Miniature sheet of 4, #395-398	4.00	4.00	
399	A69	29c	multicolored	58	58	
400	A70	29c	Red-footed booby	58	58	

A79

A80

A81

A82

A83

A84

A85

Scott No.	Illus. No.	Description	Unused Value	Used Value	//////
401	A70	29c Great frigate bird (7-2)....	58	58	
402	A70	29c Brown booby.................	58	58	
403	A70	29c White tern......................	58	58	
404	A70	29c Great frigate bird (7-5)....	58	58	
405	A70	29c Black noddy	58	58	
406	A70	$1 White-tailed tropic bird...	2.00	2.00	
a.		Booklet pane of 7, #400-406	5.50	—	
407	A71	12c Dornier 228	20	20	
408	A71	29c Douglas DC-8	50	50	
409	A71	50c Hawker Siddeley 748......	85	85	
410	A71	50c Saab 2000	85	85	
411	A72	29c multicolored	65	65	
412	A73	30c multicolored	75	75	
413	A74	29c multicolored	58	58	

1992

Scott No.	Illus. No.	Description	Unused Value	Used Value	//////
414	A75	29c multicolored	45	45	
415	A75	29c multicolored	45	45	
416	A75	29c multicolored	45	45	
417	A75	29c multicolored	45	45	
a.		Strip of 4, #414-417	2.00	2.00	
418	A76	50c multicolored	1.00	1.00	
419	A76	50c multicolored	1.00	1.00	
420	A76	50c multicolored	1.00	1.00	
421	A76	50c multicolored	1.00	1.00	
422	A76	50c multicolored	1.00	1.00	
423	A76	50c multicolored	1.00	1.00	
424	A76	$1 multicolored	2.00	2.00	
a.		Booklet pane of 7, #418-424	8.00	—	
425	A77	29c Basket weaving	58	58	
426	A77	29c Canoe models.................	58	58	
427	A77	29c Wood carving.................	58	58	
428	A77	29c Fan making.....................	58	58	
a.		Strip of 4, #425-428	2.32	2.32	
429	A78	29c multicolored	58	58	
430	A59	9c Whimbrel	18	18	
431	A59	22c Greater scaup..................	44	44	
432	A59	28c Sharp-tailed sandpiper	56	56	
433	A59	45c Common teal..................	90	90	

1993

Scott No.	Illus. No.	Description	Unused Value	Used Value	//////
434	A79	50c Butterflyfish....................	1.00	1.00	
435	A79	50c Soldierfish	1.00	1.00	
436	A79	50c Damselfish......................	1.00	1.00	
437	A79	50c Filefish............................	1.00	1.00	
438	A79	50c Hawkfish........................	1.00	1.00	
439	A79	50c Surgeonfish.....................	1.00	1.00	
440	A79	$1 Parrotfish	2.00	2.00	
a.		Booklet pane of 7, #434-440	8.00	—	

A86

A87

A88

Scott No.	Illus. No.	Description	Unused Value	Used Value	/ / / / / /
443	A80	10c multicolored	20	20	
444	A80	15c multicolored	30	30	
446	A80	19c multicolored	38	38	
447	A80	23c multicolored	45	45	
448	A80	24c multicolored	48	48	
452	A80	29c multicolored	58	58	
453	A80	30c multicolored	60	60	
454	A80	35c multicolored	70	70	
456	A80	50c multicolored	1.00	1.00	
457	A80	52c multicolored	1.10	1.10	
458	A80	75c multicolored	1.50	1.50	
460	A80	$1 multicolored	2.00	2.00	
462	A80	$2 multicolored	4.00	4.00	
462A	A80	$2.90 multicolored	5.75	5.75	
463	A80	$5 multicolored	10.00	10.00	
464	A81	Sheet of 4, #a.-d.	3.50	3.50	
1993					
467	A46	52c W60 (4-1)	1.05	1.05	
468	A46	52c W60 (4-2)	1.05	1.05	
469	A46	52c W60 (4-3)	1.05	1.05	
470	A46	52c W60 (4-4)	1.05	1.05	
a.		Block of 4, #467-470	4.00	4.00	

Scott No.	Illus. No.		Description	Unused Value	Used Value	//////
471	A46	50c	W61	1.00	1.00	
472	A47	29c	W62	58	58	
473	A46	29c	W63	58	58	
474	A46	50c	W64	1.00	1.00	
475	A47	52c	W65	1.10	1.10	
476	A46	29c	W66 (2-1)	60	60	
477	A46	29c	W66 (2-2)	60	60	
a.			Pair, #476-476	1.20	1.20	

1994

478	A46	29c	W67	60	60	
479	A46	50c	W68	1.00	1.00	
480	A46	52c	W69	1.10	1.10	
481	A46	29c	W70	60	60	
482	A47	29c	W71	60	60	
483	A46	52c	W72	1.10	1.10	
484	A47	50c	W73	1.00	1.00	
485	A46	75c	W74 (4-1)	1.50	1.50	
486	A46	75c	W74 (4-2)	1.50	1.50	
487	A46	75c	W74 (4-3)	1.50	1.50	
488	A46	75c	W74 (4-4)	1.50	1.50	
a.			Block of 4, #485-488	6.00	6.00	
489	A46	50c	W75	1.00	1.00	
490	A46	29c	W76	60	60	
491	A46	50c	W77	1.00	1.00	

1993

567	A82	29c	multicolored (4-1)	58	58	
568	A82	29c	multicolored (4-2)	58	58	
569	A82	29c	multicolored (4-3)	58	58	
570	A82	29c	multicolored (4-4)	58	58	
571	A83	50c	multicolored	1.00	1.00	
572	A84	29c	Woman, breadfruit (4-1)	58	58	
573	A84	29c	Canoes, warrior (4-2)	58	58	
574	A84	29c	Young chief (4-3)	58	58	
575	A84	29c	Drummer, dancers (4-4)	58	58	
a.			Block of 4, #572-575	2.35	2.35	
576	A85	29c	multicolored	60	60	
577	A86	$2.90	multicolored, souvenir sheet	5.75	5.75	
578	A87	29c	multicolored, souvenir sheet	60	60	
579	A88	50c	red & multicolored (2-1)	1.00	1.00	
580	A88	50c	blue & multicolored (2-2)	1.00	1.00	
a.			Pair, #579-580	2.00	2.00	

AP1

AP2

AP3

AP4

AP5

HOW TO USE THIS BOOK

The number in the first column is its Scott number or identifying number. The letter and number that come next (A41) indicate the design and refer to the illustration so designated. Following that is the denomination of the stamp and its color. Finally, the value, unused and used is shown.

Scott No.	Illus. No.		Description	Unused Value	Used Value	/ / / / / /

MARSHALL ISLANDS, AIR POST STAMPS

1985

C1	A11	44c	Booby Gannet, vert.	88	88	
C2	A11	44c	Esquimaux Curlew, vert.	88	88	
a.			Pair, #C1-C2....................	1.80	1.80	

1986

C3	A20	44c	multicolored	95	95	
C4	A20	44c	multicolored	95	95	
C5	A20	44c	multicolored	95	95	
C6	A20	44c	multicolored	95	95	
a.			Block of 4, #C3-C6.........	3.80	3.80	
C7	A21	44c	USS Saratoga, souvenir sheet	*4.50*	*4.50*	
C8	AP1	44c	multicolored	95	95	
C9	AP2	44c	Community service.........	85	85	
C10	AP2	44c	Salute...............................	85	85	
C11	AP2	44c	Health care	85	85	
C12	AP2	44c	Learning skills.................	85	85	
a.			Block of 4, #C9-C12.......	3.40	3.40	

1987

C13	AP3	44c	Wedge-tailed shearwater	85	85	
C14	AP3	44c	Red-footed booby	85	85	
C15	AP3	44c	Red-tailed tropic-bird......	85	85	
C16	AP3	44c	Great frigatebird..............	85	85	
a.			Block of 4, #C13-C16.....	3.40	3.40	
C17	AP4	44c	multicolored	85	85	
C18	AP4	44c	multicolored	85	85	
C19	AP4	44c	multicolored	85	85	
C20	AP4	44c	multicolored	85	85	
a.			Block of 4, #C17-C20.....	3.40	3.40	

1988

C21	A38	45c	Astronaut, shuttle over Rongelap	90	90	

1989

C22	AP5	12c	Dornier Do228	25	25	
a.			Booklet pane of 10..........	3.00	—	
C23	AP5	36c	Boeing 737	75	75	
a.			Booklet pane of 10..........	8.00	—	
C24	AP5	39c	Hawker Siddeley 748......	90	90	
a.			Booklet pane of 10..........	9.00	—	
C25	AP5	45c	Boeing 727	1.00	1.00	
a.			Booklet pane of 10..........	10.00	—	
b.			Booklet pane, 5 each 36c, 45c	8.75	—	

A2

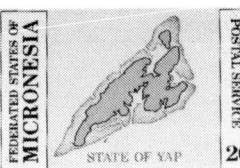
A1

A3

A4

A5

A6

A7

A8

A10

A9

A11

Scott No.	Illus. No.		Description	Unused Value	Used Value

MICRONESIA
1984

Scott No.	Illus. No.		Description	Unused Value	Used Value
1	A1	20c	Yap	50	50
2	A1	20c	Truk	50	50
3	A1	20c	Pohnpei	50	50
4	A1	20c	Kosrae	50	50
a.			Block of 4, #1-4	2.00	2.00
5	A2	1c	Prussian blue	15	15
6	A2	2c	deep claret	15	15
7	A2	3c	dark blue	15	15
8	A2	4c	green	15	15
9	A3	5c	yellow brown	15	15
10	A3	10c	dark violet	16	16
11	A3	13c	dark blue	20	20
12	A3	17c	brown lake	25	25
13	A2	19c	dark violet	28	28
14	A2	20c	olive green	30	30
15	A2	30c	rose lake	45	45
16	A2	37c	deep violet	55	55
17	A3	50c	brown	75	75
18	A3	$1	olive	1.50	1.50
19	A3	$2	Prussian blue	3.00	3.00
20	A3	$5	brown lake	7.00	7.00
21	A4	20c	Truk Post Office	48	48
22	A5	20c	Child in manger	55	55

1985

Scott No.	Illus. No.		Description	Unused Value	Used Value
23	A6	22c	U.S.S. Jamestown	60	60
24	A7	22c	Lelu Protestant Church, Kosrae	60	60
25	A8	22c	Noddy tern	75	75
26	A8	22c	Turnstone	75	75
27	A8	22c	Golden plover	75	75
28	A8	22c	Black-bellied plover	75	75
a.			Block of 4, #25-28	3.00	3.00

1985-88

Scott No.	Illus. No.		Description	Unused Value	Used Value
31	A9	3c	Long-billed white-eye	15	15
32	A9	14c	Truk monarch	28	28
33	A3	15c	Liduduhriap Waterfall, Pohnpei	30	30
a.			Booklet pane of 10	3.00	—
34	A10	22c	bright blue green	35	35
35	A9	22c	Pohnpei mountain starling	44	44
36	A3	25c	Tonachau Peak, Truk	50	50
a.			Booklet pane of 10	5.00	—
b.			Booklet pane, 5 each 15c, 25c	4.00	—
37	A10	36c	ultramarine	72	72
38	A3	45c	Sleeping Lady, Kosrae	90	90
39	A11	$10	bright ultra	15.00	15.00

A16

A17

A18

A19

A20

A21

A22

A23

A24

A25

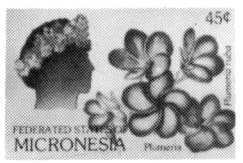
A27

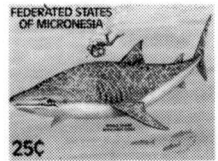
A29

A26

A28

HOW TO USE THIS BOOK

The number in the first column is its Scott number or identifying number. The letter and number that come next (A41) indicate the design and refer to the illustration so designated. Following that is the denomination of the stamp and its color. Finally, the value, unused and used is shown.

Scott No.	Illus. No.		Description	Unused Value	Used Value	/ / / / / /
1985						
45	A16	22c	Land of the Sacred Masonry	60	60	☐☐☐☐☐
1986						
46	A17	22c	multicolored	60	60	☐☐☐☐☐
48	A1	22c	on 20c No. 1	45	45	☐☐☐☐☐
49	A1	22c	on 20c No. 2	45	45	☐☐☐☐☐
50	A1	22c	on 20c No. 3	45	45	☐☐☐☐☐
51	A1	22c	on 20c No. 4	45	45	☐☐☐☐☐
a.			Block of 4, #48-51	1.90	1.90	☐☐☐☐☐
52	A18	22c	At ships helm	65	65	☐☐☐☐☐
53	A19	22c	multicolored	75	75	☐☐☐☐☐
54	A20	5c	multicolored	25	25	☐☐☐☐☐
55	A20	22c	multicolored	75	75	☐☐☐☐☐
1987						
56	A21	22c	Intl. Year of Shelter for the Homeless	65	65	☐☐☐☐☐
57	A21	$1	CAPEX 87	3.00	3.00	☐☐☐☐☐
58	A22	22c	multicolored	60	60	☐☐☐☐☐
1988						
59	A23	22c	German	60	60	☐☐☐☐☐
60	A23	22c	Spanish	60	60	☐☐☐☐☐
61	A23	22c	Japanese	60	60	☐☐☐☐☐
62	A23	22c	US Trust Territory	60	60	☐☐☐☐☐
a.			Block of 4, #59-62	2.40	2.40	☐☐☐☐☐
63	A24	25c	Running	55	55	☐☐☐☐☐
64	A24	25c	Womens hurdles	55	55	☐☐☐☐☐
a.			Pair, #63-64	1.10	1.10	☐☐☐☐☐
65	A24	45c	Basketball	90	90	☐☐☐☐☐
66	A24	45c	Womens volleyball	90	90	☐☐☐☐☐
a.			Pair, #65-66	1.80	1.80	☐☐☐☐☐
67	A25	25c	multicolored	45	45	☐☐☐☐☐
68	A25	25c	multicolored	45	45	☐☐☐☐☐
69	A25	25c	multicolored	45	45	☐☐☐☐☐
70	A25	25c	multicolored	45	45	☐☐☐☐☐
a.			Block of 4, #67-70	2.00	2.00	☐☐☐☐☐
71			Sheet of 18	7.50	7.50	☐☐☐☐☐
a.-r.	A26	25c	any single	40	40	☐☐☐☐☐
1989						
72	A27	45c	Plumeria	70	70	☐☐☐☐☐
73	A27	45c	Hibiscus	70	70	☐☐☐☐☐
74	A27	45c	Jasmine	70	70	☐☐☐☐☐
75	A27	45c	Bougainvillea	70	70	☐☐☐☐☐
a.			Block of 4, #72-75	3.00	3.00	☐☐☐☐☐
76	A28	$1	multicolored, souvenir sheet	1.65	1.65	☐☐☐☐☐

A36

A37

A38

A39

A40

A41

A42

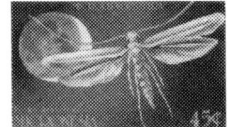
A43

A44

Scott No.	Illus. No.		Description	Unused Value	Used Value	/ / / / / /
77	A29	25c	Whale	40	40	
78	A29	25c	Hammerhead	40	40	
a.			Pair, #77-78	80	80	
79	A29	45c	Tiger, vert.	75	75	
80	A29	45c	Great white, vert.	75	75	
a.			Pair, #79-80	1.50	1.50	
81	A30		Sheet of 9	3.50	3.50	
a.-i.		25c	any single	38	38	
82	A31	$2.40	multicolored	3.50	3.50	
83	A32	1c	Horses hoof	15	15	
84	A32	3c	Rare spotted cowrie	15	15	
85	A32	15c	Commercial trochus	22	22	
a.			Booklet pane of 10	2.75	—	
87	A32	20c	General cone	30	30	
88	A32	25c	Tritons trumpet	38	38	
a.			Booklet pane of 10	4.75	—	
b.			Booklet pane, 5 each 15c, 25c	3.75	—	
90	A32	30c	Laciniated conch	45	45	
91	A32	36c	Red-mouthed olive	55	55	
93	A32	45c	Map cowrie	70	70	
95	A32	50c	Textile cone	75	75	
100	A32	$1	Orange spider conch	1.50	1.50	
101	A32	$2	Golden cowrie	3.00	3.00	
102	A32	$5	Episcopal miter	7.50	7.50	
103			Sheet of 18	9.50	9.50	
a.-r.	A33	25c	any single	50	50	
104	A34	25c	Heralding angel	40	40	
105	A34	45c	Three wise men	80	80	

1990

Scott No.	Illus. No.		Description	Unused Value	Used Value	
106	A35	10c	Kingfisher (juvenile)	20	20	
107	A35	15c	Kingfisher (adult)	30	30	
108	A35	20c	Pigeon	40	40	
109	A35	25c	Pigeon, diff.	50	50	
110	A36	45c	multicolored	70	70	
111	A36	45c	multicolored	70	70	
112	A36	45c	multicolored	70	70	
113	A36	45c	multicolored	70	70	
a.			Block of 4, #110-113	2.80	2.80	
114	A36	$1	multicolored, souvenir sheet	1.65	1.65	
115	A37	$1	Great Britain No. 1, souvenir sheet	1.65	1.65	
116	A38	25c	multicolored	40	40	
117	A38	25c	multicolored	40	40	
118	A39	25c	multicolored	40	40	
119	A38	25c	multicolored	40	40	
120	A38	25c	multicolored	40	40	
a.			Strip of 5, #116-120	2.00	2.00	

A45

A46

A47

A48

A49

A50

A51

Scott No.	Illus. No.		Description	Unused Value	Used Value
121	A40	$1	multicolored	1.80	1.80
122	A41	25c	multicolored	55	55
123	A41	45c	multicolored	1.00	1.00
124	A42	25c	multicolored	55	55
125	A42	25c	multicolored	55	55
126	A42	25c	multicolored	55	55
a.			Strip of 3, #124-126	1.65	1.65
127	A43	45c	Gracillariidae	75	75
128	A43	45c	Yponomeatidae	75	75
129	A43	45c	shown	75	75
130	A43	45c	Cosmopterigidae, diff.	75	75
a.			Block of 4, #127-130	3.00	3.00
131			Sheet of 9	3.50	3.50
a.-i.	A44	25c	any single	40	40

1991

132			Sheet of 2	1.40	1.40
a.	A45	25c	Executive Branch	50	50
b.	A45	45c	Legislative, Judicial Branches	90	90
133	A45	$1	New Capitol, souvenir sheet	2.00	2.00
134	A47	29c	Hawksbill on beach	70	70
135	A47	29c	Green	70	70
a.			Pair, #134-135	1.40	1.40
136	A47	50c	Hawksbill	1.15	1.15
137	A47	50c	Leatherback	1.15	1.15
a.			Pair, #136-137	2.30	2.30
138	A47	29c	Battleship Missouri	60	60
139	A47	29c	Multiple launch rocket system	60	60
140	A47	29c	F-14 Tomcat	60	60
141	A47	29c	E-3 Sentry (AWACS)	60	60
a.			Block of 4, #138-141	2.40	2.40
142	A47	$2.90	Frigatebird, flag	5.80	5.80
a.			Souvenir sheet of 1	5.80	5.80
143			Sheet of 3	1.25	1.25
a.-c.	A48	29c	any single	40	40
144			Sheet of 3	2.25	2.25
a.-c.	A48	50c	any single	75	75
145	A48	$1	multicolored, souvenir sheet	1.65	1.65
146	A49	29c	multicolored	45	45
147	A49	40c	multicolored	60	60
148	A49	50c	multicolored	75	75
149			Sheet of 18	8.00	8.00
a.-r.	A50	29c	any single	48	48

1992

150	A51	29c	Strip of 5, #a.-e.	2.25	2.25
151	A52	29c	Strip of 3, #a.-c.	1.75	1.75
152	A53	29c	multicolored	58	58

A52

A53

A54

A55

A56

A57

A59

A60

A61

Scott No.	Illus. No.		Description	Unused Value	Used Value	/ / / / / /
153	A53	50c	multicolored	1.00	1.00	
a.			Souvenir sheet of 2, #152-153	1.50	1.50	
154	A54	29c	multicolored	58	58	

1993-94

155	A55	29c	Block of 8, #a.-h.............	4.65	4.65	
157	A56	10c	Bigscale soldierfish	20	20	
159	A56	19c	Bennet's butterflyfish	38	38	
159A	A56	20c	Peacock grouper..............	40	40	
160	A56	22c	Great barracuda	44	44	
161	A56	29c	Regal angelfish................	58	58	
162	A56	30c	Bleeker's parrotfish	60	60	
162A	A56	35c	Picassofish	70	70	
163	A56	40c	Mandarinfish	80	80	
163A	A56	45c	Blue banded surgeonfish.	90	90	
164	A56	50c	Orange-striped triggerfish	1.00	1.00	
165	A56	$1	Zebra moray	2.00	2.00	
166	A56	$2.90	Orangespine unicornfish.	6.00	6.00	

1993

168	A57	29c	Sheet of 12, #a.-i.	7.00	7.00	
172	A59	29c	multicolored	58	58	
173	A60	29c	Yap	58	58	
174	A60	29c	Kosrae	58	58	
175	A60	29c	Pohnpei...........................	58	58	
176	A60	29c	Chuuk	58	58	
a.			Block of 4, #173-176	2.35	2.35	
177	A61	29c	Strip of 4, #a.-d.	2.35	2.35	
178	A55	50c	Block of 8, #a.-h..............	8.00	8.00	
179	A62	29c	Kepirohi Falls..................	58	58	
180	A62	50c	Spanish Wall	1.00	1.00	
181	A62	$1	Sokehs Rock, souvenir sheet	2.00	2.00	
182	A63	29c	Pair, #a.-b.	1.25	1.25	
183	A63	50c	Pair, #a.-b.	2.00	2.00	
184	A64	29c	We Three Kings	60	60	
185	A64	50c	Silent Night, Holy Night.	1.00	1.00	
186	A65	29c	Sheet of 18, #a.-r.	11.00	11.00	

1994

187	A62	29c	Sleeping Lady Mountain.	60	60	
188	A62	40c	Walung	80	80	
189	A62	50c	Lelu Ruins	1.00	1.00	
190	A63		Sheet of 4, #a.-d.	3.25	3.25	
191	A55	29c	Block of 8, #a.-h..............	4.75	4.75	
192	A66	29c	Block of 4, #a.-d.............	2.50	2.50	
193	A67	29c	Block of 4, #a.-d.............	2.50	2.50	
194	A68	29c	multicolored	60	60	
195	A69	29c	Strip of 4, #a.-d.	2.50	2.50	

A62

A63

A64

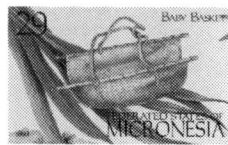
A65

A66

A67

A68

A69

A70

A74

A75

A76

Scott No.	Illus. No.	Description	Unused Value	Used Value
196	A70	50c red & multicolored	1.00	1.00
197	A70	50c blue & multicolored	1.00	1.00
a.		Pair, #196-197	2.00	2.00

AP1

AP3

AP2

AP4

AP5

HOW TO USE THIS BOOK
The number in the first column is its Scott number or identifying number. The letter and number that come next (A41) indicate the design and refer to the illustration so designated. Following that is the denomination of the stamp and its color. Finally, the value, unused and used is shown.

Scott No.	Illus. No.	Description	Unused Value	Used Value	/ / / / / /

MICRONESIA, AIR POST STAMPS

1984

C1	AP1	28c shown	55	55	
C2	AP1	35c SA-16 Albatross, 1960....	70	70	
C3	AP1	40c PBY-5A Catalina, 1951..	80	80	
C4	A4	28c multicolored	70	70	
C5	A4	35c multicolored	90	90	
C6	A4	40c multicolored	1.20	1.20	
C7	A5	28c Illustrated Christmas text	70	70	
C8	A5	35c Decorated palm tree	90	90	
C9	A5	40c Feast preparation	1.20	1.20	

1985

C10	A6	33c LAstrolabe........................	70	70	
C11	A6	39c La Coquille.......................	1.00	1.00	
C12	A6	44c Shenandoah......................	1.25	1.25	
C13	A7	33c Dublon Protestant Church	70	70	
C14	A7	44c Pohnpei Catholic Church	90	90	
C15	A8	44c Sooty tern	1.20	1.20	
C16	A16	33c Nan Tauas inner courtyard	70	70	
C17	A16	39c Outer wall........................	80	80	
C18	A16	44c Tomb	90	90	

1986

C19	AP2	44c dark blue, blue & black...	1.25	1.25	
C20	AP3	44c Ship in port......................	1.25	1.25	
C21	A18	33c Forging Hawaiian stamp.	75	75	
C22	A18	39c Sinking of the Leonora, Kosrae	90	90	
C23	A18	44c Hayes escapes capture	1.00	1.00	
C24	A18	75c Biography, by Louis Becke	1.90	1.90	
C25	A18	$1 Hayes ransoming chief, souvenir sheet...............	4.00	4.00	
C26	A20	33c multicolored	1.00	1.00	
C27	A20	44c multicolored	1.40	1.40	

1987

C28	A21	33c US currency, bicent.........	80	80	
C29	A21	39c 1st American in orbit, 25th anniv.	1.25	1.25	
C30	A21	44c US Constitution, bicent...	1.40	1.40	
C31	A22	33c Holy Family	80	80	
C32	A22	39c Shepherds........................	90	90	
C33	A22	44c Three Wise Men..............	1.00	1.00	

1988

C34	A9	33c Great truk white-eye	55	55	
C35	A9	44c Blue-faced parrotfinch	70	70	
C36	A9	$1 Yap monarch...................	1.75	1.75	
C37	A23	44c Traditional skills (boat-building)	95	95	

Scott No.	Illus. No.		Description	Unused Value	Used Value	//////
C38	A23	44c	Modern Micronesia (tourism)	95	95	
a.			Pair, #C37-C38	1.90	1.90	

1989

C39	AP4	45c	Pohnpei............................	90	90	
C40	AP4	45c	Truk	90	90	
C41	AP4	45c	Kosrae	90	90	
C42	AP4	45c	Yap...................................	90	90	
a.			Block of 4, #C39-C42.....	3.60	3.60	

1990

C43	AP5	22c	shown	45	45	
C44	AP5	36c	multi, diff........................	72	72	
C45	AP5	39c	multi, diff........................	80	80	
C46	AP5	45c	multi, diff........................	90	90	

1992

C47	AP5	40c	Propeller plane, outrigger canoe	75	75	
C48	AP5	50c	Passenger jet, sailboat	90	90	

Scott No.	Illus. No.	Description	Unused Value	Used Value	/ / / / / /

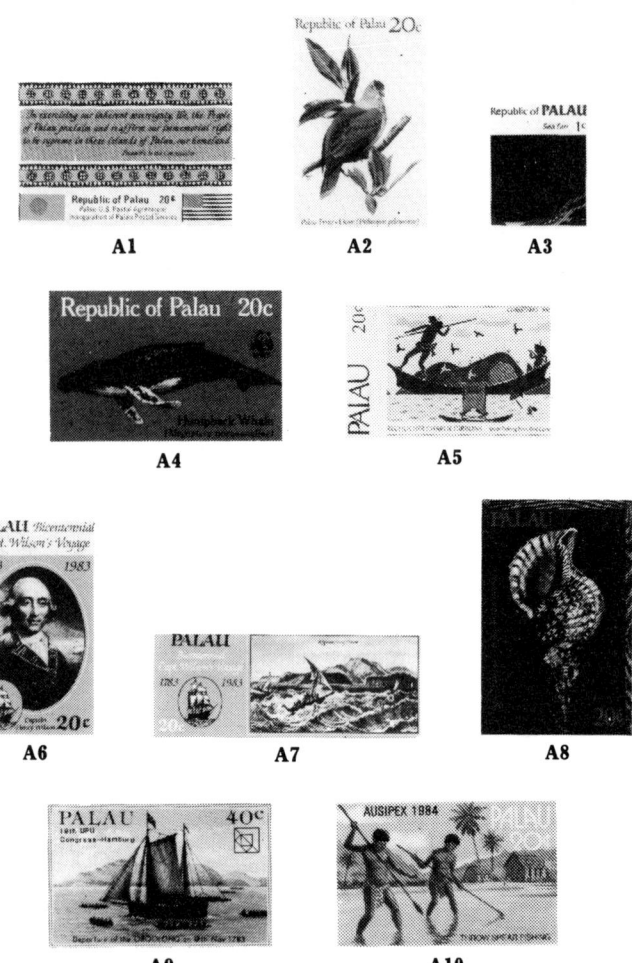

HOW TO USE THIS BOOK

The number in the first column is its Scott number or identifying number. The letter and number that come next (A41) indicate the design and refer to the illustration so designated. Following that is the denomination of the stamp and its color. Finally, the value, unused and used is shown.

Scott No.	Illus. No.		Description	Unused Value	Used Value	/ / / / / /
PALAU						
1983						
1	A1	20c	Constitution preamble.....	55	55	
2	A1	20c	Hunters	55	55	
3	A1	20c	Fish	55	55	
4	A1	20c	Preamble, diff................	55	55	
a.			Block of 4, #1-4	2.20	2.20	
5	A2	20c	shown	40	40	
6	A2	20c	Palau morningbird..........	40	40	
7	A2	20c	Giant white-eye..............	40	40	
8	A2	20c	Palau fantail...................	40	40	
a.			Block of 4, #5-8	1.65	1.65	
1983-84						
9	A3	1c	shown	15	15	
10	A3	3c	Map cowrie	15	15	
11	A3	5c	Jellyfish	15	15	
12	A3	10c	Hawksbill turtle..............	16	16	
13	A3	13c	Giant Clam	20	20	
a.			Booklet pane of 10	9.00	—	
b.			Bklt. pane of 10 (5 #13, 5 #14)	9.00	—	
14	A3	20c	Parrotfish	35	35	
b.			Booklet pane of 10	*10.00*	—	
15	A3	28c	Chambered Nautilus	45	45	
16	A3	30c	Dappled sea cucumber....	50	50	
17	A3	37c	Sea Urchin......................	55	55	
18	A3	50c	Starfish..........................	85	85	
19	A3	$1	Squid.............................	1.60	1.60	
20	A3	$2	Dugong.........................	5.00	5.00	
21	A3	$5	Pink sponge...................	11.00	11.00	
1983						
24	A4	20c	shown	40	40	
25	A4	20c	Blue whale.....................	40	40	
26	A4	20c	Fin whale.......................	40	40	
27	A4	20c	Great sperm whale	40	40	
a.			Block of 4, #24-27	1.60	1.60	
28	A5	20c	First Child ceremony	50	50	
29	A5	20c	Spearfishing from Red Canoe	50	50	
30	A5	20c	Traditional feast at the Bai	50	50	
31	A5	20c	Taro gardening	50	50	
32	A5	20c	Spearfishing at New Moon	50	50	
a.			Strip of 5, #28-32	2.50	2.50	
33	A6	20c	Capt. Henry Wilson	50	50	
34	A7	20c	Approaching Pelew.........	50	50	
35	A7	20c	Englishmans Camp on Ulong	50	50	
36	A6	20c	Prince Lee Boo...............	50	50	
37	A6	20c	King Abba Thulle	50	50	

A12

A11

A13

A14

A15

A16

A17

A18

A19

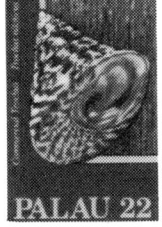
A20

Scott No.	Illus. No.		Description	Unused Value	Used Value	/ / / / / /
38	A7	20c	Mooring in Koror............	50	50	
39	A7	20c	Village scene of Pelew Islands	50	50	
40	A6	20c	Ludee................................	50	50	
a.			Block or strip of 8, #33-40	4.00	4.00	

1984

Scott No.	Illus. No.		Description	Unused Value	Used Value	/ / / / / /
41	A8	20c	Triton trumpet, d.	40	40	
42	A8	20c	Horned helmet, d.............	40	40	
43	A8	20c	Giant clam, d.	40	40	
44	A8	20c	Laciniate conch, d.	40	40	
45	A8	20c	Royal cloak scallop, d.....	40	40	
46	A8	20c	Triton trumpet, v.	40	40	
47	A8	20c	Horned helmet, v.............	40	40	
48	A8	20c	Giant clam, v...................	40	40	
49	A8	20c	Laciniate conch, v.	40	40	
50	A8	20c	Royal cloak scallop, v.....	40	40	
a.			Block of 10, #41-50	4.00	4.00	
51	A9	40c	Oroolong, 1783	95	95	
52	A9	40c	Duff, 1797	95	95	
53	A9	40c	Peiho, 1908......................	95	95	
54	A9	40c	Albatross, 1885	95	95	
a.			Block of 4, #51-54	3.80	3.80	
55	A10	20c	Throw spear fishing	45	45	
56	A10	20c	Kite fishing......................	45	45	
57	A10	20c	Underwater spear fishing	45	45	
58	A10	20c	Net fishing......................	45	45	
a.			Block of 4, #55-58	1.90	1.90	
59	A11	20c	Mountain Apple	45	45	
60	A11	20c	Beach Morning Glory	45	45	
61	A11	20c	Turmeric...........................	45	45	
62	A11	20c	Plumeria	45	45	
a.			Block of 4, #59-62	1.90	1.90	

1985

Scott No.	Illus. No.		Description	Unused Value	Used Value	/ / / / / /
63	A12	22c	Shearwater chick.............	60	60	
64	A12	22c	Shearwaters head	60	60	
65	A12	22c	Shearwater in flight.........	60	60	
66	A12	22c	Swimming	60	60	
a.			Block of 4, #63-66	2.40	2.40	
67	A13	22c	Cargo canoe.....................	50	50	
68	A13	22c	War canoe	50	50	
69	A13	22c	Bamboo raft.....................	50	50	
70	A13	22c	Racing/sailing canoe	50	50	
a.			Block of 4, #67-70	2.00	2.00	
75	A3	14c	Trumpet triton	20	20	
a.			Booklet pane of 10...........	*6.00*	—	
76	A3	22c	Bumphead parrotfish.......	35	35	
a.			Booklet pane of 10	*10.00*	—	
b.			Booklet pane, 5 14c, 5 22c	*9.00*	—	

A21

A22

A23

A24

A23a

A25

A26

A27

A28

Scott No.	Illus. No.	Description	Unused Value	Used Value	//////
77	A3	25c Soft coral, damsel fish.....	40	40	
79	A3	33c Sea anemone, clownfish..	55	55	
80	A3	39c Green sea turtle	65	65	
81	A3	44c Pacific sailfish	70	70	
85	A3	$10 Spinner dolphins	15.00	15.00	
86	A14	44c multicolored	75	75	
87	A14	44c multicolored	75	75	
88	A14	44c multicolored	75	75	
89	A14	44c multicolored	75	75	
a.		Block of 4, #86-89	3.00	3.00	
90	A15	14c multicolored	40	40	
91	A15	22c multicolored	55	55	
92	A15	33c multicolored	85	85	
93	A15	44c multicolored	1.15	1.15	
94	A16	$1 multicolored, souvenir sheet	2.75	2.75	
95	A17	44c Kaeb canoe, 1758............	85	85	
96	A17	44c U.S.S. Vincennes, 1835..	85	85	
97	A17	44c S.M.S. Scharnhorst, 1910	85	85	
98	A17	44c Yacht, 1986......................	85	85	
a.		Block of 4, #95-98	3.40	3.40	

1986

Scott No.	Illus. No.	Description	Unused Value	Used Value	//////
99	A18	44c Mangrove flycatcher	90	90	
100	A18	44c Cardinal honeyeater	90	90	
101	A18	44c Blue-faced parrotfinch	90	90	
102	A18	44c Dusky and bridled white-eyes	90	90	
a.		Block of 4, #99-102	3.60	3.60	
103		Sheet of 40......................	37.50		
a.	A19	14c any single	25	25	
104	A20	22c Commercial trochus........	55	55	
105	A20	22c Marble cone.....................	55	55	
106	A20	22c Fluted giant clam.............	55	55	
107	A20	22c Bullmouth helmet	55	55	
108	A20	22c Golden cowrie.................	55	55	
a.		Strip of 5, #104-108	2.75	2.75	
109	A21	22c Soldiers helmet................	55	55	
110	A21	22c Plane wreckage	55	55	
111	A21	22c Woman playing guitar	55	55	
112	A21	22c Airai vista	55	55	
a.		Block of 4, #109-112	2.20	2.20	
113	A22	22c Gecko	50	50	
114	A22	22c Emerald tree skink	50	50	
115	A22	22c Estuarine crocodile..........	50	50	
116	A22	22c Leatherback turtle	50	50	
a.		Block of 4, # 113-116	2.00	2.00	
117	A23	22c multicolored.....................	35	35	
118	A23	22c multicolored.....................	35	35	
119	A23	22c multicolored.....................	35	35	

A30

A31

A32

A33

A34

A35

A36

A37

A38

Scott No.	Illus. No.		Description	Unused Value	Used Value	//////
120	A23	22c	multicolored	35	35	
121	A23	22c	multicolored	35	35	
a.			Strip of 5, #117-121	1.75	1.75	

1987

121B	A23a	44c	Tangadik, soursop	85	85	
121C	A23a	44c	Dira amartal, sweet orange	85	85	
121D	A23a	44c	Ilhuochel, swamp cabbage	85	85	
121E	A23a	44c	Bauosech, fig	85	85	
f.			Block of 4, #121B-121E.	3.40	3.40	
122	A24	44c	In flight	90	90	
123	A24	44c	Hanging	90	90	
124	A24	44c	Eating	90	90	
125	A24	44c	Head	90	90	
a.			Block of 4, #122-125	3.60	3.60	

1987-88

126	A25	1c	Ixora casei	15	15	
127	A25	3c	Lumnitzera littorea	15	15	
128	A25	5c	Sonneratia alba	15	15	
129	A25	10c	Tristellateria australasiae	16	16	
130	A25	14c	Bikkia palauensis	20	20	
a.			Booklet pane of 10	3.00	—	
131	A25	15c	Limnophila aromatica	22	22	
a.			Booklet pane of 10	2.25	—	
132	A25	22c	Bruguiera gymnorhiza	35	35	
a.			Booklet pane of 10	4.00	—	
b.			Booklet pane, 5 each 14c, 22c	4.00	—	
133	A25	25c	Fagraea ksid	40	40	
a.			Booklet pane of 10	4.00	—	
b.			Booklet pane, 5 each 15c, 25c	4.00	—	
134	A25	36c	Ophiorrhiza palauensis ...	55	55	
135	A25	39c	Cerbera manghas	60	60	
136	A25	44c	Sandera indica	70	70	
137	A25	45c	Maesa canfieldiae	72	72	
138	A25	50c	Dolichandrone spathacea	85	85	
139	A25	$1	Barringtonia racemosa	1.60	1.60	
140	A25	$2	Nepenthes mirabilis	3.25	3.25	
141	A25	$5	Dendrobium palawense ..	8.00	8.00	
142	A25	$10	Bouquet	15.00	15.00	

1987

146	A26	22c	Babeldaob Is.	50	50	
147	A26	22c	Floating Garden Isls.	50	50	
148	A26	22c	Rock Is.	50	50	
149	A26	22c	Koror	50	50	
a.			Block of 4, #146-149	2.00	2.00	
150	A20	22c	Black-striped triton	55	55	

A39

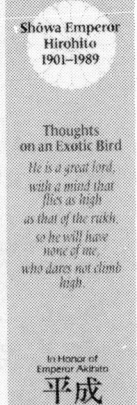

A41

A42

A44

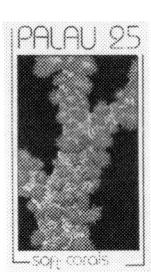

A45

A46

A49

A47

Scott No.	Illus. No.		Description	Unused Value	Used Value	/ / / / / /
151	A20	22c	Tapestry turban.................	55	55	
152	A20	22c	Adusta murex....................	55	55	
153	A20	22c	Little fox miter................	55	55	
154	A20	22c	Cardinal miter	55	55	
a.			Strip of 5, #150-154	2.75	2.75	
155	A27	14c	Art. VIII, Sec. 1, Palau.....	20	20	
156	A27	14c	Presidential seals.............	20	20	
157	A27	14c	Art. II, Sec. 1, US............	20	20	
a.			Strip of 3, #155-157 + label	60	60	
158	A27	22c	Art. IX, Sec. 1, Palau	35	35	
159	A27	22c	Legislative seals..............	35	35	
160	A27	22c	Art. I, Sec. 1, US	35	35	
a.			Strip of 3, #158-160 + label	1.05	1.05	
161	A27	44c	Art X, Sec. 1, Palau.........	70	70	
162	A27	44c	Supreme Court seals	70	70	
163	A27	44c	Art. III, Sec. 1, US	70	70	
a.			Strip of 3, #161-163 + label	2.10	2.10	
164	A28	14c	multicolored	30	30	
165	A28	22c	multicolored	45	45	
166	A28	33c	multicolored	70	70	
167	A28	44c	multicolored	85	85	
168	A28	$1	multicolored, souvenir sheet	2.30	2.30	
173	A30	22c	I saw....	55	55	
174	A30	22c	And what was................	55	55	
175	A30	22c	Twas Joseph....................	55	55	
176	A30	22c	Saint Michael...	55	55	
177	A30	22c	And all the bells...	55	55	
a.			Strip of 5, #173-177........	2.75	2.75	
178	A31	22c	multicolored	55	55	
179	A31	22c	multicolored	55	55	
180	A31	22c	multicolored	55	55	
181	A31	22c	multicolored	55	55	
182	A31	22c	multicolored	55	55	
a.			Strip of 5, #178-182	2.75	2.75	

1988

Scott No.	Illus. No.		Description	Unused Value	Used Value	
183	A23a	44c	multicolored	85	85	
184	A23a	44c	multicolored	85	85	
185	A23a	44c	multicolored	85	85	
186	A23a	44c	multicolored	85	85	
a.			Block of 4, #183-186	3.40	3.40	
187	A32	44c	Whimbrel	85	85	
188	A32	44c	Yellow bittern	85	85	
189	A32	44c	Rufous night-heron	85	85	
190	A32	44c	Banded rail	85	85	
a.			Block of 4, #187-190	3.40	3.40	
191	A20	25c	Striped engina	55	55	
192	A20	25c	Ivory cone.......................	55	55	

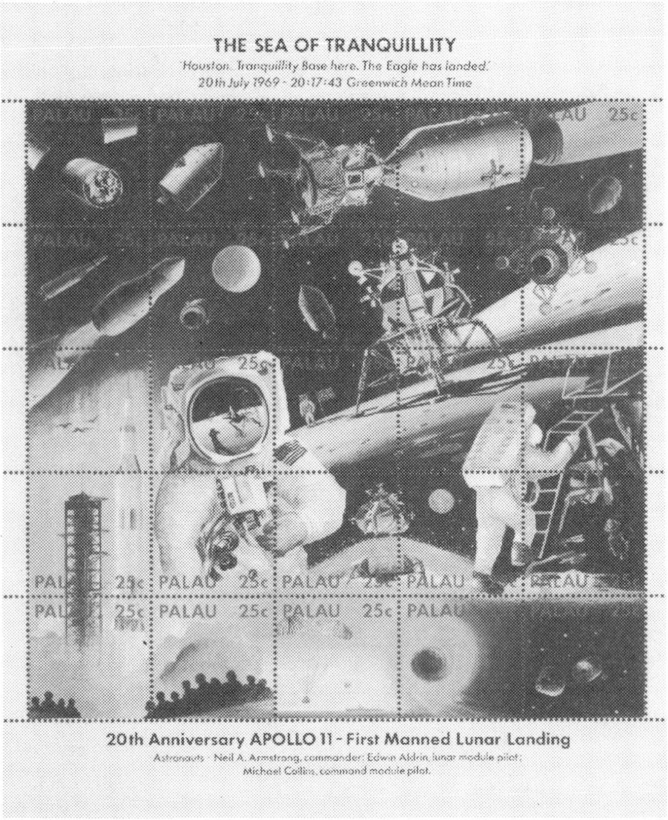
THE SEA OF TRANQUILLITY
'Houston, Tranquillity Base here. The Eagle has landed.'
20th July 1969 - 20:17:43 Greenwich Mean Time
PALAU 25c
20th Anniversary APOLLO 11 - First Manned Lunar Landing
Astronauts - Neil A. Armstrong, commander; Edwin Aldrin, lunar module pilot;
Michael Collins, command module pilot.

A40

PALAU
$1
PALAU

A48

45c
PALAU

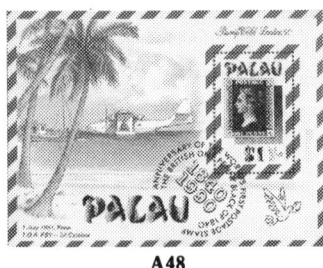

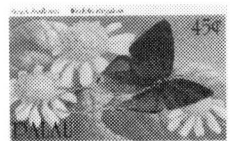

A50

Scott No.	Illus. No.		Description	Unused Value	Used Value	/ / / / / /
193	A20	25c	Plaited miter	55	55	
194	A20	25c	Episcopal miter	55	55	
195	A20	25c	Isabelle cowrie	55	55	
a.			Strip of 5, #191-195	2.75	2.75	
196			Sheet of 6	3.00	3.00	
a.-f.	A33	25c	multicolored	50	50	
197	A34		Sheet of 6	4.80	4.80	
a.-f.		45c	any single	80	80	
198	A35	25c	multicolored	50	50	
199	A35	25c	multicolored	50	50	
200	A35	25c	multicolored	50	50	
201	A35	25c	multicolored	50	50	
202	A35	25c	multicolored	50	50	
a.			Strip of 5, #199-202	2.50	2.50	
203	A36		Sheet of 5	2.75	2.75	
a.-e.		25c	multicolored	55	55	
1989						
204	A37	45c	Nicobar pigeon	85	85	
205	A37	45c	Ground dove	85	85	
206	A37	45c	Micronesian megapode	85	85	
207	A37	45c	Owl	85	85	
a.			Block of 4, #204-207	3.40	3.40	
208	A38	45c	Gilled auricularia	85	85	
209	A38	45c	Rock mushroom	85	85	
210	A38	45c	Polyporous	85	85	
211	A38	45c	Veiled stinkhorn	85	85	
a.			Block of 4, #208-211	3.40	3.40	
212	A20	25c	Robin redbreast triton	55	55	
213	A20	25c	Hebrew cone	55	55	
214	A20	25c	Tadpole triton	55	55	
215	A20	25c	Lettered cone	55	55	
216	A20	25c	Rugose miter	55	55	
a.			Strip of 5, #212-216	2.75	2.75	
217	A39	$1	multicolored, souvenir sheet	2.00	2.00	
218	A40		Sheet of 25	10.00	10.00	
a.-y.		25c	any single	40	40	
219	A41	$2.40	multicolored	4.00	4.00	
220			Block of 10	4.00	4.00	
a.-j.	A42	25c	any single	40	40	
221	A43		Block of 20	7.75	7.75	
a.-t.		25c	any single	40	40	
222	A44	25c	multicolored	50	50	
223	A44	25c	multicolored	50	50	
224	A44	25c	multicolored	50	50	
225	A44	25c	multicolored	50	50	
226	A44	25c	multicolored	50	50	
a.			Strip of 5, #222-226	2.50	2.50	

A43

A52

A53

A54

Scott No.	Illus. No.	Description	Unused Value	Used Value	/ / / / / /
1990					
227	A45	25c Pink coral	50	50	
228	A45	25c Pink & violet coral	50	50	
229	A45	25c Yellow coral	50	50	
230	A45	25c Red coral	50	50	
a.		Block of 4, #227-230	2.00	2.00	
231	A46	45c Siberian rubythroat	80	80	
232	A46	45c Palau bush-warbler	80	80	
233	A46	45c Micronesian starling	80	80	
234	A46	45c Cicadabird	80	80	
a.		Block of 4, #231-234	3.20	3.20	
235		Sheet of 9........................	3.50	3.50	
a.-i.	A47	25c any single	38	38	
236	A48	$1 Great Britain #1, souvenir sheet	1.75	1.75	
237	A49	45c *Corymborkis veratrifolia*	70	70	
238	A49	45c *Malaxis setipes*................	70	70	
239	A49	45c *Dipodium freycinetianum*	70	70	
240	A49	45c *Bulbophyllum micronesiacum*	70	70	
241	A49	45c *Vanda teres* and *hookeriana*	70	70	
a.		Strip of 5, #237-241	3.50	3.50	
242	A50	45c *Wedelia strigulosa*...........	70	70	
243	A50	45c *Erthrina variegata*............	70	70	
244	A50	45c *Clerodendrum inerme*	70	70	
245	A50	45c *Vigna marina*...................	70	70	
a.		Block of 4, #242-245	2.80	2.80	
246	A51	25c Sheet of 25, #a.-y.	10.50	10.50	
247	A52	45c Mailship, 1890	1.00	1.00	
248	A52	45c US #803 on cover, forklift, plane	1.00	1.00	
a.		Pair, #247-248.................	2.00	2.00	
249	A53	25c multicolored	40	40	
250	A53	25c multicolored	40	40	
251	A53	25c multicolored	40	40	
252	A53	25c multicolored	40	40	
253	A53	25c multicolored	40	40	
a.		Strip of 5, #249-253	2.00	2.00	
254	A54	45c multicolored	75	75	
255	A54	45c multicolored	75	75	
256	A54	45c multicolored	75	75	
257	A54	45c multicolored	75	75	
a.		Block of 4, #254-257	3.00	3.00	
258	A54	$1 multicolored, souvenir sheet	1.75	1.75	
1991					
259	A55	30c Staghorn	60	60	
260	A55	30c Velvet Leather	60	60	
261	A55	30c Van Goghs Cypress	60	60	
262	A55	30c Violet Lace	60	60	
a.		Block of 4, #259-262	2.40	2.40	
263	A56	30c Sheet of 16, #a.-p.	7.50	7.50	

A51

A56

Scott No.	Illus. No.		Description	Unused Value	Used Value	/ / / / / /
1991-92						
264	A57	1c	Palau bush-warbler	15	15	
266	A57	4c	Common moorhen	15	15	
267	A57	6c	Banded rail	15	15	
270	A57	19c	Palau fantail	38	38	
270A	A57	20c	Mangrove flycatcher	40	40	
271	A57	23c	Purple swamphen	46	46	
272	A57	29c	Palau fruit dove	58	58	
274	A57	35c	Great crested tern	70	70	
275	A57	40c	Pacific reef heron	80	80	
276	A57	45c	Micronesian pigeon	90	90	
277	A57	50c	Great frigatebird	1.00	1.00	
278	A57	52c	Little pied cormorant	1.05	1.05	
280	A57	75c	Jungle night jar	1.50	1.50	
281	A57	95c	Cattle egret	1.90	1.90	
283	A57	$1.34	Great sulphur-crested cockatoo	2.68	2.68	
285	A57	$2	Blue-faced parrotfinch	4.00	4.00	
286	A57	$5	Eclectus parrot	10.00	10.00	
287	A57	$10	Palau bush warbler	20.00	20.00	
1991						
288	A58	29c	Sheet of 6, #a.-f.	3.00	3.00	
289	A59	29c	Sheet of 20, #a.-t.	11.00	11.00	
290	A60	20c	Sheet of 9, #a.-i.	3.50	3.50	
291	A60	$2.90	Fairy tern, yellow ribbon	4.25	4.25	
292	A60	$2.90	like #291, souvenir sheet	4.25	4.25	
293	A61	29c	Sheet of 8, #a.-h.	4.00	4.00	
294	A62	50c	Sheet of 5, #a.-e	4.00	4.00	
1991						
295	A63	29c	Sheet of 6, #a.-f.	2.75	2.75	
296	A63	$1	multicolored, souvenir sheet	1.75	1.75	
297	A64	29c	Sheet of 6, #a.-f.	3.00	3.00	
298	A65	29c	Strip of 5, #a.-e.	2.25	2.25	
299	A66	29c	Sheet of 10, #a.-j.	4.25	4.25	
1992						
300	A67	50c	Block of 4, #a.-d	2.50	2.50	
301	A68	29c	Strip of 5, #a.-e	2.65	2.65	
302	A69	29c	Sheet of 20, #a.-t.	11.60	11.60	
303	A70	29c	Sheet of 24, #a.-x.	14.00	14.00	
304	A71	50c	Dawn Fraser	1.00	1.00	
305	A71	50c	Olga Korbut	1.00	1.00	
306	A71	50c	Bob Beamon	1.00	1.00	
307	A71	50c	Carl Lewis	1.00	1.00	
308	A71	50c	Dick Fosbury	1.00	1.00	
309	A71	50c	Greg Louganis	1.00	1.00	
310	A72	29c	Sheet of 9, #a.-i.	5.25	5.25	

A55   **A57**

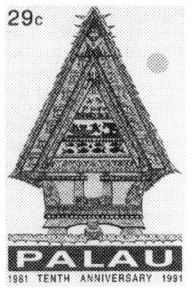

A58

A60

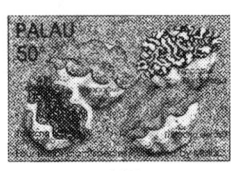

A62

A61

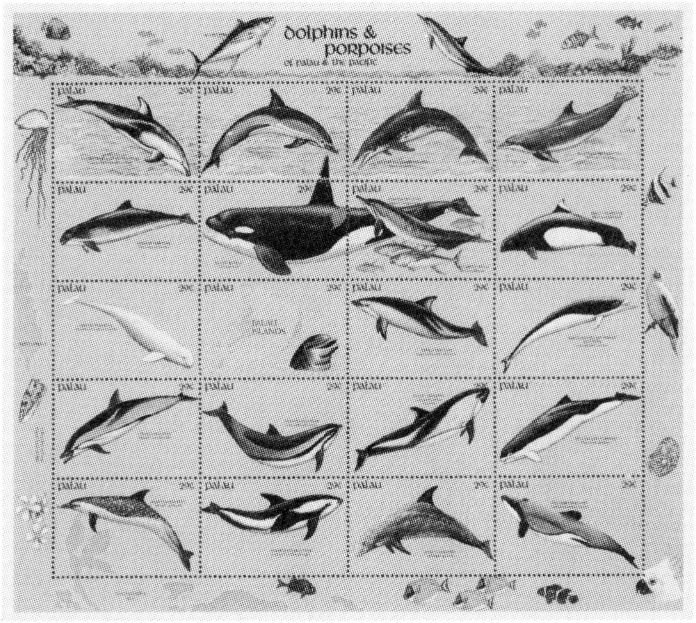

A59

A63

A64

A65

A66

A67

A68

A71

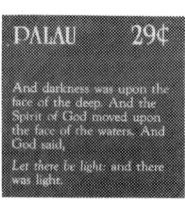

A70

A72

A73

 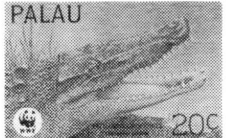 

A82   **A83**   **A84**

HOW TO USE THIS BOOK

The number in the first column is its Scott number or identifying number. The letter and number that come next (A41) indicate the design and refer to the illustration so designsted. Following that is the denomination of the stamp and its color. Finally, the value, unused and used is shown.

Scott No.	Illus. No.		Description	Unused Value	Used Value	/ / / / / /
311	A66	50c	Sheet of 10, #a.-j.	10.00	10.00	
312	A73	29c	Strip of 5, #a.-e................	2.65	2.65	

1993

313	A74	50c	Block of 4, #a.-d..............	3.75	3.75	
314	A75	29c	Block of 4, #a.-d..............	2.15	2.15	
315	A76	50c	Block of 4, #a.-d..............	4.00	4.00	
316	A77	50c	Sheet of 10, #a.-j.+label..	10.00	10.00	
317	A78	29c	Strip of 5, #a.-e................	3.50	3.50	
318	A79	29c	Sheet of 25, #a.-y.	15.00	15.00	
319	A80	29c	Sheet of 2 each, #a.-b......	2.50	2.50	
320	A80	$2.90	multicolored, souvenir sheet	5.75	5.75	
321	A81	29c	Sheet of 25, #a.-y.	15.00	15.00	

1994

322	A82	40c	Block of 4, #a.-d..............	3.00	3.00	
323	A83	20c	Block of 4, #a.-d..............	1.75	1.75	
324	A84	50c	Block of 4, #a.-d..............	4.00	4.00	
325	A77	29c	Sheet of 10, #a.-j.+label..	5.75	5.75	
326	A77	50c	Sheet of 10, #a.-j.+label..	10.00	10.00	

SP1

Scott No.	Illus. No.		Description	Unused Value	Used Value	/ / / / / /

PALAU, SEMI-POSTAL STAMPS

1988

B1	SP1	25c	+5c Baseball glove, player	50	50	
B2	SP1	25c	+5c Running shoe, athlete	50	50	
a.			Pair, #B1-B2...................	1.00	1.00	
B3	SP1	45c	+5c Goggles, swimmer...	1.00	1.00	
B4	SP1	45c	+5c Gold medal, diver	1.00	1.00	
a.			Pair, #B3-B4...................	2.00	2.00	

AP1

AP2

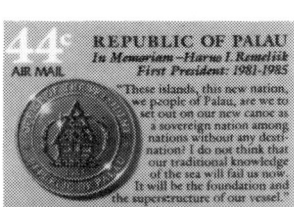
AP3

AP4

AP5

HOW TO USE THIS BOOK

The number in the first column is its Scott number or identifying number. The letter and number that come next (A41) indicate the design and refer to the illustration so designated. Following that is the denomination of the stamp and its color. Finally, the value, unused and used is shown.

Scott No.	Illus. No.		Description	Unused Value	Used Value	//////
PALAU, AIR POST STAMPS						
1984						
C1	AP1	40c	shown	75	75	
C2	AP1	40c	Fairy tern	75	75	
C3	AP1	40c	Black noddy	75	75	
C4	AP1	40c	Black-naped tern	75	75	
a.			Block of 4, #C1-C4	3.00	3.00	
1985						
C5	A12	44c	Audubons Shearwater	70	70	
C6	AP2	44c	multicolored	90	90	
C7	AP2	44c	multicolored	90	90	
C8	AP2	44c	multicolored	90	90	
C9	AP2	44c	multicolored	90	90	
a.			Block of 4, #C6-C9	3.60	3.60	
C10	A16	44c	multicolored	80	80	
C11	A16	44c	multicolored	80	80	
C12	A16	44c	multicolored	80	80	
C13	A16	44c	multicolored	80	80	
a.			Block of 4, #C10-C13	3.20	3.20	
1986						
C14	AP3	44c	multicolored	1.00	1.00	
C15	AP3	44c	multicolored	1.00	1.00	
C16	AP3	44c	multicolored	1.00	1.00	
a.			Strip of 3, #C14-C16	3.00	3.00	
C17	AP4	44c	multicolored	90	90	
1989						
C18	AP5	36c	Cessna 207 Skywagon	70	70	
a.			Booklet pane of 10	7.00	—	
C19	AP5	39c	Embraer EMB-110 Bandeirante	80	80	
a.			Booklet pane of 10	8.00	—	
C20	AP5	45c	Boeing 727	90	90	
a.			Booklet pane of 10	9.00	—	
b.			Booklet pane, 5 each 36c, 45c	8.00	—	
1991						
C21	A61	50c	like #293a	1.10	1.10	

Scott No.	Illus. No.	Description	Unused Value	Used Value	/ / / / / /

Scott No.	Illus. No.	Description	Unused Value	Used Value	/ / / / / /

INDEX TO ADVERTISERS

ADVERTISER	PAGE

—A—

The American Philatelic Society 21A

—D—

Dale Enterprises, Inc. 18A
Lowell H. Donald Co. 17A
Dutch Country Auctions 7A

—G—

Henry Gitner Philatelists, Inc. 11A

—K—

Joseph Kardwell, Inc. 6A
Kenmore 4A

—M—

Mystic Stamp Co. 13A

—P—

The Plate Block Stamp Company 247

—S—

Stamp Center • Dutch Country Auctions 7A

—V—

Vidiforms Co., Inc. 9A
Vidiforms Co., Inc. 12A

—W—

The Washington Press 2A
Wilton Stamp Company, Inc. 15A

★ ★ ★ ★ ★ ★ ★ ★ ★ ★ ★ ★

Scott Advertising Opportunities

DEALERS...take advantage of Scott's leadership position in the North American market by promoting your products and services in Scott publications...

- Scott U.S. Pocket Catalogue
- Scott Stamp Monthly Magazine
- Scott U.S. FDC Catalogue
- Scott Catalogues
  Vol. 1A (US, UN, Canada, Br. America)
  Vol. 1B (GB, Br.Eur., Br.Afr., Br.Asia, Australia, Pacific Islands)
  Vol. 2 (Countries A-C)
  Vol. 3 (Countries D-I)
  Vol. 4 (Countries J-Q)
  Vol. 5 (Countries R-Z)
  Classic (World 1840-1940)
  U.S. Specialized (Inc. UN)

To receive information about advertising in next year's Scott U.S. Pocket Catalogue or any other Scott product, contact Scott Publishing Co., P.O. Box 828, Sidney, OH 45365 USA. Phone 513-498-0832, FAX 513-498-0807.